W9-ADE-060

THE HUNDRED FLOWERS CAMPAIGN AND THE CHINESE INTELLECTUALS

"Let a hundred flowers bloom,
let a hundred schools contend."

—Mao Tse-tung, February 27, 1957.

THE HUNDRED FLOWERS CAMPAIGN and the Chinese Intellectuals

By

RODERICK MacFARQUHAR

with an Epilogue by

G. F. HUDSON

FREDERICK A. PRAEGER, *Publishers*
NEW YORK

First published in 1960
by Stevens & Sons Limited
of 11 New Fetter Lane
in the City of London
and printed in Great Britain
by Wembley Press Ltd.
Perivale, Middlesex

Published in the U.S.A. by
Frederick A. Praeger Inc.
of 64 University Place
New York 3, N.Y., U.S.A.

Library of Congress catalog card number 60–10877

To

MY PARENTS

CONTENTS

REACTION

EPILOGUE

PREFACE

ONLY once has a Communist ruler invited his subjects to criticise his régime. This was in 1957 in China when Mao Tse-tung, to use his own phrase, called for a hundred flowers to bloom. The response of the Chinese intelligentsia—the first section of the population to be asked to air views—provides a unique description of Communist Chinese totalitarianism from the inside. The aim of this book is to record that description.

Virtually all the material used is translated from the Chinese Press—no Western journalists were present at the forums at which the criticisms were made, probably no foreign journalists at all. It is, in effect, largely an official documentary record; most of the reports were carried by the Communist Party newspaper, the *People's Daily*, or the state's New China News Agency (normally abbreviated to NCNA). But it will soon become obvious to the reader that the material is divided into two sharply contrasted categories. Criticisms printed at the time they were made are usually reported "straight." Many criticisms, however, were only published after the Communist Party decided to halt the outburst it had brought upon itself. In these cases, while the critics are still quoted, their remarks are often surrounded by highly adverse comment made by the journalist. Unsatisfactory though it is in some ways, I have used both kinds of material together. If it is not completely obvious from the text, the reader can distinguish between the two categories by the date of publication. Anything printed before June 8 can be taken to have been straight reporting, June 8 being the day on which the *People's Daily* initiated the counter-attack.

I have arranged the material according to the kind of person uttering it—*i.e.*, under such headings as scholars, students, etc. This gives some idea of how the same general criticisms were voiced by different sections of the intelligentsia; it also permits the grouping together of criticisms relating only to the treatment of particular sections of the intelligentsia. I have thought it helpful to provide a brief introduction to each subdivision; in these introductions I have noted features of particular interest in the criticisms, provided background or discussed the role of that particular section during the six-week period of criticism. I have attempted to keep these introductory notes as factual as possible; but they include a measure of comment and interpretation, and the reader who wishes to form his own opinion without preliminary instruction can simply read the translations. Much of the material speaks for itself.

To put the period of criticism (roughly May 1 to June 8) in perspective I have added a prelude and a postface. The former traces the development of events from the time of Mao Tse-tung's speech on contradictions in February 1957 (the event which started the episode) to May 1. The aftermath describes the fate of the critics after the counter-attack started on June 8.

Representativeness has been a major criterion for the selection of criticisms. I have also selected some for their unusual violence and others for their detailed enumeration of defects. Some criticisms have been recorded because those who made them were interesting personalities.

A great deal of the material has been drawn from the excellent and voluminous translation service provided by the United States Consulate-General in Hongkong. Where I have thought it necessary, I have made the English more idiomatic. Wherever possible, I have checked doubtful points with the original.

A considerable amount of material has been specially translated from the *Kuang Ming Daily* and magazines such as the *Wen Yi Pao* (*Journal of Literature and Arts*) not covered by these American translations. I have to thank Dr. Y. S. Ch'en for enabling me to get this material translated. Unfortunately, cartoons I had photostatted could not be reproduced.

Much of the criticism was voiced at forums summoned by various bodies such as Communist Party committees, professional organisations, etc. At the head of reports of such meetings are the place at which it was convened and the name of the Convening body, *e.g.*, SIAN: *Kuang Ming Daily*. I have occasionally departed from this rule where another method of describing the forum seemed more appropriate. Sources are indicated at the end of the extracts.

Apart from the Shanghai *Wen Hui Pao*, newspapers are published in Peking unless otherwise indicated. NCNA reports emanate from the place they are talking about unless otherwise indicated.

I have attempted to ensure that all names are transliterated in accordance with the Wade-Giles system, but I trust Sinologists will pardon cases of missing apostrophes and umlauts.

I am particularly indebted to Mr. G. F. Hudson for providing an epilogue that describes the whole Communist " thaw " and the place of China's " Hundred Flowers " period in it. My introduction attempts to answer the question: Why did Mao do it?

My thanks are due to various people and organisations who have kindly provided me with material: Reuter permitted me to use the dispatches of David Chipp from Peking; Radio Free Europe provided me with data on East European reactions to Chinese developments; CBS Radio and Television provided me with the script of " Face the Nation " for June 2, 1957; the Union Research Institute, Hongkong, sent me photostats of *Man Hua*, the Chinese cartoon magazine; Macmillan & Co. allowed me to quote from Edgar Faure's book, *The Serpent and the Tortoise*; Pierre Montader of the Commission Internationale contre le Régime Concentrationnaire supplied me with much Chinese material; Prof. Hawkes of Oxford University allowed me to use his file of the *Kuang Ming Daily*. My greatest debt is to the staff of the United States Consulate-General, Hongkong, for their excellent translation service.

I am indebted to Sheila MacCrindle and Gina Monk for typing a first draft from illegibly annotated texts. Finally, I must thank the Congress for Cultural Freedom which commissioned the project, encouraged its growth and patiently waited for it to mature.

R. MacF.

ABBREVIATIONS

ACFDW	All-China Federation of Democratic Women.
ACFIC	All-China Federation of Industry and Commerce.
CAPD	China Association for Promoting Democracy.
CCKT	China Chih Kung [Tang] Party.
CDL	China Democratic League.
CDNCA	China Democratic National Construction Association.
CP	Communist Party.
CPPCC	Chinese People's Political Consultative Conference.
CPWDP	China Peasants' and Workers' Democratic Party.
CSS	Chiu San Society.
KMTRC	Kuomintang Revolutionary Committee.
NCNA	New China News Agency.
NPC	National People's Congress.
the Party	The Communist Party.
UFWD	United Front Work Department (of the Communist Party).

INTRODUCTION

1

THE END OF AN ILLUSION

For a brief six weeks in the early summer of 1957, Mao Tse-tung, Chairman of the Chinese People's Republic and of its Communist Party, invited his country's academic, artistic and managerial intelligentsia to criticise his régime. To the outside world, the episode has come to be known as the " Hundred Flowers " period after Mao's earlier slogan " Let a hundred flowers bloom, let a hundred schools contend." Chinese Communists could be pardoned if they were to remember it as the period of the 1,000 weeds. Certainly the intelligentsia responded enthusiastically; as one non-Communist put it in a wry reference to economic slogans, they over-fulfilled their plan. But their response was hardly on the desired lines. Mao had asked for well-intentioned criticisms, to be expressed as gently as " a breeze or mild rain." But many critics spoke forcefully and bitterly and the attack by some on the fundamental tenets of the régime could hardly be regarded by Communists as well-intentioned. Soon the critics had to be silenced and counter-attacked. But why did Mao do it? Why should the leader of a totalitarian state open such an obvious Pandora's box?

A full answer must begin with Mao Tse-tung's own views on how to rule China, for his were the formative ideas behind the " liberal " policies of 1956–57 which culminated in the decision to invite criticisms. Mao clearly believes that the Communist Party governs China on behalf of the vast majority of the Chinese people and not just on behalf of the workers whose vanguard it theoretically is. It is enabled to do so because the desires and needs of that vast majority are basically the same.

The all-pervading theme of Mao's writings is unity—the basic unity of the Chinese people triumphing over the less vital, though by no means superficial, class interests which divide them. The most advanced class—the proletariat—must lead because it alone has the requisite knowledge and revolutionary ardour. But the direction it takes is acceptable to the other classes—the peasants, the small traders and artisans (petty bourgeoisie), and the patriotic business men (national business men)—though they find it difficult to see and follow of their own accord.

Of course all Communist Parties claim to speak for the whole people. But Mao had reasonable grounds for thinking in 1949 that his own broad aims would be acceptable to most Chinese. When he and his colleagues became Communists in the early twenties, China was at the mercy of foreign Powers who had exacted from her humiliating concessions. All politically articulate Chinese sought means to end the interminable strife of the warlords and unite the country under a strong government; the latter could then expel the imperialists and initiate the economic development that would enable the country to hold its own with foreign Powers and its people to put an end to their poverty. Rightly or wrongly, a large number of Chinese, regardless of political affiliation, attributed the plight of China entirely to foreign oppression; Chiang Kai-shek's book, *China's Destiny*, published during the last war is an outstanding example of this thinking. Those who turned to Communism did so as nationalists because it seemed to offer a means of ending that oppression. Its economic theory and social philosophy were, at the start anyway, quite secondary; Marxism was hardly discussed in China before 1917. It was the Russian Revolution which inspired Mao and other intellectuals because it showed them how an intellectual élite might achieve power and unite the country; and Lenin's doctrine of imperialism and the strongly anti-imperialist declarations of the Soviet Government convinced them that this was the philosophy with which China's humiliations might be ended.

It is undoubtedly this continuing substratum of nationalism in Mao's own approach to Marxism-Leninism that permits him to believe that the Communist Party can command universal support. During the thirties he would have noted the enthusiastic response of non-Communists to his appeals for national unity in the face of the Japanese invader. And when he came to set up his government in 1949, it must have been clear to him, as it was to Western observers on the spot, that the Chinese intelligentsia were prepared to support the Communist Party because, as nationalists, they hoped and believed it would solve China's problems. From his point of view, their support certainly had practical advantages. Their skills and knowledge were valuable to the régime; and the prestige of the latter would be increased by the adherence of men of considerable standing in the country. Thus self-interest would have increased his desire to stress the factor of unity.

The firmness of Mao's belief in the existence of such a unity based on nationalism and patriotism was exhibited both in theory and practice. On the theoretical plane, Mao has shunned the conventional Marxist-Leninist term " proletarian dictatorship " when describing the structure of the Chinese State. As the American scholar Benjamin Schwartz has pointed out, it was only in 1956 that the Chinese finally identified that term with the Maoist designation of China as a " People's Democratic Dictatorship." This was done, almost in passing, as a concession to Sino-Soviet solidarity in the ideological sphere; and it did not prevent Mao from omitting all mention of the term " proletarian dictatorship " in his speech on contradictions ten months later. His own term " People's Democratic Dictatorship " signifies a joint dictatorship of workers, peasants, petty bourgeoisie and national bourgeoisie, over the small minority of counter-revolutionaries and criminals who, by their activities, excluded themselves from definition as members of the people.

It might well be argued that what was a People's Democratic Dictatorship in theory was a proletarian dictatorship in practice. It was. As the criticisms of the " Hundred Flowers " period show, the " united front " government set up by Mao in 1949 which included a number of non-Communist parties was but a façade. All real power was in the hands of the Communist Party and no attempt was made to disguise its leading role. But Marxist-Leninists do not insist on theoretical formulations, however meaningless, for nothing. The pre-1949 united front could be dismissed as a typical tactic of Communist Parties in opposition; united front in the initial years of a Communist state might be merely a means of quietly consolidating power as in Eastern Europe. But the theory of Communist China's united front has been kept alive for a decade and there is no sign of its being abandoned—even though the abolition of private property has effectively removed what for a Marxist is the necessary economic justification for the existence of parties professing capitalist ideologies. One can only assume that for Mao, the underlying unity of the Chinese people persists and that therefore the theory of the People's Democratic Dictatorship must be preserved.

But while assuming this broad underlying unity, Mao as a Marxist-Leninist also devoted great attention to class differences and the question of class struggle. He was fully aware that many of his policies would meet with opposition. The Chinese peasant's desire to have his own plot of land would be an obstacle to collectivisation; business men would object to nationalisation. To achieve such policies and to ensure unquestioning acceptance of Communist Party leadership and Marxist-Leninist doctrine from an intelligentsia trained for the most part in Western democratic ideals, there had to be class struggle. But—and this is the major practical implication of Mao's general views—this class struggle did not need to be carried to the lengths it was in Russia with the slaughter and deportation of dissenting peasants and bourgeoisie on a large scale. Because of the basic unity of aims of the Chinese people, individual class interests could be overcome by education. Nationalist agents and other actively " counter-revolutionary " opponents of the régime would be executed or imprisoned. But the vast majority of the population could be won over by persuasion. This is the argument behind the relentless ideological " remoulding " campaigns, the political study courses, the endless sessions of criticism and self-criticism. For Mao Tse-tung, " brain-washing " is not a bad term; it is the desirable and humane alternative to physical elimination, an assault on the mind rather than on the body. But even if the motives were good, " brain-washing " in practice, as the critics of the " Hundred Flowers " period made clear, was far from humane. Under its pressure, many committed suicide; those who survived were embittered rather than educated.

This process of education lasted six years until the end of 1955 when the Chinese " thaw " began. The Communists had no illusions that they had by then instilled the principles of Marxism-Leninism in the minds of the intellectuals; only 40 per cent. were described as progressive and active supporters of socialism by Chou En-lai, the Chinese Premier, in 1956. Nor did they think that they had eradicated the peasants' " spontaneous tendency to capitalism "; but what they had done was to herd them into collective farms. In the autumn of 1955, at a signal from Mao, the pace of collectivisation had been increased. Within three months the process was all but completed, probably much to the surprise of Mao himself who had not anticipated success until well into the 1960s. But as soon as he saw how well rural collectivisation was going, he started a similar movement among handicraftsmen and quickly nationalised private commerce and industry. A vast property revolution was accomplished virtually overnight without the major dislocation that had accompanied similar changes in the Soviet Union. These were the institutional reforms which for reasons of dogma and political and economic control Mao deemed basic; above all, rural collectivisation was necessary to enable the government securely to control the grain surpluses that helped to pay for industrialisation.

At the same time they were the changes that had been most likely to arouse popular opposition. Once they had been engineered, Mao could relax the pressure on his subjects. And since the Communist Party was now to devote all its efforts to economic development, a task for which Mao could anticipate popular support, class differences and class struggle could be put into the background and the underlying unity of the people brought into full play. Such were the original motives for initiating the Chinese " thaw." In January 1956, political pressure was relaxed from the go-ahead rich peasants who had been the prime object of class struggle in the latter phases of collectivisation and even ex-landlords seemed destined for gentler treatment. In the same month, Chou En-lai promised the intellectuals a better standard of living and less political study. Ultimately, they would still have to undergo complete thought reform; but the Party was now prepared to await the " gradual awakening of their consciousness."

The problem of the intellectuals was particularly pressing. Thought reform had reduced scholarship to recitation from approved textbooks; and the demand that writers should adhere to the norms of "socialist realism" had effectively stifled artistic creation. Bearing in mind the shortage of intellectuals in general—officially estimated at 3·8 million—and of highly qualified ones in particular—100,000—the problem was clearly serious. In May, Mao Tse-tung attempted to encourage greater initiative in the cultural sphere with the slogan "Let a hundred flowers bloom, let a hundred schools contend." (Mao's speech was never published, but it was publicly interpreted by Lu Ting-yi, head of the Party's propaganda department.) "Let a hundred flowers bloom" referred primarily to the literary field, though in China and abroad it later took on a wider connotation; it was a phrase apparently coined by Mao himself. With it Mao gave permission for artists to disregard socialist realism provided their art served the people; even writing about fairies was permissible so long as one's books were read. The slogan "Let a hundred schools contend" was less original. The "hundred schools" is the name, derived from the Taoist sage Chuangtze, usually given to the flourishing of philosophical speculation in China during the third and fourth centuries B.C. Mao's adaptation of it was designed to encourage scholarship. The natural sciences were declared to have no class character—in other words it was permissible to study Western scientific achievements. The position was made less clear on the sensitive field of the social sciences. But Party members were warned against monopolising it and it was indicated that the Chinese Communists would not copy Stalin in producing a textbook of distorted Party history to which historians would have to make their material conform. In general for all intellectual activity the prescription was: the aim of converting all to Marxism-Leninism stands, but for the moment non-Marxist ideas can be held and propagated so long as they do not mean active counter-revolutionary activity.

The policy did bring some results, mainly in the literary field; but on the whole the intellectuals were cautious after the mental batterings they had sustained over the previous six years for saying the wrong thing and holding non-Marxist beliefs. It must have been clear to Mao that a more radical policy was necessary if cultural "liberalisation" was to mean anything. Indeed, from the beginning of 1956, Mao was clearly examining the whole question of how totalitarian rule might be made less oppressive. The January changes were, as has been suggested, part of an overall shift, of a strategic rather than a tactical nature, from " hard " to " soft " policies. But from the point of view of non-members of the Party, this was not obvious. Even Party members could take it merely as a tactical change; their own position had not suffered. They had substituted the carrot for the stick, but the latter was always handy.

As early as June 1956, with the revelations of Mr. Khrushchev's secret speech before him to spur him on, Mao had ordered his Party officials to examine their methods of work. But it was the Hungarian revolt that brought home to him the vital necessity of bettering relations between Party and people. Though he did not believe the situation in China to be so serious as it had been in Hungary—the Chinese " thaw " was in no sense a retreat in the face of popular pressure—strikes by workers and students had shown him that the Chinese people would not indefinitely tolerate brutal and high-handed officials. Mao certainly had always been aware of the shortcomings of Party members; the methods of some were even officially compared to those of the Chinese Nationalists, the worst possible criticism by Communist standards. But while the Party was disciplining the people in the class struggle, Mao could not attempt a major reform of methods for fear of disrupting that work by diminishing self-confidence. After collectivisation it was possible; and the economic difficulties and shortages of consumer goods in the winter of 1956–57 made it even more imperative that the people should be treated correctly to prevent popular demonstrations. Indeed, the rectification campaign was put forward by a year from 1958, so important were its tasks considered.

Mao's speech on contradictions (or conflicts) among the people, made on February 27, 1957, was designed to provide the essential theoretical underpinning for a lasting " liberal " policy that would prevent tensions within China increasing to the point where revolution of the Hungarian type might break out. After China's support for the suppression of the Hungarian revolt it was a necessary guarantee to non-Communists that " liberalism " was to be a permanent feature of the Chinese scene. And without such a theoretical formulation, Party officials would have been unlikely to treat the new line with the respect Mao desired.

The main message of his speech was simple. Even in a Communist country, conflicts of interest must arise; in particular the interests of the government, for all that it truly represented the people, might conflict with those of the people. The state might

---

"Certain limits" are necessary—Edgar Faure interviews Mao

PEKING May 30

. . . In appearance Mao Tse-tung seemed not so young, not so full-faced, not quite so supple as in his current photographs. He is powerful in build with a vigorous bearing. . . . His manners are of extreme and pleasing simplicity. . . .

What can be expected from the "cheng-feng" [rectification movement], the Hundred Flowers and the Hundred Schools? I told the President of the intense interest that we had in these campaigns which might be held to show—though from a very different angle—a "liberalising" tendency.

"Yes, criticisms must be allowed. If not, centres of irritation and incomprehension are created. Men must be allowed to say what they have in their hearts."

He confirmed that the two movements are linked, and that they are inspired by a similar tendency.

But: "One must take account of special conditions. With a people like this it is necessary to observe certain limits."

The comments and tone of the President on this matter confirmed me in the view that I had already formed. Certainly these two campaigns are not a negligible matter, but it would be a great mistake to see in them a major turning point from the Western angle. We have not gone beyond the varying limits allowed by the Communist régimes. Moreover, we are coming once again towards the middle line which has always been that of Mao Tse-tung: careful handling of the non-Communists, the incorporation of different sectors of the country's life into the régime, and education of the Communists themselves in order to make them understand these aims. . . .

[From "The Serpent and the Tortoise." London, 1958

want more centralism, the people more democracy. The state might pay more attention to overall and long-term interests, the people to their immediate wants. Autocratic officials enforcing state policies might anger the people by their behaviour. All this was inevitable and should not cause worry; the essential thing to remember was that when such conflicts arose, they must be solved without force because they were " among the people." In other words, officials should not treat strikers as counter-revolutionaries and the people should not regard Communist officials as being no better than the Nationalists. Discussion, not force, was to be the method by which disputes were to be solved. There was nothing in Mao's theme of democracy or any suggestion that any basic aims had been abandoned. His aim was to retain his system intact, but to ensure permanent modification of the severity of its impact on the people. At best Mao is a benevolent despot. Neither his Chinese background nor his Comintern training provided him with any of the genuinely democratic ideals which seem to have given Lenin cause for self-reproach in his later years for the system he had created.

The rectification campaign that was launched two months after Mao had made this speech was designed to make the new theoretical line part of the practice of Party officials. It was entitled the movement to " rectify the style of work " (cheng-tun tso-feng, or cheng-feng for short) after a similar campaign launched in 1942. The latter was mainly concerned with brutal methods in intra-Party struggle, a heritage from the period of Comintern domination prior to Mao's assuming the leadership in 1935. Now he wished to eliminate the same methods as applied against outsiders. It was in order to find out how the Party had misused its powers that Mao gave non-Communists, who were in the best position to know, the chance to voice criticisms. The Party would then reform on the basis of them.

But as the criticisms soon revealed, Mao had made a major mistake when he started his speech on contradictions with the words: " Never has our country been as united as it is today." As far as the intelligentsia was concerned this was no longer true. One cannot tell whether Mao's theory of the People's Democratic

Dictatorship had in fact meant fewer deaths than Stalin's proletarian dictatorship. But certainly the criticisms suggest that in the three-anti and five-anti movements and the campaign against counter-revolutionaries, violence played a more important part than theory allowed. The most alarming aspect from Mao's point of view was the complete disenchantment that large numbers of students showed with the régime. These youths had been largely educated under Communism, had been courted and told the future was theirs; yet they were the most violent among those who turned on the régime. Indeed, it was probably the student unrest that led Mao to halt the flow of criticisms. With the bad economic conditions then prevailing, he may have feared they could incite a wave of strikes. There were suggestions by non-Communist Chinese that Mao had been forced to agree to a reversal under pressure by less "liberal" Party officials led by Liu Shao-ch'i, second in the Party hierarchy. But it is doubtful if Mao could have wanted to pursue the policy under the circumstances. Students and other critics had voiced demands for genuine democracy to prevent future abuses. Mao could never tolerate such demands.

How did Mao come to make this colossal mistake? How did a man who has shown himself a skilled politician and a shrewd observer of the people fail to realise the vast reservoir of discontent that had been built up? The Communist Party later claimed that there had been no mistake, that all along it had aimed to provoke such critics to come into the open. But it could scarcely have done otherwise. As the custodian of Marxism-Leninism, it could never admit that events took it by surprise. On balance it is most unlikely that Mao set a trap. There were no indications before the invitation to critics that he had abandoned his major principles, though some intellectuals were clearly hazy as to the amount of freedom they had to criticise them. It is certainly unlikely that Mao would have gone to all the trouble of formulating his doctrine on contradictions to unearth bourgeois thoughts of whose existence he was already aware.

It is perhaps easy to say that Mao was the victim of his own propaganda, but there is some truth in the suggestion. No non-Communist was willing to step out of line so long as he was likely to be subjected to endless attacks for doing so. Since he parroted the official line there was no way of knowing how he really felt; Mao might correctly guess that an intellectual still harboured bourgeois thoughts. But he would have no way of knowing the degree of bitterness that had been built up inside him.

Probably it would be more correct to say Mao was the victim of his own ideas and illusions. He really believed in the fundamental unity of the Chinese people and believed that the methods he had employed had preserved that unity. He knew mistakes had been made; the whole object of the rectification campaign was to prevent their recurrence. But he firmly believed that the conventional Communist formula—often criticised during the " Hundred Flowers " period—that achievements were primary and defects secondary really corresponded to the facts.

Some students attacked Mao's ideas as metaphysical. There is a certain truth in the accusation. The fundamental assumption of the rectification campaign was that one could make a totalitarian régime acceptable simply by rectifying the conduct of those who held power. This is a very Chinese idea. Only one thing modified the despotism of imperial China outside of its imperfect methods of control. And that Confucian tenet that government should be by good example, that if the ruler's conduct is correct the state will be well run, would seem to lurk in Mao's mind. Both in imperial times and today, such literally idealistic notions take no account of the facts of despotic institutions. Mao was using all the devices of control perfected under Stalin; and the normal corrupting influence of power was aggravated by the fact that a large proportion of the Party's twelve million members had jumped on the band-wagon after 1949 simply for the sake of the privileges Party membership would bring.

Mao continues to try to rectify the Party's conduct. Officials are now ordered to do regular spells of manual labour to bring them closer to the people. But at the same time other officials are permitted to drive the peasants remorselessly in the new communes to fulfil the grandiose plans of the economic " leap forward." Attempts to ameliorate Communist totalitarianism will always founder on reasons of state in this way. An élite which is firmly confident of its rightness in delineating policy and which has no institutional checks upon its exercise of power will not fail ultimately to force through its aims. Mao may rectify individual situations; but he can never solve the underlying contradiction between the desire to use power and the temptation to abuse it.

The idea that free discussion can take place in a totalitarian society is equally metaphysical. The original " Hundred Schools " contended at a time of such political disunity that it is known as the Warring States period. With the creation of the centralised empire, disputation was stopped. In this century, a hundred schools did contend in the turbulent period between the fall of the Manchus and the triumph of the Communists. During those four decades, Chinese intellectuals eagerly investigated diverse foreign doctrines. Such freedom could hardly be envisaged when the state was again unified and one doctrine proclaimed supreme. Mao had everything in his favour—immense prestige, a disciplined and loyal Party, a stable state. Yet he still found genuine intellectual freedom too dangerous. His reaction was to castigate the intellectuals and turn back to his old allies, the peasants. The 1958 " great leap forward " was launched on the premiss that manual labourers working all-out could do anything intellectuals could do better. Eventually the régime will need its intellectuals again. Scholars will be excused from their long hours of " practical " work and manual labour, and academic life will return to normal. But neither Mao Tse-tung nor his successors are likely to call again for a hundred flowers to bloom.

PRELUDE

"If a ruler rectifies his own conduct, government is an easy matter, and if he does not rectify his own conduct, how can he rectify others?"

—Confucius: *The Analects*

2

A FEELING OF EARLY SPRING

On the afternoon of February 27, 1957, Mao Tse-tung addressed a closed session of the Supreme State Conference in Peking on the conflicts and tensions existing in China. His speech was entitled: "On the correct handling of contradictions among the people." On the following two days, it was discussed by the 1,800 participants in the conference who comprised the cream of China's Communist and non-Communist élite.

During March and April, Mao's words were carried further. The vast corps of Party propagandists related and explained them to people at all levels throughout the country. Then, on April 30, the Communist Party launched a campaign to rectify its "style of work," taking the principles outlined by Mao as its guide. To find out the mistakes it had made, the Party invited non-Communist officials and intellectuals to proffer criticisms. A trickle at first, the criticisms soon grew to a torrent forcing the Communist Party to call a halt, and on June 8 the official Party paper, the *People's Daily*, published the first of a series of editorials counter-attacking the critics.

It is the criticisms made of the Party that make up the bulk of the documentary section of this book. Some of them are denunciations of the foundations of Communist rule; more are bitter attacks on the abuses of Communist officialdom. To understand how such views could be put forward in a totalitarian state, it is essential to understand the situation created by Mao's speech, the atmosphere within China during the two months that preceded the invitation to critics to speak up.

Unfortunately, we cannot be sure that we know exactly what Mao Tse-tung said on February 27. The announcement of his speech was bereft of all details of its content. When a text was finally published on June 18, it was admitted to contain additions.

We shall see that these additions were almost certainly very important ones.

However, during the two months preceding the launching of the "rectification campaign" on April 30, the *People's Daily* explained the most important points of the speech. At this stage, before the outpouring of criticism, there was clearly no need for amending Mao's original text and we can take it that the paper's editorials correspond fairly closely to the original theme.

Contradictions, the paper explained on April 13, exist within all things and processes and are indeed the motive force of development and progress. In class societies, contradictions (or conflicts) between the rival classes are extremely bitter and are called antagonistic. That between the Chinese Communists and Nationalists had had to be solved by force; but as a result of Communist victory in the civil war and the subsequent collectivisation of agriculture and nationalisation of industry, antagonistic class contradictions within China had been eliminated. Such contradictions as remained were non-antagonistic and could be resolved by discussion and persuasion. This was because the interests of the people were fundamentally the same.

Many of the contradictions among the people take the form of conflicts between the leaders and the masses whom they lead. This is because all the various policies and principles are decided on at the top and then have to be performed by the people. Since the leaders are concerned with broad programmes and long-term policies, they are apt to neglect the immediate interests of the people; on the other hand, the people immersed in physical labour with little time to take part in government are inclined to attach too much importance to their own particular local problems.

In present-day China, the editorial went on, it is the bureaucratic approach of the leaders that is the main cause of contradictions between them and the people. Some leaders neither understand the masses nor pay any attention to their opinions. They shelve their problems and even wantonly suppress their demands.

To solve this problem, the *People's Daily* advocated two things; greater supervision of the leadership through regular meetings of factory workers and collective farmers and, secondly, more intensive educational and propaganda work to explain to the people why their needs could not be met, to help them understand the general situation in the country and see their problems in a wider perspective.

Four days later, the *People's Daily* again took up the theme of how to eliminate the bureaucratic habits of leaders. The practice of criticism and self-criticism should be greatly encouraged. No one, however exalted, should be immune. Criticism and self-criticism should be looked on as being as much a part of the daily routine as washing one's face or cleaning one's house. If Party and state organisations accepted correct criticisms and rectified their mistakes, their prestige in the eyes of the people could only be enhanced.

If this was the basic message of Mao's speech, it is hardly surprising that he made a good impression on the non-Communists in his audience. One was said to have been " so stimulated by Chairman Mao's address that he could not sleep for one whole night! " The element of exaggeration in this report from a Hongkong Communist newspaper is obvious; but later events do indicate that many non-Communists were cheered and misled by Mao's " benevolence." After all, he had admitted that the Communist Party, clearly the principal element in the national leadership, was to blame for many of the tensions within China by its authoritarian behaviour. The Party was now to accept criticism and attempt to reform. To " the led " this could only be pleasing.

Certainly there were enough problems requiring solution. At the session of the Chinese People's Political Consultative Conference in March, Lo Lung-chi, Minister of the Timber Industry and Deputy Chairman of the Democratic League, outlined the grievances of the scholars, soon to be in the forefront of the régime's critics. At the same session, Chang Po-chun, Minister of Communications, also a Deputy Chairman of the Democratic League, put forward his suggestion as to how the democratic parties might play the greater role demanded of them under the new policy of " long-term coexistence and mutual supervision " with the Communist Party. A month later, David Chipp, Reuter's Peking correspondent, sent home a dispatch which accurately summed up the explosive situation in the universities. His report and

Lo Lung-chi's speech provide an excellent background for the understanding of later developments.

Lo Lung-chi speaks for the intellectuals

" At present, what still constitute the problems relating to the intellectuals? In the matter of arrangement and employment, some conditions need still to be further readjusted. There are students of philosophy who work on the compilation of catalogues in libraries, students of law who take up book-keeping work in offices, students of dye chemistry who teach languages in middle schools, and students of mechanical engineering who teach history in middle schools. Many higher intellectuals who study social sciences, particularly those who study political science and law and finance and economics, have no class to teach although they are on school pay-rolls. Among the higher intellectuals, there are also returned students from Britain who earn their living as cart-pullers and returned students from the United States who run cigarette stalls. These are of course only instances that are found in individual places and units. . . .

". . . the teaching work of the primary school teachers is heavy enough. Notwithstanding this, they are required by the cadres in some places to do odd jobs, to work as copyists in offices, to sell books for book-stores, to drill wells and build dykes in the countryside, and to dry grain and to keep watch on granaries. The primary school teachers are tired of these orders. . . .

" The key problem lies today in how to eliminate the chasm between the Party and the non-Party personnel. . . . Premier Chou En-lai pointed out one year ago that ' the chasm frequently owes its existence to both sides.' At the same time, he laid it down that the Party member cadres ' must take the initiative of exerting themselves to have the chasm eliminated.' I consider this view is absolutely correct. . . .

" Take some specific instances. . . . A small number of professors have complained about the unfairness of adopting the grading system to improve the treatment of the higher intellectuals on the grounds that more weight has been attached to political standing than academic attainment and that Party and Youth League members have been graded higher than the non-Party personnel. . . . This reflects of course the one-sided view of the minority. Nevertheless it calls for the leadership cadres to take the initiative and exert themselves so that investigations may be conducted to find out whether there is insufficient consultation made in administrative work, whether there is the shortcoming of insufficient democracy, and whether the defect of sectarianism has been inadvertently committed. . . .

" During the past year, not many flowers bloomed and few schools of thought contended in the academic and ideological fields . . . the basic cause lies in the fact that the higher intellectuals are still suspicious and are still plagued by misgivings. . . . In my opinion, the occurrence of this phenomenon is primarily due to the lack of a correct appreciation and comprehension of these two slogans on the part of some Party member cadres and the small number of progressive intellectuals outside the Party. They feel that since the advancement of these slogans, the society has swarmed with heresies. They are therefore over-eager with the work of defending the faith. . . ."

[Speech to the CPPCC, March 18, Peking. People's Daily. March 23

Chang Po-chun speaks for the democratic parties

" Some people are worried that with all schools contended, idealism and bourgeois ideas will twist and distort Marxism. . . . It is my hope that . . . each and all will show some tolerance and will not be over-zealous to be ' defenders of the faith.' It is not right to jump on intellectuals when they start to speak, intellectuals who seek progress. . . .

" Next there is a sort of contrary view that democracy is not enough. Inasmuch as democracy is to be developed, why stress the leadership of the Communist Party, why stress democratic centralism? This way of speaking is welcome in a capitalist society, but we are not following the capitalist road but a socialist democratic road under the guidance of the working class. Democratised political life has been getting ever richer during past years; it has not declined.

" Finally permit me to say something about the Chinese People's Political Consultative Conference. The enlargement and consolidation of the people's democratic united front demands a continual increase in the tasks and work of the People's Political Consultative Conference and growing perfection and enrichment of the content and methods of the People's Political Consultative Conference's work. Capitalist countries have a two-chamber parliamentary system; socialist countries like the Soviet Union and Yugoslavia also have a two-chamber system; the Council of the Union and the Council of Nationalities in the case of the former and Federal Assembly and the House of Producers in the case of the latter. With our own actual conditions, we need not be the same as others, now can we force ourselves to be the same as others. The role and development of the People's Political Consultative Conference are being strengthened. I think that beginning from its 3rd plenary session, more political tasks for the People's Political Consultative Conference should be considered. Its power, for instance, to hold consultations, make proposals and exercise supervision could be strengthened. The People's Political Consultative Conference could gradually be turned, in the course of political life, into a democratic link in the parliamentary system required for the Chinese people's democracy. After this plenary session, we should strengthen the work of the People's Political Consultative Conference at all levels from the central to the local. . . ."

[*Speech to the CPPCC, March 18, Peking People's Daily. March 19*

Dry tinder in the schools

Dissatisfaction with educational facilities and career prospects among school children, students and parents is causing considerable concern to the Chinese Government. . . . According to one Chinese who attended the Supreme State Conference on February 27, Mao Tse-tung, Chairman of the central committee of the Communist Party, revealed that there had been unrest amounting to token strikes in two institutes of higher education in south-west China, while some students in a cadre (activist) training school at Cheng Ting, about 150 miles south of Peking, actually began a march on the capital. These students were apparently complaining that they had been told that they were among the cream of the nation's youth and yet were often directed to second-rate jobs . . . young people are beginning to judge the situation on its merits instead of by mere comparison with the past. If something is wrong or inefficient, they are no longer so likely to accept the explanation that it is all the fault of the imperialists or the Kuomintang's maladministration. . . .

Added to this, the great majority of students, more than 80 per cent. of the total in universities, come from middle class families and are thus "apt to cling to their bourgeois ideologies." This was the explanation given for the doubts felt by some Chinese students about the official policy in regard to recent events in Hungary. . . .

Some of the students' doubts are believed to have been increased, and possibly fostered, by discussion with students from Eastern Europe, particularly Hungary and Poland, and with overseas Chinese. . . .

Large amounts have been spent on education since the Communists came to power in 1949. . . . But in spite of these improvements it has recently been stated that about four million school children leaving primary schools this year will not be able to get into junior middle schools, about 800,000 leaving junior middle schools will not be able to go on to the senior grade, and 90,000 will not find places in institutes of higher education, including the universities. . . . Practically every school is overcrowded and some are working the two-shift system, which means that children have half the day idle. This has led to complaints of unruly classmates roaming the streets and getting up to all sorts of mischief when they are not in school.

There have also been complaints that too much time is taken up with political studies, discussion groups, and frequent attendance at mass rallies and meetings. The government is now telling those who cannot find places to start work, particularly in the countryside. . . . But this solution does not appear to appeal to many who have begun their education and hoped to complete it and get better jobs.

[*David Chipp, Reuter, Peking. April 13*

The speeches of Lo Lung-chi and Chang Po-chun are interesting for their caution. Lo Lung-chi is careful to justify his remarks by quoting from Chou En-lai and by adopting the conventional formula that shortcomings are only minor blemishes on the face of a basically healthy situation. In the same speech, he attempted (in vain as it turned out) to safeguard critics who might be less cautious by suggesting that attacks on individual Party members should not be construed as attacks on the Party itself, far less as counter-revolution.

Chang Po-chun's suggestion for the People's Political Consultative Conference is an obvious attempt to make the most of the official Communist policy of giving a greater role to the democratic parties. But his almost fawning emphasis on Communist Party leadership indicates that he has no illusions that there is any chance of real independence for them. Clearly, both he and Lo Lung-chi were aware of the limits of Mao's new policy. Yet three months later they were to be accused of leading a nation-wide plot against the Communist Party. This is a curious affair to which we will return again.

Certainly if Mao's speech had misled people they should have been able to see the new line in perspective from the tone of official comment in the months preceding the launching of the rectification campaign. Even if the *People's Daily* encouraged critics to speak out, it indicated that improper criticisms and attacks on fundamental Party policies would be repulsed. The writers were warned against promoting art for art's sake by their famous colleague Mao Tun, who had become the Communists' Minister of Culture. Editorially, the paper warned business men who hankered after capitalism, and advocated more intensive political studies for teachers and students so that they might better understand current problems.

There was no contradiction in this; it was the reverse side of the coin. While mistakes were more likely to arise from bureaucracy at the top, " one-sided " popular views were also possible. But these had to be eradicated not by force—since the contradiction was among the people and thus " non-antagonistic "—but by persuasion; in practice, this would naturally mean greater attention to propagandising Marxism-Leninism.

Some Party members, reluctant to submit themselves to criticism, clearly took heart from these reassertions of familiar doctrines and methods. The *People's Daily* warned them that they were " in danger " politically and encouraged the democratic parties to press on with their duty of criticising and supervising the Communist Party. A leading Party official, while again emphasising the need for Marxist studies, stated that the important thing was for the Party to learn from the intellectuals.

With the *People's Daily* inviting criticisms and rebuking doctrinaire Communists on the one hand and reaffirming the need for Party leadership and Marxism-Leninism on the other, it is perhaps not surprising that many were confused and apprehensive. At the paper's own forum some quite bold views were expressed, including the allegation that Marxism had not developed since 1895. But among Shanghai intellectuals there were apprehensions that the proffering of criticisms would leave one open to counter-attack. The prevailing mood was summed up in the phrase " Early Spring Weather," first coined by the noted sociologist Fei Hsiao-t'ung in an article published in March. His article had in fact been written before Mao's speech had ushered in warmer weather; but another intellectual thought the phrase was still applicable in April.

Early spring is cool; summer is in the offing, but it is too early for most flowers to bloom. Those that do may be trapped by a sudden frost. The analogy is obvious—if the hundred flowers were to bloom, if the intellectuals were to speak up, there must be an assurance that there would be no sudden reversal of policy that would find them exposed to counter-attack. In the absence of that assurance, the intellectuals would not consider the atmosphere suitable for airing their views. Past experience had made them cautious; future events were shortly to prove how right they were to be so.

But some non-Communists were beginning to swing the other way, interpreting Mao's speech in more liberal terms than intended. In rebutting these views, Teng Ch'u-min, a member of the Democratic League's standing committee, made some very significant remarks. For by suggesting that critics should be guided by "four circles," he indicated fairly conclusively that Mao had laid down no specific criteria for criticism in his February speech. After all, if the six criteria that appeared in the text published in June had been a part of the original speech, Teng would not have needed, nor indeed had the effrontery, to suggest his own criteria.

But if in China an air of uncertainty prevailed on the eve of the rectification campaign, in Poland Chinese events were already being watched with approval. Even Pavel Yudin, the Soviet Ambassador to China, admitted in fraternal mood that Russia, too, had internal contradictions—an odd slip for a noted ideologist to make and one which Mr. Khrushchev would contradict. Chou En-lai's own contribution to the conversation at Hangchow illustrates the mood of comradely *bonhomie* that the top leadership was trying to infuse into the populace, an endeavour which, as we have seen, was meeting with mixed success.

The People's Daily holds a forum

TIENTSIN

Li Chien-hsun [Vice-President, Tientsin Normal College]:

"Is Marxism-Leninism to be considered the guiding ideology in the process of contending? If it is, it may stop other schools of thought from contending; if it is not, a state of ideological confusion may result.

. . . In my opinion, Marxism-Leninism should be taken as a weapon in contending to voice one's views, but should not be definitely laid down as the guiding standard. Since Marxism-Leninism will eventually win in the contention, it is the same as taking Marxism-Leninism as the guiding ideology. . . ."

Hu Yi [President, Hopei Tientsin Normal College]:

" When questions are under discussion, there are people who seldom base their analysis on facts or their arguments on reason, but often suppress others by quoting from classical writings [*e.g.*, Marxist classics—*Ed.*] or by 'dubbing hats'[1] on others. Such a way of doing things is rather dogmatic. For it is not required that objective facts submit to classical works, but it is required that classical works be combined with objective facts. Hence we must base ourselves upon facts, and convince others by reasoning. . ."

Wang Kan-yu [Professor, Nankai Un.]:

" After the liberation, people who had in the past studied social sciences suffered a certain mental blow, because some of the social sciences were abolished and some lost their independence. . . . Much of the curricula of the past was abolished simply because there were no such curricula in the Soviet Union. . . . Take sociology for example. This is a study which is very broad in scope. When this department was abolished, many specialised fields—such as demography, ethnology, and social thought—were ignored and no one studied them. . . ."

Lei Hai-tsung [Professor, head of world history teaching research group, Nankai Un.]:

" . . . in regard to the new social science established by Marx and Engels, all people are unanimously agreed in theory that Marxism-Leninism should continue to develop. Actually, however, it ceased to develop long ago, and has remained as it was when Engels died in 1895. After 1895, Lenin and Stalin put forward certain new ideas about the problems of revolution facing them at that time. As far as the understanding and sorting of mankind's several thousand years of historical experiences, and the establishment of a new social science is concerned, Marxism has been on the whole stagnant since 1895. . . .

" Marx and Engels constantly revised their own theories when they were alive, keeping an eye on the conditions of development in every

[1] *i.e.*, labelling critics as anti-Marxist, etc.

branch of social science, and grasping the materials and fruits of scientific research. But their successors thought Marx and Engels had solved all problems and that social science could develop no further. This was not in accordance with the facts; after 1895, there were plenty of new materials in the field of social sciences and many new interpretations had been given to old materials. Our task today is to make up all the lessons we have omitted during the sixty-two years since 1895. This is a problem not of any one individual, but of the whole socialist camp, and the work is hard indeed. . . ."

[*People's Daily* editor's note:

Mr. Lei is also of the opinion that Lenin's contribution to Marxism was limited to "certain new ideas about some individual problems," and that Marxism "has on the whole been stagnant since 1895." This is, however, contrary to the facts. The social science of Marxism includes the basic Marxist theories concerning social developments, but not individual conclusions for individual cases. It was precisely in a series of basic theories in the field of social science—first of all the basic theories relating to imperialism, to the proletarian revolution and proletarian dictatorship, and to socialist construction—that Lenin developed Marxism. . . .]

Pao Chueh-min [Professor, Nankai Un.]:

"As a student of economic geography, I was always haunted with the fear of being dubbed with the hat of 'geographical determinism.' After the liberation there was a unanimous clamour for studying the advanced sciences and experiences of the Soviet Union, which phenomenon was good indeed. At the same time, however, bound by certain dogmas, I was forced to accept all things from the Soviet Union, lock, stock and barrel, despite the fact that some of the things were not convincing enough to me. . . ."

[Forum held April 14. People's Daily. April 21, 22

A feeling of "early spring"

In his article, "Why is there a feeling of 'early spring'?" *People's Daily*, April 20, Ch'ien Po-tsan wrote:

"The policy of 'Let a hundred flowers bloom, let a hundred schools contend' has been advanced for more than half a year. Why is it that there is still the feeling of 'early spring'? . . . Although the slogan . . . has been released, yet the leadership cadres in some places or establishments are limiting themselves to giving lip service to the slogan without taking action to make flowers blossom forth or relaxing their restrictions. As a result some people say: 'The thunder clap is loud, but the raindrops are small!' . . .

It is precisely because there are only thunder claps but no rain and that there is nobody coming down the staircase although footsteps can be heard that the intellectuals are still at the stage of groping their way at the moment. They have to speculate for example whether the call for flowers to bloom forth is sincere or just a gesture. They have to guess to what extent, if the call is sincere, flowers will be allowed to blossom forth and whether the call will be recalled after the flowers are in bloom. They have to guess whether the call for flowers is the end or just a means and whether the call is made for the sake of bringing prosperity to culture and science or of unearthing thoughts and rectifying individuals. They have to guess which are the problems that can be brought up for discussion and which are the problems which cannot be discussed. All these questions have been raised.

Due to the misgivings of the intellectuals, when the leadership cadres of some establishments limit themselves to the giving of lip service to the call without taking action to make flowers blossom forth, relaxing their restrictions, the intellectuals also refrain from airing their views and entering into controversy about the views aired. . . ."

[*NCNA, April 21*

An envious glance at China

POLAND

We know the slogan "Let all the flowers bloom" and we look with sorrow on the Polish meadow. The unheard-of devaluation of intellectual work which has become a fact during recent years is the practical expression of the position of the intelligentsia. There has been a violation of the normal differential between remuneration for simple and for complicated work, for unqualified and for skilled work, for manual and for intellectual work, and the results of this may be dangerous. . . .

[W. Lechoowicz, Vice-chairman, Democratic Party. Tygodnik Demokratyczny. Warsaw. April 3–9

What did Mao really say?

PEKING

There can be different interpretations of Chairman Mao's speech on the problem of "Correctly handling contradictions among the people" at the meeting of the Supreme State Conference. Teng Ch'u-min said at the forum [of the Democratic League]: "After hearing this report some people probably think that Chairman Mao only advocates 'blooming'; however, my understanding is that there is 'contraction' in 'blooming.' For instance, there should be the picking of weeds and there should be criticism of idealism. A hundred schools have to contend; but as a result of contention, there is only one truth under a fixed set of circumstances. . . ."

Teng Ch'u-min felt that four circles should be drawn with reference to the contending of the hundred schools. He said: "I do not have the audacity to say that everybody else must respect these four circles I have drawn for contending, yet for my own contending I think it will be advisable not to depart from these four circles." These four circles are:

1. "The contending of the hundred schools must have leadership, namely the leadership of Marxism-Leninism."

2. "The contending of the hundred schools must have direction, namely the direction of socialism."

3. "The contending of the hundred schools must have a boundary, namely it must be confined to the people and enemies should not be allowed to take part."

4. "The contending of the hundred schools must have a criterion. Practice is the criterion of truth and of contending."

The speech of Shen Chih-yuan [standing committee, CDL] revealed clear disagreement with Teng Ch'u-min's opinions. He said that on hearing Chairman Mao's speech, "the basic spirit underlying this report, as I understood it, lies in the word 'blooming,' that is, loosening the grip boldly and widely blooming. He held that 'loosening the grip' and 'widely blooming' were not the same thing as advocating idealism and the ideology of the capitalist class. . . . Only through the contending of the hundred schools—not the solo performance of one school, nor the pontificating of one school . . . could the real scientific truth be brought into the light of day and mastered by people. . . ."

Then Shen Chih-yuan went on to oppose views held by some people. He said: "To take this line of approach is not to associate oneself with that attitude taken by some comrades who hold that the object of letting the hundred schools contend is to unmask the bourgeois and petty-bourgeois thoughts of others so that we can attack them relentlessly and thereby strengthen Marxism-Leninism. Such an explanation which interprets the policy of letting a hundred schools contend as a device for 'inducing the enemy to fall into the trap, in order to liquidate them *en masse*' is not an appropriate one. . . ."

[*Kuang Ming Daily. April 21*

Fresh flowers and poisonous weeds

Teng Ch'u-min replies

I must first of all admit that comrade Shen Chih-yuan's views are correct and illuminating, and that his understanding of the basic spirit of Chairman Mao's speech is very close to mine. . . . When I said there was "contraction" in "blooming" I was by no means objecting to blooming; on the contrary, I was in favour of it. . . . Then what is meant by "there is contraction in blooming"?

I myself listened to Chairman Mao's speech. Chairman Mao said that there were fresh flowers and that there were also poisonous weeds. The peasants have to weed every year; it just would not work in practice if one were only to issue an order forbidding the poisonous weeds to grow. One simply weeds them with a hoe, that's all. He also said that criticisms ought to be proffered against the opposite of dialectical materialism—idealism. It was wrong not to criticise it. . . .

In addition, I would like to go on and discuss the problem of the so-called four circles . . . [they] are in essence only one circle—namely, we must not range the policy of "Let a hundred flowers bloom, let a hundred schools contend" against the leading position of the Party, equipped with the ideological weapon of Marxism-Leninism, in the ideological field. . . . The scope of "Let a hundred schools contend" definitely does not permit enemies to speak and behave irregularly. . . .

[*Kuang Ming Daily. April 26*

Russia, too, has contradictions

HANGCHOW

Premier Chou En-lai today welcomed Chairman Voroshilov at Hangchow airport. Before Chairman Voroshilov's plane landed, Premier Chou En-lai discussed the problem of correctly handling contradictions among the people and opposing bureaucratism with Deputy Chairman of the Presidium of the Supreme Soviet, Rashidov, the Soviet Minister for Higher Education, Yelyutin, and the Soviet Ambassador to China, Yudin, who had arrived first.

The conversation started with Premier Chou En-lai introducing the guests to the scenery of Hangchow's famous West Lake. Holding a map of Hangchow in his hand, the smiling Premier told the guests: "I have been to Hangchow twice this year already so I can tell you something about the place." Comrade Rashidov observed: "It's usually hard for a leading Communist to find time to get around to different places." "Yes, one should get around more," the Premier said, "bureaucratism will develop if one always stays in Peking. The high city walls of Peking are likely to separate the leadership from the masses." Jokingly, Rashidov said: "These city walls have their advantages, too. They keep bureaucracy within bounds." "There's still another advantage," quipped Premier Chou En-lai, "if people oppose bureaucracy the city walls will keep them off for a time. But they cannot be a certain guarantee," he said. "Walls can be breached. Nearly forty years ago, we Peking students broke into Peking's ancient city to oppose the bureaucrats and warlords of that day." He pointed to two children who had come to present flowers to Comrade Rashidov and Ambassador Yudin and said: "If we don't change our bureaucratic ways, some day they will break through the walls."

Comrade Rashidov said that he had heard of how China was carrying out a great struggle against bureaucracy. "Yes," Premier Chou replied, "only yesterday, I was making a report to 2,000 Government workers here, both Communist Party members and non-members, about the correct handling of contradictions among the people and the launching of another movement to rectify our style of work. . . . It is a common trait of man that when he scores the least achievement he gets conceited, and Communists are no exception especially at a time of victory, believing that even if they have shortcomings, people will make allowances for them."

Ambassador Yudin said: "Oh, yes. People think that since they have the support of the people, they cannot be bureaucratic." "Here lies the tragedy," Rashidov joined in, "one gets bureaucracy without being conscious of it. This work China is carrying on now is of great significance." At this moment, Premier Chou En-lai pointed to the two children and said: "If, ten years from now, there is still bureaucracy in the leadership, you should oppose it." Premier Chou En-lai continued:

" Bureaucracy is one of the contradictions among the people. After the class struggle has in the main been concluded, the contradictions among the people come to the fore . . . in the various social relations, contradictions between the leadership and the masses will also stand out." Ambassador Yudin said: " Yes, we also have such contradictions. . . ."

[*Conversation on April 25. People's Daily. April 26*

BLOOMING AND CONTENDING

"When one subdues men by force, they do not submit in their hearts (and submit outwardly only because) their strength is insufficient."

—*The Mencius*

3

INTRODUCTION: GENTLE BREEZES AND MILD RAINS

THE signal for the launching of the rectification campaign was the publication on April 30 of a directive of the Communist Party's central committee. The directive laid it down that the campaign should centre first on the correct handling of contradictions among the people. For this reason, Mao's February 27 speech (and the explanation of it which he gave to 800 Party propagandists in March) was prescribed as the text for the movement.

The full title of the campaign was " movement for the rectification of style of work." By " style of work " was meant the approach and methods of officials; the campaign was in no way depicted as designed to alter policies or programmes. In particular, rectification was designed to eradicate the " three evils " of " bureaucratism, subjectivism and sectarianism."

Bureaucratism involves what we call red tape—long-winded reports with a pretentious vocabulary, never moving from one's office and issuing orders without checking on their feasibility. Subjectivism embraces two failings, dogmatism and empiricism, dogmatism being the tendency to apply Marxist theory blindly without considering the practical situation, while empiricism is the opposite tendency to neglect theory altogether. Dogmatism has always been recognised by the Chinese as the most serious form of subjectivism; its prevalence can hardly be considered surprising when the canons of Marxism-Leninism are officially proclaimed to contain the solutions to all problems. Mao himself, while always upholding the need for theoretical analysis, has consistently attacked those who cannot apply their theory rationally to practical problems; for him, the exclusive reliance on the letter of the Communist classics is mechanical as opposed to dialectical materialism.

Both bureaucratism and dogmatism, especially the latter, are promoted by the privileged position of Communist officials. Since the latter have little fear of sanctions resulting from popular outcry, they must continually be tempted to take the easy way out—to work according to the book or the directive rather than sweat at trying to make policy fit objective conditions. A premium is put on this approach by the dutiful obedience to Party directives expected of Party officials.

But the most important result of the immunity from sanction of Communist officials is sectarianism—the practice of discriminating against people who are not members of the Party. This practice is encouraged by the Party's assumption that the weapon of Marxism-Leninism gives its members a decisive intellectual superiority over non-members because it enables them to understand and indeed predict the development of events. But while sectarianism springing from intellectual arrogance might lead only to bureaucratism and dogmatism, the sectarianism encouraged by unrestricted power had clearly led to more serious consequences. The directive launching the rectification campaign admitted that " some wavering elements are liable to be contaminated with remnants of the Kuomintang style of work from the old society, to think of themselves as privileged and even resort to attacks or oppression when dealing with the masses."

Basically, the rectification campaign was designed to eliminate what the central committee ingenuously disowned, while condemning with the worst adjective in its vocabulary, as the " Kuomintang style of work." Even senior officials were ordered to get literally closer to the people by doing regular spells of manual labour. The concept of privilege was not confined just to " some wavering elements," but was widespread throughout the Party. It was the Party's privileged position (as the directive implied) that was at the root of the contradiction between the leaders and the led. Leaders thinking of long-term needs of the country would naturally be encouraged to impose their policies without worrying about the cost to the individual; the truth is that in many cases the motives of the leaders were far less lofty than that.

The directive laid down that the campaign should be a movement of ideological education, to be carried out as gently as " a breeze or mild rain." Comradely heart-to-heart talks and small discussion groups were to be the medium by which criticism would be aired, not large-scale " struggle meetings." Except in cases of serious offences against law or discipline, mistakes revealed were not to be punished. Some non-Communist critics later objected to this mild treatment, so different from their own experiences. But clearly the Party leaders had no desire to allow critics to get out of hand.

The reason for this became clear when the Party's United Front Work Department invited leading members of the non-Communist parties and leading non-party officials to proffer criticisms of the Party at a series of forums in Peking. Soon Party organisations throughout the country were following suit and calling similar forums. It must have been realised that some critics would have considerable grievances against various Party members; hence the desire to avoid the type of denunciation meetings which the Party had employed against its subjects.

Even when the Communist Party started holding forums potential critics were cautious—particularly in the provinces, where Party officials appear to have been somewhat hesitant to encourage them. But as reports of the increasing number of forums in the capital appeared in the newspapers, " blooming " gradually started in cities throughout the country.

4

FORUMS OF LEADING NON-COMMUNISTS

THE major importance of the forums of leading non-Communists held by the Communist Party's United Front Work Department in Peking was that they revealed the illusory nature of China's "coalition" government. The Communists had never concealed that theirs was the leading role and indeed had written that principle into the national constitution. But by the preservation of a "united front" of Communist and non-Communist parties, they suggested that the latter were respected and their members enabled to play a useful role in the governing of the country.

These democratic parties (as the eight non-Communist parties are called) have varied histories, but all date back to the pre-Communist period when they made up a small and disunited "third force." The Kuomintang Revolutionary Committee (KMTRC), composed of defectors from Chiang Kai-shek's Kuomintang (Nationalist party), is somewhat different from the rest among which it is officially accorded seniority. Broadly speaking, the others drew their strength from intellectual circles (the exception is the China Democratic National Construction Association (CDNCA), largely a business men's party) and subscribed to the ideals of Western democracy. The most important was, and is, the (China) Democratic League (CDL) of which Lo Lung-chi and Chang Po-chun were Deputy Chairmen when the rectification campaign was launched. It emerged from a federation of democratic parties formed in 1941 to oppose one-party government, party armies, secret police and corruption. If the Nationalists and Communists had been able to solve their differences peacefully after the Second World War, it might have been a powerful parliamentary force. But in a state of civil war, all the democratic parties were powerless because they lacked armed forces.

It is hardly surprising that after years of Kuomintang police persecution, many members of these parties preferred life on the mainland under the new despotism which they did not know to exile in Formosa under the old which they did. Doubtless motives were mixed, but patriotism was probably more important than opportunism. Besides Chinese scholar-officials have always continued to serve under a new dynasty; since the old one is considered to have lost the " mandate of heaven " by reason of its own failings, no moral odium is incurred by such conduct.

In September 1949 representatives of these parties [1] attended a meeting of the Chinese People's Political Consultative Conference (CPPCC) summoned by the Communists which proclaimed the establishment on October 1 of the Chinese People's Republic. The CPPCC, the official organ of the united front, acted as the national legislature for five years until the election of a National People's Congress (NPC) and promulgation of a constitution in 1954. (It is now a " consultative body.") The democratic parties were also granted representation in the new legislature.

In the initial administrative organisation, non-Communists occupied half of the deputy chairmanships and ordinary seats on the supreme Central People's Government Council. In the Government Administrative Council (or cabinet) they held two of five deputy premierships and a proportionate number of ministries. Their representation in the new administrative organs set up in 1954 was roughly the same, though as Ch'u An-p'ing, editor of the *Kuang Ming Daily*, pointed out [2] they no longer held any deputy premierships.

But in fact the proportion of offices allocated to the democratic parties is quite irrelevant when only Communist office holders wield power. These Peking forums make it quite clear that the democratic parties have no power at all and their members little if any authority, whatever their official title. The standing committee of the National People's Congress on which many of them serve is exposed as a mere rubber stamp for Communist Party

[1] The others are the China Association for Promoting Democracy (CAPD), the Chinese Peasants and Workers' Democratic Party (CPWDP), the China Chih Kung Tang (CCKT), the Chiu San Society (CSS), and the Taiwan (Formosa) Democratic Self-government League.

[2] See below, forum on June 1, pp. 52–53.

policies; the equivalent bodies at the lower levels are shown to be as little respected.

The reasons for the preservation of this façade of a united front government have been discussed in the introduction; the argument there is largely confirmed by Ch'u An-p'ing's contribution to the forums in which he suggests that it is good for uniting the country and keeping up appearances. It is important to note that his suggestion was concerned solely with repairing the façade by giving the non-Communists more positions; he did not, as was later alleged, indicate any desire to do away with Communist Party leadership.

It was at these forums that Chang Po-chun and Lo Lung-chi made the suggestions later to be used as evidence against them when they were accused of allying to lead a nation-wide anti-Communist plot. As early as May 10, Lo Lung-chi was being reproved by Mme. Shih Liang, Minister of Justice, who was later to be in the forefront of the democratic party leaders who rounded on him and Chang Po-chun. It was at these forums, too, that Ch'en Ming-shu made the first suggestion that Communist Party control of the universities should be brought to an end.

Similar forums of leading local non-Communists were held by the Communist Party organisations in Shanghai and Tientsin, those at the latter city producing some startlingly outspoken views on removing the Communist Party from its position of undisputed leadership.

Leading non-Communists invited to criticise the Party

PEKING: *UFWD forums* **May 8**

Vice-Chairman of the Democratic League, Chang Po-chun:

According to some members of the Democratic League, some adult members of the democratic parties and groups had not had a chance to play their due role in state affairs during the past several years. . . . While some Communist cadres got promoted very fast, non-Party cadres rarely had similar opportunities. Chang also alluded to the duties and authority of the state administrative organs and of the Party organisations and the necessity of drawing a clear line between them . . . at present the Party's organisation exercised control over virtually everything. . . . Leading non-Party figures who were assigned an office and invested with authority should be held responsible for it. But the present situation was that a Party organisation was held responsible for work entrusted to non-Party people. . . .

In his speech, Ch'en Ming-shu [Standing Committee, KMTRC] insisted on the abolition of the Party Committee system now existing in schools [" schools " includes universities—*Ed.*], saying that leading non-Party figures should be invited to take part in discussions on the major problems of the organs in which they worked. . . .

Chang Nai-ch'i [Vice-President, CDNCA; Minister of Food] . . . said that some of the Party's members advocated one set of truths inside the Party, but another outside the Party. They made obvious mistakes, but refused to admit them, trying to show their partisanship. . . .

Chang said that he himself had power corresponding to his official position. He maintained normal relations with the Party organisation of the Ministry of Food. But he had acquired that power only through a series of struggles, he added. . . .

Commenting on the April 22 editorial of the *People's Daily* entitled " Industrialists and Merchants Should Continue Reforming Themselves and Actively Work," Chang Nai-ch'i put forward the opinion that the editorial's emphasis on " the necessity of submission to State Leadership " was a one-sided view; for if they acted that way, the leading personnel representing capitalist interests would have none of the authority and the responsibility required for the fulfilment of their official duties.

He raised strong objections to the editorial's demand that the national bourgeois elements should be subject to thorough ideological remoulding.

[*NCNA. May 8*

The " eyebrows " of the Communist Party

May 9

Wang Kun-lun (Standing Committee, KMTRC] cited the case of the standing committee of the National People's Congress. . . .

Wang indicated that because the standing committee men did not understand fully the condition of state work, they could raise some problems or some general opinions only when the standing committee was discussing such bills as the state budget and the yearly economic plans. Thus their discussion on major policies as well as their approval was only a gesture. . . .

On many occasions when major matters were under discussion often only the democratic personages spoke, whereas the Party members declined to utter a word. " Does this indicate that the Party has already discussed and made its decision on the matters concerned," Wang Kun-lun asked. . . . He said that some people described the democratic parties as the eyebrows, but not the nose and eyes of the Party. . . .

Chen Chi-yu [Chairman, CCKT] commented on how reactionaries were suppressed. He said that the democratic parties and groups were not notified of the reason when some of their individual adult members were arrested at the time of the purge of reactionaries. He asked whether this was due to the fact that the democratic parties and groups were not trusted or regarded as organisations having no relations with their members. Whatever the reason, such a way of doing things was not proper. . . .

[*NCNA. May 9*

Lo Lung-chi clashes with Shih Liang

May 10

Shao Li-tse [Standing Committee, KMTRC]:

" The Party has replaced the Government " in the past, especially among the leadership organs of the hsien level and below. The general public attached little importance to the hsien people's council. The Communist Party hsien committee, however, exercised very great power. . . .

Lo-Lung-chi [Vice-Chairman, CDL; Minister of the Timber Industry] . . . laid stress on the problem of " long-term coexistence and mutual supervision," saying that if the democratic parties and groups hoped to exist together with the Communist Party in the long run, three problems should be tackled: how to develop their organisations, how to take part in policy-making conferences and how to strengthen the role of their basic level organisations. . . .

As to the problem of " long-term coexistence," Lo Lung-chi took the stand that in the organisation of the democratic parties and groups one might find the conditions for coexistence, but added that it was too early to talk about the problem of coexistence. The Communist Party recruited members from the masses of the workers and the peasants, whereas the democratic parties and groups were not allowed to. The latter might recruit members from among the intellectuals and, what was more, only from among the old-style [*i.e.*, Western-trained—Ed.] intellectuals who were quite old now. Since the way to socialism was a long one, the restriction of their recruitment to the middle-aged and older persons would deprive them of the longevity required for "long-term coexistence." . . . When allowed to join the Party, the old-style intellectuals lost interest in the democratic parties and groups which were restricted to recruiting members from among them. . . . What embarrassed the democratic parties and groups most was the lack of the information required for the study of policies. At the standing committee meetings of the National People's Congress and the People's Political Consultative Conference, the democratic parties and groups could not voice any effective opinion on matters under discussion because they were not informed in advance of the matters to be discussed, and they had no time to study them at the moment of discussion. He therefore proposed that when any major policy was to be decided, the democratic parties and groups should be provided in advance with the information and materials related to it and should be allowed the chance to discuss it at the same time as the members of the Communist Party. . . .

Lo Lung-chi voiced opposition to the running of schools by Communist Party committees, saying that it was not compatible with the spirit of the present political system. For, since the people's democratic dictatorship in China was led by the Communist Party and based on the worker-peasant alliance, with the democratic parties and groups taking part in government work, the schools should not be left to the control of the Party committees . . . one had to decide how to bring into play the role of the basic-level organisations of the democratic parties and groups and how to separate the Party from the governmental administration. . . .

Shih Liang [Vice Chairman, CDL; Minister of Justice] voiced disagreement with some of Lo Lung-chi's views, saying that the chief basis on which the democratic parties and groups could exist along with the Communist Party in the long run, lay in long-term ideological remoulding, not in the number of recruits. . . .

"It is not right," she said, "to regard the rapid growth of the Communist Party as a check on the 'life' of the democratic parties and groups, nor is it right to restrict all intellectuals to affiliation with the Democratic League." . . .

After Shih Liang's speech, Lo Lung-chi said that he did not say that the members of the democratic parties and groups should not join the Communist Party, but said there was a contradiction in this respect. . . .

Ch'en Ming-shu [Standing Committee, KMTRC] made two points supplementary to his speech of the other day [May 8]: (1) He hoped that unqualified Party members would be removed from their present position in institutions of higher education. . . .

[*NCNA. May 10*

Criticisms of United Front work

May 11

Hsiung Ko-wu [Vice Chairman, KMTRC] advanced his opinion on the question of the legal system, saying that . . . a man had been under arrest since the time of the three-anti campaign, but so far there had been no definite announcement made as to the conclusion of his case. "This case," said he, "makes the masses of the people realise it is necessary to improve the legal system. The time is ripe for us to put forward this problem."

Ch'ien Chia-chu [Deputy Secretary-General of CDL] pointed out that the Communist Party discriminated against non-Party cadres when promoting and emphasised political standing to the neglect of intellectual level and working ability. He said that the Communist Party did not abide closely by the principle of employing men with talent and virtue. . . .

Wang Ting-chen [Standing Committee member, CCKT] said that the overseas Chinese were the people dealt with by the China Chih Kung Tang. Despite the fact that the Government attached importance to overseas Chinese affairs, the United Front Department did not care much about the work of the Chih Kung Tang and extended it little assistance. . . .

On the relations between Party members and non-Party people, Wang Yao-nien [Standing Committee, CDL] said that . . . Sometimes a Party member made a mistake, but it was taken as right; and a non-Party man did right, but it was taken as wrong. The Party member might get promoted over three classes a year; but the non-Party men, however assiduous in work, were not promoted for three to five years. When a Party member committed a mistake, his case was dealt with behind closed doors. If not punished by the Party organisation, he was reinstated with the same powers. When a non-Party man committed a mistake, the Party organisation did not let him know where he was wrong, nor extended him assistance, but let him drift along, and punished the organisation to which he belonged. . . .

Wang Yao-nien also commented on the United Front Department's work, saying that first the department made no wide contact with the outside—which aroused criticism from various circles and for which the department had made self-criticism. But after this was over, everything had remained the same. It seemed that the department acted somewhat like this: "We sincerely accept your criticism but have decided not to make any change."

[*NCNA. May 11*

Dogma—their sole blueprint, their only support

May 13

Chang Hsi-jo [non-party, Minister of Education] analysed the sources of sectarianism from two sides. . . . Some members of the Communist Party considered that "the empire has been conquered by us" and so they thought they were the first people on earth, and treated themselves as meritorious contributors to the revolution. . . . In this way there grew in them the thought of authority, and they acted like those with authority in the days of old, "once authority is in his hands, he starts issuing orders." Secondly, dealings with the masses; when it was absolutely necessary they sought the co-operation of the masses. In critical moments, they adopted the Confucian philosophy, "tell them what to do, but not why to do it."

Chang Hsi-jo thought that in addition to the above three "isms," the Communist Party had one more fault—doctrinairism. Some members of the Communist Party, with a low level of knowledge and a lack of experience, resorted to the use of doctrinairism in their effort to do a good job. They looked upon dogmas as their sole blueprint, their sole dictionary, all their capital, and their only support. . . .

[*NCNA. May 13*

Too many jobs, too little authority

May 15

Shen Yen-ping (Mao Tun) [non-party; Minister of Culture; Secretary, Writers' Union] said . . . quite a few experts had had too many duties assigned them, and their time was taken up with the "three meetings" [long conferences, dinner parties and evening parties], so that they had no time for proper work, and were forced to become busy bureaucrats. Shen Yen-ping said that he himself was nominally a responsible leader of a people's organisation, an official, and at the same time still looked upon by many as a professional man [author]. He himself did not know what he really was. . . .

Mme. Liu Ch'ing-yang [Central Committee's Standing Committee, CDL] . . . stated that in Hopei Province some agricultural producer co-operatives had taken the trouble to train a number of women tractor drivers. But after they had married officers of the army stationed in the area, they would no longer work as tractor drivers, separated themselves from production, and lived with the army. They began to wear leather shoes and silk clothes, and go about in motor-cars. This produced an unfavourable influence on the rural cadres and the peasants. . . .

Mei Kun-pin [Secretary-General, Central Committee, KMTRC] spoke on the views on the united front held by leading personnel of the Central Committee of the Kuomintang Revolutionary Committee and cadres of its organisations of different levels.

On the question of arrangements for employment, Mei Kun-pin stated that some people had analysed the situation and arrived at the following three conditions: (1) some were given jobs but no authority; (2) some were given nominal, but not actual authority; and (3) some were given neither nominal nor actual authority. . . .

Chang Hsi-jo [non-party; Minister of Education] referred to the contempt held for the past. He said that history was a natural heritage and the wisdom of man had been accumulated over a long period. But many people neglected historical factors and applied foreign dogmas in dealing with everything. They considered the things left over from history to be feudalist and to be overthrown. . . .

[*NCNA. May 15*

A legal system is needed

May 16

Huang Shao-hung [Central Committee's Standing Committee, KMTRC] . . . suggested that systems already established must be respected. For example, in the meetings of the National People's Congress standing committee and its bills committee, quorums were generally only barely achieved. Absentees included more members of the Communist Party than any other party, and this led people to feel that these Communist Party members did not respect the supreme organ of state power. He asked whether it was because some members of the Communist Party thought that decisions were generally reached inside the Party, and that the National People's Congress standing committee merely passed them as a formality.

On the question of legislation, Huang Shao-hung stated that the country's legal machinery was not perfect, and lagged behind the development of the objective situation. The Criminal Code, the Civil Code, police regulations and regulations for the punishment of public functionaries—none of these had yet been enacted and promulgated. Economic laws and regulations were especially incomplete. The first five-year plan was about to be fulfilled, and yet the country still had not enacted regulations governing weights and measures. . . . He also recommended the timely disposal of cases involving responsible leaders whose bureaucratism and subjectivism in the past had resulted in serious losses of life and property to the people. . . . He stated that it had become a formula in work reports to say, "The achievements are the principal thing, and deviations and mistakes are only individual incidents." The inclusion of this formula in any report, according to Huang, implied an emphasis on achievements and the covering up of mistakes, and involved the danger of making greater mistakes. . . .

Chin Chih-hsuan [Central Committee's Standing Committee, CAPD] . . . stated that the rectification movement should . . . begin with the "old ladies of the house" in the central government departments, the Ministers of the different ministries who were members of the Communist Party. In the past, the central government seldom inspected their work, and the lower grades did not dare to criticise them. . . .

[*NCNA. May 16*

The suggestion for a political "design department"

May 21

Chang Po-chun [Vice Chairman, CDL; Minister of Communications] . . . pointed out that every person had by now realised that the guidance of the Communist Party was absolutely indispensable to the institutions of higher education; . . .

Chang Po-chun said that . . . Each industrial ministry of the Central Government had its own design department but there was not a single design department for political work. He said that the Communist Party should fully co-operate with the People's Political Consultative Conference national committee, the standing committee of the National People's Congress, the democratic parties and groups, and the people's organisations in discussing the important policies and problems of the state. . . .

In her speech, Hsu Kuang-p'ing [Vice Chairman, CAPD] . . . said that many Communist Party organisations in various localities had never given enough respect to middle and primary school teachers, thus discouraging many youths from becoming school teachers. . . .

Vice Chairman Lin Han-ta [Vice Chairman, CAPD] . . . held that the entire Ministry of Education existed only in name without any actual authority. The directives issued by the Ministry of Education did not mean anything to the lower-level organisations, while sometimes even a directive issued by the State Council encountered the same indifference among the lower-level organisations. He said that the lower-level organisations only observed the directives jointly issued by the Communist Party Central Committee and the State Council. . . .

[*NCNA. May 21*

A Commission to rectify injustices proposed

May 22

Lo Lung-chi [Vice Chairman, CDL; Minister of the Timber Industry] in his statement today proposed that the National People's Congress's standing committee and the People's Political Consultative Conference's standing committee should jointly establish a special organisation, of a united front nature, to inspect the deviations during the past "three-anti," "five-anti" campaigns and the movement for the suppression of counter-revolutionaries. It would at the same time provide a guarantee that people who dared to "bloom" and "contend" would not be subject to attack and retaliation. Lo considered that such an organisation should be set up immediately. . . . In the first place, every road leads to Peking. Some people think that all will be well if any wrong can be brought to the notice of the capital, since Chairman Mao and the highest organs of state power are in Peking. . . . In the second place, the leadership machinery for the "righting of past wrongs" must be clearly distinguishable from the leadership organs in charge of the past movements, the "three-anti," "the five-anti" campaign and the suppression of counter-revolutionaries. The present committee will be responsible for the inspection and handling of cases wrongly adjudged during the past three movements. At the same time it will hear charges made by the people, so that those who were wronged and who are objects of retaliation will have a place to take their troubles to. . . .

Lo Lung-chi . . . said that there were eight offices in the State Council, and in addition the State Planning Commission, the State Economic Commission, and the National Construction Commission. In the drawing up of plans, the practice was not to have the plans prepared at the lower levels and submitted to the higher levels, and then returned to the lower levels. The higher levels simply decided on the plans, and assigned tasks to the lower levels. The lower levels, including the ministries, only had to receive assignments from above and pass them on to the still lower levels and their task was fulfilled. Thus the Minister was also in a passive position and became somebody with a post but no authority. . . . He added that in the Offices of the State Council, and the several Commissions mentioned above, all the responsible cadres were members of the Communist Party. He thought these departments should take in more non-Party intellectuals with technical and field experience to work in them. . . .

[*NCNA. May 22*

" *Walls and Moats* "

May 30

Chang Yun-ch'uan [Executive Bureau, CPWDP] . . . speaking on the question of the " wall and moat " expressed the opinion that it was due to Party members' sense of particularity and sense of superiority. He said: " In leading the masses to carry through the revolution in the past, the Party stood among the masses; after the liberation, it felt the position had changed and, instead of standing among the masses, it stood on the back of the masses and ruled the masses."

Chang Yun-ch'uan was particularly dissatisfied with some so-called activists among the masses. He called them " volunteers " for building walls and digging moats. He even had this to say: " A few activists air criticism at random behind one's back, calling one progressive and another backward. They have their individual aims and ulterior motives. They put on airs and insult others. . . ."

Chang Yun-ch'uan also . . . said: " Government cadres should differ in duties, not in status. Some are deeply conscious of being officials; they occupy special positions even when taking meals and seeing operas. . . ."

Lung Yun [Vice Chairman, KMTRC] expressed the opinion in his speech that most errors and defects were displayed at the lower levels but their roots lay in the upper levels. . . . Before directives were issued,

Lung Yun pointed out, the upper levels did not weigh matters judiciously, regarding everything in the world as very simple. . . .

Lung Yun proposed a gradual reduction in the number of Han [*i.e.*, Chinese; after the Han dynasty—*Ed.*] cadres in the organs of nationalities autonomous districts. . . . Already complaints were heard that minority nationalities practised autonomy but Han cadres were the masters. . . .

Concerning the problems left over from the suppress-counter-revolution campaign, Chu Yun-shan [Central Committee's Standing Committee, KMTRC] proposed that following the forthcoming National People's Congress, its standing committee and the People's Political Consultative Conference's standing committee should call a co-ordination meeting forthwith to discuss the organisation of a provisional check-up organ to be charged with the task of thoroughly checking up and disposing of the remaining problems in connection with relevant organs in various areas. . . .

Lung Yun attacks the Soviet Union

Lung Yun's absurd views consist of the following:

1. It was unreasonable for China to bear all the expenses of the resist-America aid-Korea war.

2. During the Second World War, the United States granted loans and leases to her allies. Later, some of these allies refused to pay back the loans, and the United States excused some from repayment. It will take our country more than ten years to repay the loans from the Soviet Union, if we can ever repay them. Besides, we have to pay interest to the Soviet Union. China fought for socialism, but look at the result.

3. The Soviet Army dismantled and shipped away some of the machinery of our factories when it liberated north-east China. What was the price paid by the Soviet Union? Will the Soviet Union compensate us?

4. The foreign aid budget of our country is too large and should be curtailed.

Lung Yun presented the above-mentioned absurd views recently at an important meeting. He was criticised on the spot by many people who denounced him as an anti-Soviet and anti-socialist nationalist rightist.

[NCNA. Peking. June 18

Liu Wen-hui [Central Committee's Standing Committee, KMTRC] said, as some organs did not attach due importance to compensation for loss sustained by citizens through infringement of their civil rights and as the citizens were subjected to compulsion by some cadres at the local level, civil rights were not fully safeguarded. . . .

Liu Fei [Central Committee's Standing Committee, KMTRC] said: "At the hsien level and below, one sees only the Party and not the government and even the people's congresses are not held in a normal way. This state of affairs is attributable to the fact that, as the Republic had been founded only recently, the legal system has not been perfected and certain high-ranking cadres and many middle and lower cadres have sketchy ideas of the legal system and are not democratic in their style of work. But inadequate attention of the Communist Party central committee to this state of affairs is not without its effect."

[*NCNA*. *May 30*

Ch'u An-p'ing criticises the "old bonzes"

June 1

Speaking on the subject "Allow Me to Offer Some Opinions to Chairman Mao and Premier Chou," Ch'u An-p'ing [Editor-in-Chief, *Kuang Ming Daily*] said: "After the liberation, intellectuals warmly supported the Party and accepted the leadership of the Party. But in the past few years the relations between the Party and the masses have not been good and have become a problem of our political life that urgently needs re-adjustment. Where is the key to the problem? In my opinion, the key lies in the idea that 'the world belongs to the Party.' I think a party leading a nation is not the same thing as a party owning a nation; the public supports the Party, but members of the public have not forgotten that they are masters of the nation. . . . isn't it too much that within the scope of the nation, there must be a Party man as leader in every unit, big or small, whether section or subsection; or that nothing, big or small, can be done without a nod from a Party man? . . . For many years, the talents or capabilities of many Party men have not matched their duties. They have bungled their jobs, to the detriment of the state, and have not been able to command the respect of the masses with the result that the relations between the Party and the masses have been tense. But the fault has not lain with the Party members, but rather with the Party which has placed square pegs in round holes. I wonder if the Party acts this way because it entertains the idea that 'every place is royal territory' and therefore has created the present monochromatic, one-family-empire appearance. I think this idea that 'the world belongs to the Party' is at the bottom of all sectarianism and the root of all contradictions between the Party and non-Party people. Today, the obviousness of sectarianism and the bad relations between the Party and the masses are nation-wide phenomena. The Communist Party is a highly organised, highly disciplined party—do these defects of a nation-wide nature have anything to do with the central leadership of the Party? Recently, the public advanced many critical opinions about the young bonzes but nobody had anything to say about the old bonzes. Now I want to cite an example and ask Chairman Mao and Premier Chou about it. Before the liberation, we heard tell that Chairman Mao wanted to organise a coalition government with non-Party members. In 1949, when the new nation began, three of the six deputy chairmen of the central government were non-Party persons, and two out of the four deputy premiers were non-Party persons. It looked like a coalition government. Later, when the government was reorganised,

---

A catalogue of sins

The primary object of the rectification campaign is to drive home to the senior and junior cadres alike within the Party the truth that subjectivism, bureaucracy and sectarianism are incompatible with Marxism-Leninism, dialectical materialism and historical materialism, and that in actual life and work, self-righteousness, self-importance, subjective presumption, complacency and arrogance, much-ado-about-nothing, trumping up stories, confusing black with white and right with wrong, hypocrisy, boastfulness, claiming false credit, distorting facts, concealing facts, denying facts, fabricating facts, stirring up trouble on false pretexts, ostentation and extravagance, suspiciousness, two-faced attitudes, sham observance of rules, spreading rumours to create incidents, sowing discord among friends, vindictiveness, debauchery, shielding fellow officials —to sum up, to clearly recognise that departing from reality and the masses, not worrying about the sorrows of the masses, not seeking to understand everything about the hearts of the people—are basically not part and parcel of Marxism-Leninism, dialectical materialism, or historical materialism. . . .

["My understanding of the Party's rectification campaign" by Teng Ch'u-min. *Kuang Ming Daily*. June 7

there was only one deputy chairman of the People's Republic of China, and the seats of the non-Party deputy chairmen were moved to the standing committee of the People's Congress. That is not all. Now there are twelve deputy premiers in the State Council, not one of whom is a non-Party man. Could it be that there is not a single person among the non-Party people who can sit in a deputy premier's chair, or that none of them can be groomed to hold this chair? From the point of view of unifying non-Party men and of unifying the nation, and with an eye to domestic and international appearances, doesn't this arrangement seem to need further study? . . ."

[*People's Daily. June 2*

Ch'en Ch'i-yuan [Central Committee's Standing Committee, KMTRC] . . . stated that some people had an impure style of work; some people, on becoming the head of a department, had to appoint their wives chiefs of personnel sections. It was of course permissible for husband and wife to work together, but if her only qualification was being his wife and nothing else, then the situation was bad. . . .

[*NCNA. June 1*

The first mention of "rightists"

Mme. Ho Hsiang-ning [Vice Chairman, KMTRC; Chairman, Overseas Chinese Affairs Commission] in her written statement . . . criticised those responsible cadres in the Overseas Chinese Affairs Commission who were Party members. She said that she was responsible for the work of the Commission, and during the past seven years had repeatedly stressed production activities among dependants of overseas Chinese, the organisation of returned overseas Chinese and returned overseas refugees for production for self salvation, and the promotion of the writing of letters by dependants of overseas Chinese to their kinfolk abroad to publicise conditions in the country. Though she might have repeated these matters scores of times, her wishes had not aroused attention. She was especially dissatisfied with Chang Kan-cheng, Director of the General Office of the Commission. She pointed out that sometimes some overseas Chinese wanted to see her, and though she had explained that such people had come from thousands of miles away and she would see them even when she was ill, Chang still prevented the callers from meeting her. When questions arose in the home districts of overseas

Chinese, the reports she received often told only the good side news and omitted the bad. There were, for instance, cases of encroachment and corruption connected with remittances from overseas, and the reports were not brought to her until she had learned about them and had asked for them repeatedly. . . .

She believed that . . . there were a very small minority of people who paid lip-service to socialism, but actually admired capitalism; their minds were filled with admiration for the Euro-American type of government. She considered that these people were obviously rightists. . . .

Teng Ch'u-min [Central Committee's Standing Committee, CDL] . . . stated that some people, as soon as they become officials, assumed the air of officials, and adopted the style of work of an overlord. Such people were not only to be found among members of the Party but also to be found outside the Party. . . .

Yang Ming-hsuan [Central Committee's Standing Committee, CDL]: . . . if the non-Party people acted like some of the Communist Party members now criticised, doing nothing all day long other than getting fed, or were arrogant and conceited and particular over personal gains and losses, they would fail to make a good job of their work, and naturally would not win the confidence of the Communist Party and the people. . . .

[*NCNA. June 1*

Many criticisms are mistaken

June 3

Li Wei-han [Director, CP United Front Work Department] addressed the session of the forum this afternoon. . . .

"We have through consultation decided on the inauguration of fortnightly forums of democratic parties and groups and non-party personages, and discussion meetings on the work of democratic parties and groups. . . .

"Generally speaking, we consider many of the criticisms and views brought forward by various quarters to be correct, and to be earnestly accepted and dealt with. A considerable portion of these criticisms and views are mistaken, and call for further study and analysis.

"I now declare this forum closed. . . ."

[*NCNA. June 3. People's Daily, June 4*

*

"Storm Over Shanghai"

SHANGHAI **May 19**

Tsou Cheng-lu, research member of the Biological Research Institute of the Chinese Academy of Sciences, presented the demand that scientists must run the Academy and asked for the breaking down of the system of ruling classes in the Academy. . . . He pointed out that of the scientists who now held leadership posts in the Academy and its departments, the majority had been separated from scientific research work for a long time, and for a period of from eight to ten years they had not undertaken research activities. To the outside world, they were still scientists, but to the inside world of science, they had already become outsiders. . . .

Grey-haired Huang Ming-lung, research member of the Organic Chemistry Research Institute of the Academy of Sciences . . . stated that three years ago he went to Tsingtao for a rest, and lived in a house which a high-ranking Communist Party cadre had reserved, but had subsequently not taken up. There were three persons who waited on him: a cook, a nurse and a manservant. All the three addressed him as "leading official." Later he learned that all people who took up the villas in the vicinity for rest were high-ranking cadres of different government departments, and all of them were addressed as "leading officials." Huang pointed out that this was tantamount to the old practice in which all servants addressed their employers and all the bureaucratic gentry as "Lao Yeh" [venerable master], or "Ta Jen" [excellency]. Such a situation was not to be found even in capitalist countries. . . .

The unanimous cry of the actors and actresses was for more chances to play on the stage, more appearances before audiences. . . .

Yen Hui-chu, Peking opera actress, stated that the conditions which existed in the dramatic troupes could be used as material for the writing of a play which might be entitled *Three Unwilling Parties*; the audience was unwilling, the players were unwilling and the government was also unwilling to continue operating the troupes. The Peking Opera Troupe was losing money every year.

A joint written statement was issued by thirteen players of seven kinds of local operas under the new State Owned Dramatic Troupes. The statement said: "The Bureau of Culture, in approving the scheme for the state ownership of the troupes, had not considered the matter fully, taking up the proposal only on the spur of the moment out of enthusiasm for socialism. After the troupes became state owned, the traditional systems in force in the private troupes for decades were abolished, but a rational new system was not established in their place. Instead many unreasonable restrictions were added, and so since the state took over, conditions have grown worse. . . ."

[*NCNA. May 19*

*

Allow non-Communist parties to rule

TIENTSIN

The secretariat of the Communist Party Tientsin Municipal Committee and the relevant departments of the committee held forty meetings and forums. . . . Over 400 people delivered speeches. . . .

Huang Hsin-p'ing, a teacher in the Third Girls' Middle School of Tientsin . . . said: "Although the democratic parties are allowed to

---

Cadres accused of violating the law

SHANGHAI

In mid-May, at the Propaganda Conference convened by the municipal Party committee and thereafter, a few people took the opportunity of blooming and contending to disseminate a number of statements that were hostile to socialism. . . . Professor Yang Chao-lung of Futan University . . . was of the opinion that the Communist Party merely advocated democratic centralism and that, in practice, there was only centralism but no democracy. . . . Vice Chairman Ch'en Jen-ping of the Shanghai Municipal Committee of the China Democratic League and Professor Wang Tsao-shih of the Futan University advocated publicly that the onus of blooming and contending be placed on the basic-levels. In the capacity of a "representative" of workers and peasants, Wang Tsao-shih described the basic-levels as dark places, where the cadres acted in violation of the law and in disregard of discipline, and suggested that blooming and contending be carried out there first. Ch'en Jen-ping suggested it was necessary to "settle old accounts" in the rectification movement and to punish a few "questionable persons." Otherwise, he said, the people would not have confidence in the rectification movement. Ch'en Jen-ping even went to gather "materials" everywhere and to incite the movie actors to cast away their "stumbling-block." . . .

[NCNA. June 20

exist and the political platform of those parties is to advance in the direction of Communism, why could not the method of rotating the democratic parties in power be adopted? If we cast away one-party rule by the Communist Party and let the Communist Party and all other parties put forward their different political platforms, leaving the decision to free election by the masses of the people, the Communist Party and all the democratic parties would work harder to overcome their shortcomings in order to solicit more votes on the basis of their service to the people. . . ."

Yang Yueh, member of the Chiu San Society and Engineer of the Tientsin Civil Housing Designing Board of the Ministry of City Construction, stated: "The government must not be in the hands of one Party, the Communist Party. It should be a coalition government participated in by all democratic parties." Clerk Hu Tsung-han of the Tientsin Municipal Power Industry Bureau suggested that the Chinese Communist Party should let the democratic parties rule one province, one municipality or one ch'u complete with their own law codes and police force. . . .

[*NCNA. June 9*

Worse than a change of dynasties

Is our socialist country sound?

Su P'ei-ying, member of the China Democratic League and Engineer of the Tientsin Civil Housing Designing Board, said: "When the Communists first entered Tientsin, they said this was a revolution and our revolution was not a change of dynasties. The way I look at it now is that the revolution was worse than a change of dynasties and living in such a society is heart-breaking. The intellectuals are more and more timid every day, and they are living less peacefully than during the Japanese occupation or Kuomintang rule. . . ." Another engineer, Yang Yueh, of the board remarked: ". . . Before the Constitution was promulgated, the government looked like a coalition government. But now, all the democratic parties have been kicked away."

Is it necessary to have Party leadership in technological departments? . . .

Chief Engineer Wang Kai-ch'ing of the Tientsin Civil Housing Designing Board of the Ministry of City Construction . . . made a concrete suggestion on three possible outlets for Communist Party members. (1) The section chiefs and directors should step down to work their way up as clerks from the bottom. Their salaries need not be adjusted as their seniority should be respected. (2) Party schools at all levels must be turned into cultural supplementary schools for old cadres so that they could come back to positions of leadership when they had completed their studies. (3) If both the above two outlets were unfeasible, they must then be mobilised to return to production in the countryside.

If the Communist Party withdraws its leadership from the technological departments, what will be the arrangements for those leadership Party members? . . . a doctor, Chang Ch'un-cheng, put forward a method of treatment. He said: "Let the Communists go back to the period of production when they worked with the people. . . . If he is the president of a hospital, but cannot look after the patients, he must try to scrub floors and make beds. In this way, he will learn through common labour that he is not qualified to be the president. . . ."

[*NCNA. June 9*

5

THE PRESS

THE criticisms raised by journalists about restrictions on their own work need no comment; they clearly indicate the amount of freedom permitted to the Chinese Press. It is interesting to note, however, that even Communist journalists resented their role and used this brief opportunity to attempt to gain greater freedom.

The question that does need some elucidation is the role of the Press during the period of blooming and contending. Certainly the few formally non-Communist papers do not seem to have pursued an anti-Communist editorial policy in the sense of printing anti-régime editorials much as a liberal paper might criticise a conservative government in a democratic country. What they were attacked for was printing highly critical views uttered by people at forums. One might argue that this was a cunning way of being anti-Communist without appearing to be; but in fact the official Press was printing similar views. Ch'u An-p'ing, editor of the *Kuang Ming Daily* (whose criticism of Mao Tse-tung and Chou En-lai is printed in the section on the forums of leading non-Communists), is accused of deliberately inciting people by sending out his reporters to nine cities to hold special forums at which malcontents were encouraged to speak up. That Ch'u An-p'ing later confessed that this interpretation was correct is, of course, no real indication of its truth when one bears in mind the pressure brought to bear on the (bourgeois) rightists during the anti-rightist campaign.

What is interesting in his confession is that he mentions the damage done by the printing of these reports both at home and abroad. They created " ideological confusion " and prevented some people from seeing the truth for a time. This is the crux of the matter. The reports in the papers spread unrest. Potential critics and in particular the students were encouraged by what they read was going on in the capital. They read these reports in the *People's Daily* as well as in the *Kuang Ming Daily*; but obviously the official Party paper could not be accused of spreading unrest (but the *People's Daily* was later criticised for " liberalism " and some staff changes were made) and the *Kuang Ming Daily*, having been bold enough to hold its own forums, was a convenient scapegoat. Ch'u An-p'ing's real motive, however, was probably not to incite people against the Party—he would have known, whatever his hopes, that he could never get away with that. But he probably did want to make sure—and this was a legitimate objective in line with the aims of rectification—that no injustices remained unrighted simply because people would not speak up for fear of retaliation from the Party backwoodsmen.

Even so, it is quite clear that he realised there were limits beyond which he could not go. There is no other way to account for the fact that he only printed one report of the university unrest which was clearly so very important. Later revelations indicate that Party members on the paper objected even to the report on the " Democratic Wall " at Peking University as being inflammatory and managed to suppress other reports. We are also told that copies of the magazine *Hsin Kuan-ch'a* were suppressed because of a report on university activities.

This curious omission of reports on university activities is significant because it shows that the Press was not as unbridled as the Communists have suggested. The likelihood is that the censorship was compulsory rather than voluntary; there is a passage in the confession of another non-Communist editor which suggests that the Shanghai Press was warned about what to print as early as the middle of May. The importance of this point is obvious; it means that the criticism that we have to hand may in fact only be the top of the iceberg, that there may be much more that remains unrevealed below the surface. Indeed, the *Chinese Youth Newspaper* admitted that the " erroneous and reactionary articles withheld from publication . . . were many more and more serious than those which appeared in our paper."

Restrictions on journalists

SHANGHAI: *Wen Hui Pao* May 8

More often than not, reporters would suffer various set-backs, sometimes serious and sometimes minor ones. . . .

When a *Hsin Wen Daily* photographer tried to snap workers engaged in pipe-laying work on Nanking Road, he was stopped by a comrade at the construction site for security reasons. When the relevant unit was contacted, approval of picture-taking was given on condition that the prints were submitted for screening before they were released. The reporter argued that since tens of thousands of pedestrians on Nanking Road had seen what was going on, security was hardly necessary. . . .

Despite the Communist Party Central Committee's announced design urging newspapers to unveil criticisms and self-criticisms, some units have still tried to resist and challenge such criticisms. . . .

Ching Nien Pao criticised the metal workshop of Wu Tung Ship Building Works for failure to support young workers' rational suggestions. When the reporter of that newspaper called up that factory again, he was subject to three hours of tirade by the Party, trade union and Youth League cadres of the workshop. . . .

The reporter of *Hsin Wen Daily* disclosed that commercial departments often looked up reporters for help to promote the sales of merchandise not very much in demand. Under such circumstances, they paid compliments to newspaper workers and credited them with the promotion of sales. A reporter of *Chieh Fang Daily* said that many units looked upon that newspaper as a good medium for inserting various notices. . . . The New China News Agency reporter added that some units only informed the New China News Agency and *Chieh Fang Daily* whenever important events came up, and ignored the other newspapers. In their eyes, these newspapers were not operated by the Party and the people. . . .

1. It was requested that the spokesmen of various government organs would hold Press conferences at regular intervals to describe work done and answer questions raised by reporters.

2. It was hoped that the Communist Party Central Committee would instruct its subordinate committees to pay more attention to newspaper work, strengthen contacts, and accord reporters news-gathering facilities.

3. It was requested that the Communist Party Central Committee would instruct its subordinate committees to safeguard the right of

correspondents to write articles for newspapers and to describe conditions truthfully.

4. It was proposed that relevant departments would revise the excessive restrictions on news coverage of foreign visitors. . . .

[*Wen Hui Pao. May 10*

*

" Obstructions, Restrictions, Discrimination "

PEKING May 12

Dear readers, you have often read about newspaper reporters' accounts of happenings here and there. But many of you have not been familiar with the hardships associated with journalistic work. It is true that many departments and comrades have been very helpful to us and we are very grateful for their assistance. But we have also come across numerous unreasonable obstructions and restrictions, and even rough treatment in the course of carrying out our duties. This newspaper particularly, being a non-Party organ, sometimes has been subject to some discrimination, while non-Party reporters of this newspaper have been subject to greater discrimination. These are not just isolated instances although infrequent. . . .

The Chungking correspondent of this newspaper once called on the jointly operated Chungking Paint Factory to find out the progress of the remoulding of personnel representing private interests. Comrade Kang Lin, director of the factory, considered the *Ta Kung Pao* introduction " not valid," and asked for an introduction from the United Front Department of the Communist Party ch'u committee. Later, the correspondent had to spend two hours getting the required certificate from the Communist Party municipal committee. . . .

On one occasion when the *Ta Kung Pao* correspondent in Wuhan had read half way through a copy of a document at the industrial bureau, the bureau cadre suddenly asked: " Are you a Party member? " When the answer was negative, the document was quickly withheld. The same situation confronted a *Ta Kung Pao* correspondent who happened to be at the Yangtse River Navigation Bureau. He was reading a copy of a document marked " confidential," and was about through when the bureau cadre asked whether he was a Party member. When the answer was no, the cadre became jittery and said: " I'll take this back and show you two copies of ordinary materials. . . ."

[*Ta Kung Pao. May 12*

Newspapers are " gramophones "

PEKING: *For journalists* **May 17**

The journalists' symposium which adopted " Journalistic Work and the Contention of Diverse Schools of Thought " as the central theme for discussion was in session for two days on May 16 and 17 in Peking. . . . Present at the meeting were more than 200 journalists from Peking, Shanghai, Shansi and Liaoning. More than twenty persons spoke on the two days. . . .

Chief editor Chang Li-ch'un of the *Chinese Youth Newspaper* talked about the question of to whom should a newspaper be held responsible and how journalists should realise its role. He thought that at present newspapers were actually playing a role of a notice board, a gramophone. . . . The journalists were thus . . . incapable of thinking independently.

Teacher Mo Ju-chien of the Department of Journalism of China People's University . . . said . . . " The role of the newspaper as textbook is over-emphasised. It is always used to transmit orders from the upper echelons to the lower echelons." . . .

A correspondent of the *Ta Kung Pao* advocated that the question of how the fine traditions of the newspapers of the old days should be carried on should be studied with care. . . .

[*NCNA. May 17*

The non-Party Press—the " adopted son "

PEKING: *For journalists* **May 18**

Teng T'o [Chief Editor, *People's Daily*] thought that the newspapers today were very dreary and dull. The same was true of the *People's Daily*. . . . He considered that newspaper work should be geared towards the solving of contradictions among the people. . . .

Teng Chi-hsing [a veteran journalist] . . . said: " Some say that . . . the Party Press is like one's own son, and the non-Party Press is like an adopted son. This manifests itself in the different treatment accorded reporters. . . . This problem also exists in the allocation of newsprint and in increasing the quantity of equipment. The newsprint allocated to the *People's Daily* by the Ministry of Culture is not only large in quantity but also better in quality; whilst the quantities allocated to the other papers are restricted and its quality is inferior. . . ."

[*Kuang Ming Daily. May 19*

*

THREE KUANG MING DAILY FORUMS[1]

Ice cold or piping hot

SHANGHAI: *For democratic parties* **May 5**

Ku Shih-ling [Vice Principal, Shanghai Twelfth Girls' Middle School; CAPD]:

"The Principal of another school was a female Party member who maintained school discipline by means of punishment. I submitted views to her, but she ignored them. I then brought the matter to the notice of the Bureau of Education, whose reaction was non-committal, feeling perhaps that it was a tough nut to crack. From then onwards the Principal hated me like poison. . . . Soon, I was transferred by the Bureau of Education to some other place, and at the time was repeatedly tipped off by the Bureau not to let her know which school I was being transferred to for fear of incurring her displeasure. Is this not purposely showing prejudice in favour of the Party members? . . .

"Even now the teachers are still kept so frantically busy that they can hardly cope, what with big meetings and small meetings one after another. Meetings as a rule take place in the evenings, which means if one has to attend these meetings, one has no time left to prepare for classes, and consequently, one is unable to raise one's professional standards. . . ."

Sun Ting [Assistant Manager, State Revolving Electrical Appliances Manufacturing Co.; CAPD]:

"Learning from the Soviet Union is a royal road; but some cadres do not understand and think that it means copying. I say if we do, it will paralyse Chinese engineers. . . . I have been engaged in electrical engineering for twenty years. Some of the Soviet experiences simply do not impress me. Of course, I suffered a good deal in the five-anti movement because of these opinions. . . .

"The leading cadres of a factory are very clever indeed. They leave the solution of all difficult problems to the masses. They call a meeting and ask everybody to sign his or her name. They are thus exonerated from blame for any future misventure because they have already 'depended on the masses.' . . .

"In deciding the pay scales for the old and young workers, their 'working ages' have been completely ignored. Young workers are

[1] There are further examples of *Kuang Ming Daily* forums and reports in other sections.

promoted by leaps and bounds while the old ones always remain at the same place under the ironic pretext of protecting their wages. At the time of the Hungarian and Polish incidents, some young workers manifested wavering in their thinking while the old workers maintained a firm standpoint. Can it be said that the old workers are without 'character'? . . ."

Shih Mo-k'ang [Manager, State-Private Shanghai United Electrical Appliances Factory; CAPD]:

"I am the chief Committee Member of the Regional All-China Federation of Industry and Commerce, whose Secretary is a Party member. Normally, it has always been I who submitted views to him, never the other way round. He never came to my house, and I never dared to visit his. During the high tide of socialist reform last year, we often dined together for business reasons; sometimes he stood the treat and sometimes I did. But when the high-tide period was over, he always made some excuse or other at meal time to avoid [such a] situation. . . ."

[*Kuang Ming Daily*. *May 10*

Hsu Chung-yu [Professor, Deputy Head, Dept. of Chinese, E. China Normal Un.; Shanghai Committee, CDL]:

"As a matter of fact it is not true that people in our circles can't get on well with all Party members—certainly not. Old friends . . . still confide in each other when they meet . . . one can't help thinking how nice it would be if only those Party members in one's department or profession were all like some of these old friends. But the regrettable fact is that those Party members never come to us unless they want something from us and when they do come to us they frighten us out of our wits. They do not cultivate friendship with us in daily life and when occasionally they come to us, it is either to find out which way the wind blows or to enlighten our thoughts, or to carry out education or else to demand a self-scrutiny . . . on the one hand they squat on their high horses with bows at the ready, bent on finding fault; on the other hand they tread gingerly as if skating on thin ice, all humble and obliging, lest they overstep the bounds. . . .

"The Party members, due to their occupying positions of leadership and being favourably situated, seem to enjoy in all respects excessive privileges. Take theatres for instance; a certain Party member pointed out in his self-examination that he was never happy unless he was offered a seat in the first ten rows. Why did he feel like that? Because he was used to seats in the first ten front rows. . . . Some of the names that appeared on the list of elected executive members of the Shanghai Writers' Union seemed never to have been associated with any periodical at all, some of them can only be reckoned as learner-writers. Yet some of the old writers who have been engaged in literary work for twenty to thirty years have been left out. . . . Another problem which has many people muddled is the so-called problem of having to protect the prestige of Party members. During the past few campaigns, one by one the people have had the skin of their faces torn to pieces, and the intellectuals have had their authority knocked for six, all of which may, should and indeed does have certain advantages. But why is it that the rectification of Party members must be done behind closed doors, and why is it that the masses are not allowed to probe into things if and when a Party member makes a mistake. . . . Never treat a person as if he were worse than dog's excreta one moment and regard him as worth ten thousand ounces of gold the next. The intellectuals cannot stomach the ice cold, nor can they swallow the piping hot."

[*Written statement. Kuang Ming Daily. May 11*

Professor T'an Ch'i-hsiang [History Department, Futan Un.; CSS]:

"In 1954, Ch'en T'ung-sheng, Deputy Director of the United Front Department, invited a number of teachers to a meeting and told them that they should have no reservations in presenting their views to the Party and encouraged all to 'bloom.' But those teachers who 'bloomed' during the meeting were all later rectified during the campaign against counter-revolutionaries and the remarks they made at the meeting were used as material evidence for rectification. . . ."

[*Kuang Ming Daily. May 11*

*

A clay buddha

NANKING: *For scholars* May 13

Chou Shu-wen [Adviser, Nanking Agricultural College; KMTRC]: "It is said that the reason why the No. 3 bus in Nanking has to make a detour through Kiangsu Road instead of following the direct route through Ninghai Road is because a V.I.P.'s residence happens to be there. It is also at that place that big-wigs played tennis under thousands of lights glittering like daylight at a time when power was in short supply during February, March and April last year. . . ."

Ch'en Ling [Principal, Nanking School of Physical Training: CAPD]:

"I am Principal of the Nanking School of Physical Training. . . . The secretary of the Party faction is the head of the executive office of the school and can deal with many matters on his own. . . . People are being transferred in and out and I am kept in the dark; I did not even know of the arrival of a new secretary in the office. This man has all along mistaken me for the Deputy Principal and whenever he receives an official letter he hands it direct to the Party-member Deputy Principal. Only recently has he tumbled to the fact that I am the Principal. . . ."

Fan Kuang [Nanking Committee, CDL]:

"I suggest that we make a study of our current personnel system. Under the system we use today, all the assignments and transfers are centrally controlled. Everything and everyone obeys the organisation and there is no room for individual freedom . . . in cases where husband and wife work in different areas, it is very difficult to have one of them transferred to join the other. Since the liberation, many husbands and wives, in deference to the needs of the country, have worked in different localities and have remained separated for many years. . . ."

[*Kuang Ming Daily. May 21*

*

"Employ only one's relatives and Party members"

TSINGTAO: *For democratic parties* May 23

Huang Yuan-chi [Chairman, Tsingtao ACFIC; Manager, Tsingtao State-Private Bank; CDNCA]:

The lack of a reliable basis for plans and the considerable discrepancy between them and the raw material supplies which arrive from the provinces leads to stoppages and slow-downs, especially in basic construction. Take basic construction in Tsingtao for instance; work did not commence in the second and third quarters with the result that they had to put on a spurt in the fourth quarter in order to complete the task. Therefore, shoddy workmanship and waste of material necessarily occur. Such instances were numerous last winter, and repairs and overhauling became necessary the following year, the waste being incalculable.

"Secondly, we must investigate subjectivity in production and policy standards. . . . This year a plywood factory was started. It has led to a shortage of fuel in the whole town; and the townspeople were discontented, but they had no option but to chop up old chairs as substitute for fuel. Who is this man who is in charge of all these matters, that whatever he says goes? Has anyone ever studied these points? . . ."

Ch'en Yang-chih [CDL]:

" In the matter of promoting cadres, the Party members come off best every time. Some of those who have become Principals know absolutely nothing about education. Quite a few ignoramuses who cannot even read simple documents without difficulty have been appointed to positions of leadership. Such, I am told, is the Party's policy for cadres. . . .

" I consider that the Party cadre policy is completely correct. But in promoting cadres, virtue and wisdom are the only factors taken into consideration by all establishments. Talent rarely counts. . . . I have heard it said that the maxim ' employ only the good and the talented ' is superseded by ' employ only one's relatives and Party members.' . . ."

Hsu I-kuan [KMTRC]:

" Since 1952, campaign has succeeded campaign each one leaving a great wall in its wake, a wall which estranges one man from another. In such circumstances, no one dares to let off steam even privately in the company of intimate friends, let alone speak his mind in public. Everyone has now learnt the technique of double-talk; what one says is one thing, what one thinks is another. . . ."

[*Kuang Ming Daily*. *June 5*

* * *

Party journalists attack a municipal committee

ANSHAN

On May 14 this year, the journalists in Anshan convened a forum to request the Communist Party Anshan municipal committee to support reporters in their news-gathering activities. After the meeting, however, Li Hui-chung [deputy chief editor, *Anshan Daily*; Communist Party member] and his accomplices and followers jointly plotted and wrote a news story which criticised many cadres, giving their names. This, in essence, amounted to an attack on the Anshan municipal committee. With malicious intent, this report slanderously charged that certain agencies regarded the reporters as " spies," and wantonly abused certain leading cadres as "lacking the minimum of common sense for journalism."

Meanwhile, Editor Chang Shih [Party member] of the *Anshan Daily* had also decided to write an article for publication in co-ordination with this report. The article stated that "the reporters are now faced with many restrictions. Wherever they go, they are questioned about their background, as far back as three generations—and are subjected to many obstructions."

Leading members of the Anshan municipal Party committee pointed out that the report contained excessive criticism and suggested revision before publication. However, reporter Chang Chung-huan returned to the newspaper office and distorted the meaning of "revision before publication," calling it disapproval of publication. He made certain inappropriate criticisms, saying that leading comrades of the municipal committee had rejected the report, because their own personal reputations were involved.

Li Hui-chung, who was then attending the rectification mobilisation meeting, convened by the municipal committee, hurriedly rushed to the newspaper office and stated that "if the municipal committee does not approve publication, I will not come to work tomorrow." Editor Hou Shao followed with the statement: "Since the municipal committee has not approved publication, I myself will approve of publication!" Chang Shih added: "If publication of this report is not approved, then we will submit no more manuscripts and leave a big hole in the newspaper."

Chang Shih then asked Yu Ching-hsin, director of the office of chief editor: "Will you dare to publish it?" Yu Ching-hsin readily replied: "I will do so if someone will assure a livelihood for my wife and my children." . . .

The same evening, the leading member of the municipal committee considered visiting the newspaper office to explain the views of the municipal committee and to listen to everyone's opinions. However, Liu Mu, secretary of the Party branch and deputy head of the government and education section, Kao Wei, of the supplementary edition section, editors Hsueh Ai and Yu Ching-hsin, Yu Cheng-chi, editorial committee member and head of the economic section, and others who were then enthusiastically discussing the matter, all left the scene when they heard that the leading member of the municipal committee was coming to see them.

The municipal committee fails to discipline the Anshan Daily

The following morning the municipal committee convened a conference of the standing committee to discuss the *Anshan Daily* incident; it also decided to convene a meeting of the newspaper office editorial committee in the morning, and to invite the Party branch secretary to attend the meeting. However, at the time of the meeting, of the five editorial committee members, only the chief editor and the first deputy chief editor arrived. Li Hui-chung, Yu Ching-hsin and Yu Cheng-chi all refused to attend.

Li Hui-chung stated: "I am a member of the Chinese Communist Party, and not a member of the Anshan municipal committee. I will not subject myself to all their restrictions!" He also slanderously charged that the Anshan municipal committee was a "bureaucratic clique." Liu Mu was at first reluctant to attend the conference. After much persuasion by the leading member of the Party committee at the agency, he finally agreed to attend.

However, after the conference was over Liu Mu returned to the newspaper office. Instead of reporting to the masses the spirit of the conference, he slanderously alleged that the municipal committee members had threatened him. He also divulged certain inner-Party information. At this time, Hou Shao, while wantonly charging that the municipal committee members were ignorant and the same as the Kuomintang, also bruited the idea of petitioning the municipal committee. He also openly incited the Party members to rebel against the Party by saying—all those who are not afraid of losing the Party ticket, follow me! Meanwhile, he proposed that three concessions be demanded from the municipal committee: (1) a change in the methods of leadership by the municipal committee over the newspaper office; (2) municipal committee support for blooming and contending and for publication of the report on the journalists' forum in its original form; and (3) replacement of the chief editor of the newspaper office.

On the evening of the same day, the leading member of the municipal committee again visited the newspaper office to explain matters and win them over. However, these rightists and their followers still persisted in their anti-Party stand.

At the conference of the editorial department cadres convened on May 17, Li Hui-chung launched an even more wanton attack against the municipal committee. He stated: "The decision of the municipal committee to oppose the criticism of certain people and the mentioning of their names was a bureaucratic decision!" He also threatened the municipal committee: "This demand of ours is a struggle through which we are striving to change our status from that of a dog to that of a man. We cannot accept the decision of the municipal committee. We will appeal to the central authorities."

At two ensuing meetings of the Party and League branches, Liu Mu spoke of members of the Party who opposed the municipal committee as being "good Party members, with strong Party character," while Yu Ching-hsin denounced those Party members who refused to join in the anti-Party activities for "refusing to uphold the truth, weakening their Party character, and giving consideration to their personal gain and loss."

Li Hui-chung and his followers also made advance preparations for the propaganda conference which the municipal committee convened early in June. At the conference, Hsueh Ai and Hou Shao delivered a joint statement in which they wantonly abused and maligned the Party. They charged that "because of the dogmatic leadership exercised by the Communist Party Anshan municipal committee, the *Anshan Daily* has acquired awesome and hateful features in the eyes of the masses. . . ."

[From a report on Anshan Daily rightists. NCNA. July 28

*

A magazine's rightist deviations

PEKING

Since last autumn, *Hsin Kuan-ch'a* [*New Observer*] has published one after another a number of articles which contained bourgeois thoughts and were unfavourable to socialism. After the rectification campaign began, the periodical went one step further by shooting a number of poisoned arrows at the Party . . . it had been intended to publish in No. 12, which was to come out on June 16 this year, an article entitled "Is trouble brewing in Peking University?" The report openly exaggerated the activities of the rightists in Peking University in a manner ten times worse than the report of "Wall of Democracy" in the *Wen Hui Pao*, and was in reality an attempt at inciting the students to make trouble. It was wholly excised by the comrade leaders of the Writers' Union when about 200,000 copies of the issue had already been printed. *Hsin kuan-ch'a* has committed the error of turning right principally because of the conspiracy between a small group of men in the editorial department, represented by rightist Huang Sha, and rightist Fei Hsiao-t'ung. . . .

Huang Sha, a favourite pupil of Fei Hsiao-t'ung and a correspondent of *Hsin Kuan-ch'a* and also deputy chief of the Social Life Group [of the magazine] . . . has kept in close touch with Fei Hsiao-t'ung and followed his every advice. Fei Hsiao-t'ung called regularly on Huang Sha, and became an "intimate friend" of the editorial department of *Hsin Kuan-ch'a*. . . .

Huang Sha . . . said "the Party is like a religion. It is not a question of whether you believe in it or not, but you simply must believe in it." He also said . . . "the Party is . . . like an evil spirit that possesses you." . . . During the summing-up of the movement for the repression of counter-revolutionaries last year, Huang Sha . . . said: "A man is not worth anything in this society. You may be a good man today, but tomorrow you may be wrongly sentenced as a counter-revolutionary." He did not think that the rectification campaign of the Party could solve any problem. He said: "It is a question not of the style of work of certain individuals but of the whole system. An attempt at solution must begin with the system itself. . . ."

He said in his confession: "After the Hungarian incident, I came to the conclusion that the Party itself should change. I wanted to join the Party in order that I might reform it with bourgeois ideology."

Huang Sha thinks that there is no "freedom of the Press" today . . . that the journalists . . . have become "ceremonial troops," and that Press reports of industrial and agricultural achievements are so much "eyewash. . . ."

A member of the Communist Youth League, Chu Hsing, also an editor of the Art Unit cried in unison with Huang Sha: "Bureaucratism is a product of socialism. Capitalism is highly efficient and doesn't produce bureaucratism. One must get down to the 'system' itself." Even when the struggle against the rightists began, Chu Hsing continued to persist in his reactionary stand, and sticking obstinately to his views, preferred to resign from the Communist Youth League.

Kung Chih-fang, chief of the Art Unit . . . described the relations between the Party and the masses as something worse than the relations between employers and their employees in the old society. He said that a man who was normally outspoken would "keep his mouth shut as soon as he joins the Party" and become a yes-man. . . .

Many who attended the meetings have concluded that the rampancy of the rightists in the editorial department and the gradual degeneration of *Hsin Kuan-ch'a* were inseparable from the serious errors of Ke Yang, presiding editor.

Many comrades pointed out at the meetings that since the Hungarian incident Ke Yang had begun to express doubts and waver on certain fundamental questions, and that her rightist opportunism became more and more serious. As a Party member and leader of the movement for the suppression of counter-revolutionaries in the editorial department of *Hsin Kuan-ch'a*, Ke Yang took a completely negative attitude toward the achievements of the movement when summing up its results. After the rectification movement began, Ke Yang declared on one occasion in the presence of many people: " Doctrinairism binds one. In the past, to be a Party member one had to regard oneself as either a lunatic or a corpse. One could speak one's own mind only in the privacy of one's own bedroom. . . ."

[Report of Hsing Kuan-ch'a (New Observer) anti-rightist forums NCNA. Peking. July 26

*

Liu Pin-yen

PEKING

Liu Pin-yen, Editorial Dept., the *Chinese Youth Newspaper* . . . joined the Party in September 1944, but he refused again and again to devote all his strength to the Party. . . .

According to him: In the whole Communist Party with the unique exception of Chairman Mao, the top consisted of a number of conservative forces—the " privileged class " of ranking cadres—the middle was in the hands of a group of outwardly submissive but inwardly rebellious " local emperors "—the leading Party cadres at provincial and municipal levels—and the bottom was a crowd of unsuspecting and ignorant " fools." . . . He further opined that the formation of this " privileged class " within the Party was brought about by the system in its entirety. He frantically expressed his disagreement with Premier Chou who said that bureaucratism had its origin in history. He considered this to be an excuse. . . . He more than once sardonically and sarcastically described the Party cadres to other people as a group of characters who played cards all day long, who read light publications, but not literary books, who had no interest in literature. . . .

Liu Pin-yen's estimate of the present conditions inside the Party was embodied in the words " a mess." He opined that there was little democracy in the Party, that there were few criticisms in the Party, that elections in the Party were a formality. . . . He said: "For the past few years, the Party has been increasingly estranged from the masses. Most of the people absorbed by the Party have been flatterers, sycophants and yes-men. . . ."

In a report which he made last year in the course of a forum called by the People's Broadcasting Station in Shanghai, he said: . . . "The mistakes were even more flagrant during the suppression of counter-revolutionaries. The movement did not respect man and regarded human dignity as negligible. . . ."

He ascribed certain defects in commercial work to the fact that the state "was trying every means to extort something from the masses." . . . he tried to bring out the point that youths had been oppressed during the past few years. . . .

[*Report on the exposure of Liu Pin-yen. People's Daily. July 20*

Another rebellious Communist journalist

PEKING

Tai Huang is a correspondent of the New China News Agency. He joined the Communist Party in 1944. . . . He opposed the Party and attempted to organise the "Revolutionary Committee of the

---

Leadership of newspapers

Ni Hung-yi, an editor of the Luta Daily . . . said . . . "The central and regional Party papers should not be run single-handedly by the Communist Party. Non-Party cadres and members of democratic parties may be invited to take part in the leadership. In the editorial department, half of the workers may be Party members and the other half may be people not affiliated with the Party. As for the other workers of the papers, there is no necessity to have an overwhelming majority of members of the Communist Party and Communist Youth League. As for the responsible persons of the papers, there is no definite need to have Communist Party members alone. One Communist Party member and one person not affiliated with the Party could fill the presidency and vice-presidency of the paper."

NCNA. Lushun-Dairen. August 7
[From a report on the unmasking of Ni Hung-yi.

Communist Party" to work for the overthrow of the Communist Party. . . .

In November last year, Tai Huang started to write his "10,000-word letter" to the Communist Party Central Committee and Chairman Mao (which has not yet been completed) to slander and attack maliciously the Central Committee and Chairman Mao. In this letter . . . he said affirmatively: "There is a privileged class in existence. Even if a national united class has not yet been formed, the embryo of this class is forming and developing."

According to the preposterous allegation of Tai Huang, the "privileged class" had become an "exploiting class" which should be brought down. He asserted that there was a "sharp difference in livelihood" between his so-called "class" and the people. To prove this fallacy, he shamelessly fabricated "facts" like: "With the exception of rice, more goods are consumed by the revolutionaries who make up 5 per cent. of the population than the peasants who form more than 80 per cent. of the population." He maliciously sought to provoke people by saying: "All the pork and edible oil have been consumed by the members of the Communist Party and the cadres." He shouted: "The lot of our peasants is too hard!" The ordinary people had been "grievously disappointed." He even clamoured: "The old ruling class has been overthrown but a new ruling class has arisen. The evolution of this will lead to an amalgamation with Taiwan. . . ."

Tai Huang directed the spearhead of his attack at the Communist Party Central Committee, Chairman Mao and the leading organs of the Party at all levels. He said: "We do not worry about the universality of bad cadres and the seriousness of their crimes. What we do worry about is the bureaucracy prevailing in the upper echelons. . . ."

Tai Huang slanderously alleged that from the Central Government down to the local authorities, the leadership at all levels thought that "they themselves are above everything" and sought to "deify themselves." . . . He tried to kill all the cadres in the country at a blow by asserting: "The high ranking cadres violate the law and discipline while the cadres of the lower echelons have little regard for the law. They do not hesitate to perpetrate any evil save manslaughter and arson." He emphasised that "the Central Government should be held responsible" for all this. . . . He said that after the 20th Congress of the Soviet Communist Party he "began to suspect that Chairman Mao had committed errors. . . ."

After the outbreak of the Hungarian Incident, Tai Huang disapproved of the dispatch of Soviet troops to help Hungary to suppress its counter-revolutionary rebellion. He said that "there was no case" for the Soviet Union to send in troops "on the ground of justice and morality" . . . "If it was right for the Soviet Union to send its troops, then it would also be right for the United States to help Chiang Kai-shek." . . . He slandered the people's journalistic enterprises as a "policy to make the people ignorant." He maliciously attacked the leaders of the New China News Agency everywhere. . . .

[*NCNA. Peking. August 7*

6

SCHOLARS

University Teachers

WHEN the Communists came to power in 1949, Chinese academic life had been under the influence of the West for some thirty-odd years. The humiliation of China at the hands of foreign Powers during the nineteenth century had inevitably, and justly, been ascribed in part to the limitations of the traditional culture, and with the abandonment of Confucianism the way was open for the influx of Western ideas and techniques with which China would build herself into a modern nation able to hold her own. University syllabuses, textbooks and teaching methods were based on Western models. Over a dozen universities were sponsored by Western missionary organisations and universities and had a high proportion of foreigners on their faculties. Many Chinese students went abroad, particularly to the United States, to do post-graduate work in Western universities. English was the Chinese student's second language.

The Communists knew they could rely upon the scholars to back them in the patriotic task of industrialising China into a great Power and clearly realised their dependence on them for the training of the next generation of technicians, administrators and scholars. But to establish the Party's supremacy in the intellectual sphere and to prevent the contamination of youth, the Communists had to eradicate their " bourgeois " political and academic ideas. Ideological " remoulding " was started in 1951 and the intellectuals were forced to study Marxism-Leninism, attend criticism and self-criticism sessions, and to write confessions. A prime target was what the Communists described as their " pro-America, worship-America, fear-America " mentality. For political and practical reasons, Russian displaced English as the student's second language. Most important of all, universities were brought under the strict control of their Communist Party committees.

The effect of this policy is brought out in the criticisms included in this section. Academic work has been seriously damaged. The opinions of experienced professors are overruled or neglected because they have been trained in the West. Some professors have found themselves obliged to accept Russian ideas they consider unsound; social scientists who used to teach subjects not included in the Russian syllabuses have found themselves deprived of the opportunity to pursue their studies.

Since political reliability is regarded as more important than academic qualifications, even completely untrained Party officials can be promoted over the heads of more learned non-Communists. For fear of denunciation for "bourgeois" ideas, the latter refrain from pressing or even expressing dissenting views, language reform being a case in point. Even where political considerations have not entailed the revision of academic thinking, even natural scientists have had to hold back for fear of reprisals from jealous or autocratic Party officials. The effect of such conditions on teaching has been that teachers usually just reproduce the words of the approved textbook and students dutifully copy them down and parrot them in examinations. In sum, the whole policy of employing the valuable talents of the Western-trained scholars has been largely stultified in the implementation. Those scholars have been turned from educators into transmission belts for the purveying of approved knowledge.

Among the more general critiques of the régime included here, that of the Shenyang professors, Chang Po-sheng and Huang Chen-lu, is the most interesting and important. In spirit, these men are closest to the Communist intellectuals of Poland, the "mad fraction" now condemned as revisionists, who sparked off the Polish "October revolution" in 1956.

The material in this section is primarily arranged geographically.

"Unity, unity—but too little criticism"

PEKING: *Peking University* **April 28**

As it was known to all that Professor Feng Ting was an old Communist Party member, his speech appeared to be a piece of self-criticism made by a representative of a section of the Communist Party members.

He said smilingly: "Some of our Party comrades whenever they open their mouths purport to represent the whole Party; they will not talk of anything but politics; every moment of the day they put on a Party member's front, with its political air, making people afraid to approach them. The fact is in dealing with human beings politics apart, there are many non-political matters one can talk about. . . ."

The conversation then turned to the problem of whether some of the non-Party administrative leading cadres had both position and power or had position without power. People's thoughts naturally turned to the President of our Peking University, Ma Yin-ch'u, because he is a non-Party leading cadre. Many people thought that there were failings in this respect. Some professors said: "Looking at it from the position of a third party, the Party-member leading cadres did not in the past keep sufficiently in touch with or hold conversations with President Ma. Some of the Party-member leading cadres failed to do their work properly; for instance, at meetings called by the University in the past, due to the lack of proper consultation and study, some of the problems had not been previously agreed. The result was during meetings, after the President had made his speech, the Party-member Deputy President would as a rule, under the pretext of making some supplementary remarks, raise many views which revised those of President Ma. Of course, there is nothing wrong in studying problems together at meetings, but the impression it created in the minds of the observers was that President Ma's understanding of situations was not as good as that of the Party-member Deputy President. . . ." Professor Fung Yu-lan went on to talk of his new comprehension of the Party's policy. He said: "Chairman Mao submitted that there should be unity, criticism, unity. This is to say that we should first start with the desire for unity, passing through criticism and arrive at better unity on a new foundation. . . . If we only talk of unity, and whenever we meet we only talk of pleasant things avoiding criticisms, that will be a vulgar unity; and yet at present Peking University is faced with a situation in which there is unity, unity and again unity, but too little criticism. But only talking of unity doesn't lead to any changes in thinking. . . ."

[*Kuang Ming Daily*. *May 4*

A Party secretary admits faults

PEKING: *Peking University* May 14

The first secretary of the Communist Party committee of Peking University, Chiang Lung-chi, Deputy President of the University [said that] . . . Many comrades thought that they could only exercise the leadership of the Party by taking part in administrative leadership and by Party members monopolising everything and superseding everyone. The result was that there had emerged the phenomena of there being no differentiation between the Party and the administration. Speaking of the relationship between himself and the non-Party President of the University, Ma Yin-ch'u, he submitted that he himself had also failed to keep the Party and the administration separate. There was insufficient consultation with President Ma Yin-ch'u on work matters. With regard to university affairs, much more came under his direction than under that of President Ma.

He said that another manifestation of sectarianism was that many Party members overrated themselves and underrated the masses. . . . On the subject of subjectivism he thought that it expressed itself in two ways—dogmatism and empiricism, mainly in the former. He thought that where dogmatism was most apparent was in the study of the Soviet Union's experiences. Everything Russian was idealised, and everything European or American was negated. The Soviet Union's experiences were respected whereas Chinese traditions were neglected. The Soviet specialists were respected while Chinese specialists were ignored.

[*Kuang Ming Daily. May 15*

*

Attacks on language reform

PEKING

Etymologist T'ang Lan said at the meeting that he agreed to the need of reforming the Han characters and the road of phoneticisation. . . .

He thought that the reform of the written language should take note of its national form, and the adoption of the Latin alphabet was therefore not satisfactory. Some phonetic alphabetic letters might gradually be introduced into the Han characters. He was opposed to the unrestricted simplification of the Han characters and considered that if the process of simplification was carried on, the language would be reduced to a large heap of symbols. . . .

Historian Ch'ien Po-tsan said . . . there was a tendency to abolish the Han characters through the process of simplifying them, but many simplified characters were difficult for them to recognise. Ways and means should be devised as soon as possible to have this rectified. He felt that the present process of having 300-odd characters simplified had already aroused resentment in various quarters. This was primarily due to inadequate action being taken to have these quarters consulted on the matter and the unsatisfactory process adopted to simplify the characters. . . .

Etymologist Ch'en Meng-chia expressed his firm opposition to the coining of simplified characters and the replacement of characters with homonyms. He thought that the simplified characters had borne fruit by confusing the meaning of some characters. The Chinese Written Language Reform Committee should decree the withdrawal of simplified characters from use at the earliest possible date. . . .

Chang Teh-ch'ing of the engineering and technical circle thought that it was easier to learn a phonetic language than a hieroglyphic language. . . .

T'ao K'un, editor and translator of chemical terms, said that while there were numerous documents pertaining to the reform of the written language, he could find no reason why the Han characters were difficult to recognise and write, other languages were likewise not easy to recognise and write. The reform might make typing and cable-sending more convenient, but technology should bow to culture. . . .

Ch'ien Wen-hao of the engineering and technical circle said that . . . he thought that some people were opposed to the reform on the ground that the language stood for the accumulation of history. But he looked on the language as a medium of intercourse for mankind, so he thought the reform must be well planned. . . . The Latin alphabet was incompatible with the Han language. The Chinese Written Language Reform Committee had designed the alphabet subjectively without following objective and scientific criteria. To make the reform a success, a scheme would have to be designed with the help of new scientific developments. . . .

T'ao K'un had also had his differences with the Chinese Written Language Reform Committee. This Committee once convened a forum on scientific terms. When releasing information, it gave only the views which were in agreement with the committee. He expressed disbelief in the *Kuang Ming Daily's* special page on language reform and stated that he simply could not believe that in such a large country as China there was actually not one voice in opposition to the reform of the written language. . . .

[*Report of Chinese Written Language Reform Committee forum. NCNA. May 16*

*

Criticism of the Academy of Sciences

PEKING: *The Academy of Sciences* April 30

Many scientists sharply criticised the bureaucratisms of the Academy of Sciences. Among the examples cited that of stopping research work on the growing of mildew on electric wires aroused everybody's attention. The Bacilli Preservation Commission and various organisations concerned have been studying this subject—which was the most important problem brought up during the Second World War—for two years and have made some progress. But now the Academy has suddenly instructed them to stop this work. When research worker Fang Hsin-fang was commenting on this incident, he repeated four or five times that he could not make head or tail of it. He also said that microbiologists had no idea how the twelve-year plan for the development of microbiology was mapped out. . . .

Wu Pao-san [Deputy Director, Institute of Economics, Academy of Sciences] said . . . there were many problems that should be discussed and solved jointly by all economists. But they seldom held meetings to discuss them. Even if one was called, the old economists hardly had any opportunity to take part.

"Yesterday a research assistant told me that during recent years he had studied more Marxist and Leninist economic theories than the capitalist economic theories he had learned previously. But people still regarded him as an old intellectual. When can this label be taken off? Now there are only two roads for the old economists to take. One is to study economic history and the other to study international economy. I studied national income in the past. Now I am dealing with the history of economic thought. Although I like my present work, it is nevertheless a 'loss.' . . ."

[*Kuang Ming Daily*. *May 1*

The academic atmosphere

PEKING: *The Academy of Sciences* May 8

Chang Wen-yu [physicist] said: "I have been back from abroad for half a year and the thing that impresses me most is that the academic atmosphere in the country is not strong enough. The concrete expression of this is that many people keep their mouths shut and do not care about learning. I recall that during the anti-Japanese war, in spite of the poor material conditions then prevailing, many people delighted in the pursuit of learning. . . ."

Liu Ta-kang [chemist] pointed out in his speech: ". . . Take the development of the experimental sciences for instance. They call for special attention to be paid to equipment and accommodation, etc.; but most of the laboratory buildings of the Research Institute of Chemistry were constructed in accordance with the standards for office buildings. We have submitted many views regarding this but the result was, I hear, that we were fitted by some people with the 'cap' of capitalist class thoughts. . . ."

[Kuang Ming Daily. May 9

Difficulties of research

PEKING: *The Academy of Sciences* May 24

Lu Shu-hsiang [philologist]: "Many people engaged in research work have stated that in the last few years they don't seem to have been doing any research, but have been circling around the fringe of research work most of the time. First of all, there is the planning of work. Secondly, there is the organising of work. Thirdly, there is the preparing of work. Fourthly, there is the promoting of work. Then, no sooner has one had time to get one's breath back, than there comes the checking of work and the stocktaking of work. When work is not properly done, there is still scrutinising of work. After scrutinising, come the planning, organising . . . and so on all over again . . . for the last few years, I myself have been running round and round this circle and have become paralysed. . . ."

[Kuang Ming Daily. May 25

*

Why studying in Russia is popular

PEKING

Lei T'ien-chueh [Deputy Director, Institute of Mechanical Science] . . . said: "There is a tendency for political qualifications to override cultural and technical qualifications. Many students sent to Soviet Russia find difficulty in keeping up with their studies. . . . The stock of a student who has been to Russia rises sky-high on his return. He gets a cushy job and a princely salary and enjoys all sorts of privileges, including meals at special messes, without having to prove his worthiness. . . ."

[Forum held by 1st Ministry of the Machine Industry.
Kuang Ming Daily. May 20

*

A lack of trust

PEKING: *Tsinghua University* **May 14**

Associate Professor Fang Ch'ung-chih raised the point that . . . when foreign visitors came to the school, the teachers were compelled to use Chinese and were not permitted to speak in a foreign tongue; and when sending presents to their colleagues among the Soviet specialists, permission had to be obtained from the departmental secretaries and so on. All this revealed a lack of trust in the intellectuals. . . .

[*Kuang Ming Daily. May 15*

Marxism leads to doctrinairism

PEKING: *Tsinghua University*

Hsu Chang-pen said that he thought the adoption of Marxism as the guiding ideology was bound to give rise to doctrinairism. This was because all doctrines were born under certain historical conditions and had a contemporary relevance. If a relatively static doctrine was adopted as guiding ideology, the perpetration of doctrinairism would become inevitable. He said that even a most wise leader was liable to commit mistakes. . . . Some mistakes were inevitable, but some owed their origin to the employment of Marxist-Leninist political and economic theories. No doctrine could embody the whole truth. Men organised their economy and production themselves, and the assertion that economic environment determined man's thinking was (therefore) doctrinairism. . . .

Professor Wang Chao-lin said: " . . . Ordinarily when a meeting was convened, we knew nothing about the things for discussion beforehand. When we turned up at the meeting, we were given a pile of documents. The sponsor of the meeting spoke lengthily to prove how correct was his point of view. Because we were not acquainted with the situation in detail, it was rather difficult for us to discuss the matter. . . ."

[*People's Daily. May 25*

*

Difficulties of geologists

PEKING: *Ministry of Geology*

Feng Ching-lan [Professor, Peking Institute of Geology] and others thought that the Ministry of Geology was too vainglorious, ever emphasising quantity at the expense of quality. It showed rash adventurism in the work of prospecting. The training of cadres was a particularly extraordinary state of affairs. They said the Ministry had founded three Geological Colleges and a dozen or so Technical Schools, in spite of the shortage of qualified teachers. The result was that the teachers had become superficial and could only bring up substandard pupils. . . .

[*Forums on May 31, June 1. Kuang Ming Daily. June 3*

*

Sycophants and salaries

PEKING: *CPWDP* **May 24**

Ho T'ing-chieh [Professor, Peking Normal[1] Un.]:

"I am a professor, but what I do at Peking Normal University is not a professor's job. There is a graduate-assistant in the university, a Party member, and a former student of mine who was rapidly promoted to lectureship and eventually became my leader. . . ."

Yeh Tzu-kang [member, Peking Institute for Railroad Research]:

"The people engaged in personnel work are a crowd of kids. These kids simply don't understand the achievements and the specialisations of people like us. Our achievements and specialisations have in fact been written off with a single stroke of the brush [Chinese characters or ideographs are traditionally written with a brush—*Ed.*], and we have become merely 'rubbish being utilised.' . . ."

T'ai Shuang-ch'iu [Professor, Peking Normal Un.]:

"The assessment of grades and salaries undermines the unity of the professors. . . . Those who are entrusted with the task of assessing the salaries have not even read the academic theses of our professors—they don't know what they specialise in, so how can they make judgments? There are even a few specialists who have been assessed as fifth-grade—this is 100 per cent. subjectivism. . . ."

[*Kuang Ming Daily. May 27*

*

On control of the universities

PEKING: *Peking Normal*[1] *University*

Chu Chi-hsien proposed three principles . . .

1. Democratic rule for universities. . . .
2. The professionals and specialists to govern. It had become a

[1] A "Normal" university or college is a teacher-training institution.

nation-wide problem that the universities were not being governed by professionals.

3. Division of duties. (a) Academic Committee to be responsible for matters concerning teaching and research. (What to teach, how to teach, what merits research and how, teachers, and research workers, etc.) (b) Administrative Conference to be responsible for general administration. (c) Party Committee to be responsible for ideological work and the implementation of policies. . . .

[*Kuang Ming Daily. June 4*

✱

Kuomintang methods towards discarded rubbish

PEKING: *College of Political Science and Law*

Professor Ch'en Fang-chih:

"Methods employed by Kuomintang to deal with intellectuals have pretty well been revived today. . . ."

Yang Ho-kao, a young professor, sorrowfully pointed out that the old teachers at the College were regarded as discarded rubbish by all, from the leadership down to the undergraduates. . . .

Ch'ien Tuan-sheng [Principal of the College] pointed out that the Party comrades did not treat him with respect. He said: "Once a man wrote me a letter complaining that Principal Wu [Wu Cheng-shang, an ex-Deputy Principal] and the Dean, Mr. Liu, only looked after the old cadres, and had no concern for the old teachers. When I showed them the letter, Principal Wu said: "I have received a letter giving exactly the opposite view." But he produced no letter to show me. . . . I treated them with open-hearted sincerity, yet they did not treat me on a footing of equality. Moreover, Principal Wu often tried to pick up one-sided information about me from my chauffeur. This is reprehensible; it is a question of having or lacking confidence in me."

[*Forums reported in Kuang Ming Daily. June 7*

" A huge beehive of doctrinairism "

PEKING: *China People's University* [2]

Hsu Meng-hsiung [Professor, Department of Journalism]:

"The People's University instead of looking like a school looks like

[2] This university was set up in 1953 specially for training Party officials in Economics, Philosophy, History and Law; its curriculum was laid down by Soviet advisers. It is ironic that some of the most violent criticisms should have emerged from it.

a huge beehive of doctrinairism. The bees it produces, rather than gathering honey, spread poison and extensively at that. . . . If we say that the People's University can claim any credit, it is for the dissemination of doctrinairism—such 'credit' if allowed to continue will become 'crime.' . . ."

[*Kuang Ming Daily*. *May 25*

"The masses may overthrow you"

PEKING: *China People's University*

Ko P'ei-ch'i [lecturer, Department of Industrial Economics]:

"I think that nothing can be wider apart than the relations between the Party and the masses today compared with those of pre-liberation days. The schools as well as the common people have the same feeling in this connection. . . . A mess has been made of planned buying and marketing. As a result there are tensions in the supply of commodities. A mess has been made of the movement for the suppression of counter-revolutionaries. The Party has committed mistakes and the leaders should submit themselves for punishment. There is an acute shortage of pork, and the common people find the commodity unavailable. Some people attribute this to the elevation of living standards. Who are the people who enjoy a higher standard of living? They are the Party members and cadres who wore worn-out shoes in the past, but travel in saloon cars and put on woollen uniforms now. To tell the truth, the acute shortage of commodities is caused by the mistakes perpetrated by the people who are entrusted with the enforcement of Party policies. For instance, where has all the pork gone to? The common people are not responsible for this. The shortage is brought about by deviations committed in enforcing planned grain buying and marketing policy which make the common folk unwilling to breed hogs.

"When the Communist Party entered the city in 1949, the common people welcomed it with food and drink and looked upon it as a benevolent force. Today, the common people choose to estrange themselves from the Communist Party as if its members were gods and devils. . . . The Party members behave like plain-clothes police and place the masses under their surveillance. The Party members are not to be blamed for this for the Party organisations instruct them to gather information. . . .

"If the Communist Party distrusted me, the distrust would be mutual. China belongs to 600,000,000 people including the counter-revolutionaries. It does not belong to the Communist Party alone. . . .

If you carry on satisfactorily, well and good. If not, the masses may knock you down, kill the Communists, overthrow you. This cannot be described as unpatriotic, for the Communists no longer serve the people. The downfall of the Communist Party does not mean the downfall of China. . . ."

[*People's Daily*. *May 31*

"*Food for the fish*"

PEKING: *China People's University*

Ko P'ei-ch'i went on to make representations against the Communist Party. He said:

"The very fact that the masses are as yet not free from misgivings in regard to the airing of views is a practical instance of their distrust of the words of the Communist Party. The Communist Party should pay special attention to this. This is because 'people cannot be convinced without faith.' I want to reiterate once again that the masses want to overthrow the Communist Party and to kill the Communists. If you do not reform and make efforts and the degeneration is allowed to continue, there will come the day when you will travel that road. This also conforms with the socialist law of development, and it will be no use your emptily shouting long live so and so.

"Why do the masses distrust the Communist Party? This is because the masses have learned in the course of eight years that the Communist Party is good at changing direction. Last year the central committee directed that the higher intellectuals should be taken good care of, and public personnel were available to provide them with meals and drinks. This year, these public personnel were done away with on the grounds of simplification and economy. When the Party organisation finds a person useful, it treasures him even though he has committed the crime of murdering its friends, comrades and other people belonging to the Party. When it has no more need of him, it nonchalantly excludes him even though he has sweated and shed his blood for the Party. Some Party members disown their relatives and are estranged even from their fathers. When a Party member writes to his mother, he addresses her as comrade. All these instances indicate that it is entirely rational for the masses to distrust the Communist Party.

"The masses could not have had so many grievances against the Communist Party in 1949. The failure to remove the three evils has let loose an inundation. It is still possible to bring the flood under control by removing the three evils. The other possibility is for the Communist Party to be swept away by the flood to provide food for the fish. . . ."

[*People's Daily. June 8*

" The machine-guns may be turned round . . ."

PEKING: *China People's University*

Wang Teh-chou:

" The Party has reached a dangerously critical situation. The masses generally say that the policies of the central committee of the Party are correct, but the lower levels have done wrong. Speaking of pork, in a certain lane twelve butchers' shops have been reduced to two. When pork is unavailable, it is difficult to convince people that living standards have improved. Vegetable prices have increased by 600 per cent. compared with last year. The common people begin to lose confidence in the central committee, saying that in some matters, the situation is worse than under the Kuomintang. The present rectification movement must attain 90 per cent. success, otherwise the Communist Party will collapse. The Communist Party has been victorious, how then should it collapse in such a manner today? To say that the Party has divorced itself from the masses is not so true as to say that the masses have divorced themselves from the Party. The Party will collapse soon. More than 90 per cent. of the members of the Party indulge in sectarian activities, and some indulge in the most evil of acts. At any time, might overcomes might. It is possible to mount machine-guns to deal with trouble. But what is to be feared is that the machine-guns may be turned round for action. I recommend that the Democratic League organise all the people to assist the Party and to supervise the Party in the rectification campaign, so as to achieve the final goal of rectification through the abolition of special privileges. . . ."

[*The Chinese Youth Newspaper. June 10*

* * *

Kuang Ming Daily solicits intellectuals' opinions

SHANGHAI

Wang Tsao-shih [Professor, History Department, Futan Un.; non-party]:

" It is no use denying that the 'contend' and 'bloom' movement has not developed widely and deeply. . . . Some people are very cautious. . . . They fear 'the keeping of accounts.' They fear 'being given enough rope to hang themselves.' . . .

"Now many people are advocating the revival of sociology. I support this proposal because in the new society there are new social problems. . . ."

Liu Hsien [Professor, Biology Department, Futan Un.; CSS]:

"In discussing 'Let a 100 schools contend,' I had better start with a concrete incident. In 1950 I wrote a book entitled *The History of Development from Ape to Man.* Shortly after its publication, a certain reader published a piece of criticism in the *People's Daily*, saying that it was an idealist book. The publisher immediately took back all the copies issued and destroyed them. I wrote a letter to the *People's Daily* stating some viewpoints different from those in the criticism, in the hope that it would be published and induce discussion. But the paper returned my letter, saying that my book was based on the old biological viewpoints of Darwin and exhorting me to study more of the new biological viewpoints of Michurin. To divide biology into the old and the new was really too much for me to take. In September 1955 the Academy of Sciences called a meeting to criticise idealist thinking. My book received 'condemnation-type' criticisms. After the meeting, the *Science Gazette* asked me to write an article, hoping that I would conduct some self-examination and write about my new understanding and appreciation. In my article I accepted some criticisms, and against those unacceptable opinions I put forward my own opposing viewpoints. But the editor of the *Science Gazette* was not satisfied with the article. He said that mistakes of my book had been established and the verdict confirmed. There was no room for further discussion. He returned the article to me.

"After the judgment of the Academy of Sciences, the Research Institute, the Biology Department and the Marxism-Leninism Study Group of Futan University immediately followed suit. In the first term of 1956 they devoted the whole term, holding a discussion meeting every two weeks, to criticising my book, chapter by chapter and paragraph by paragraph. I did not regard this kind of criticism as unnecessary. A scientist who has committed mistakes is always willing to correct them. What seemed regrettable to me was that this kind of criticism was not aimed at the development of science of seeking for truth. It was criticism for criticism's sake. In the course of these criticisms false charges were made against me saying that I was an idealist. They even accused my book of having propagated a reactionary political ideology and harmed the study movement. Charges were many, but evidence was insufficient. These criticisms failed to solve the problems of ideology, but led to a conflict of feelings. Some comrades who took part in the criticisms had not studied my book and only expressed some pointless opinions. Marshalling a number of doctrines, some critics denounced all the viewpoints in my book which were not in agreement with the theory of Engels. In short, that book was torn to pieces by the critics. I accepted some observations which were correct, and had reservations on others. Some criticisms were simply unacceptable. But criticism had become a kind of spiritual pressure under which I was unable to express my own viewpoints fearlessly. If I did, some people would have accused me of resisting thought-reform. In this atmosphere, when a man's idealist ideology is subjected to criticism and regarded as reactionary, even intimate friends shy away from him. . . ."

Chu Yu-hsien [Professor, Education Department, East China Normal Un.; CAPD]:

"During the past few years the fundamental feature has been the mechanical copying of Soviet experiences. There has been a strong tinge of doctrinairism. Up to the present, Chinese institutions of higher education are still using only Russian textbooks on education. No textbook on education has been written and published by ourselves to suit the actual conditions of China. . . ."

Yang Chao-lung [Professor, Law Department, Futan Un.; CSS]:

"I think it is right to suggest that we can only 'bloom' and must not 'contract.' As a matter of fact, contracting is now out of the question. . . ."

T'an Chia-cheng [Head, Biology Department, Futan Un.; CDL]:

"It is understood that in the central government there are now about forty or fifty ministries. Every ministry has established some schools, publishing houses and research institutes. Each of them needs a number of high-grade intellectuals as leaders. Therefore, many top class intellectuals are tied down with administrative duties and very few of them are actually doing any research. This is an enormous waste. . . . Here I think it is necessary to repeat: there is a difference between science and politics. A scientist should not separate himself from politics; but sciences themselves—particularly the natural sciences—are classless."

Hsieh Hsun-ch'u [Senior Instructor, Psychology Research Group, East China Normal Un.; CAPD]:

"First of all, the policy of 'Let a 100 schools contend' has increased the burdens on teachers. . . . In the past, teachers could solve all problems by just quoting some doctrines from authoritative works. For instance, when discussing psychology, you needed only one sentence: Psychology is the reflection of external reality. In criticising idealism you just had to say that it was reactionary politically and idealist ideologically. At that time, we only spoke in accordance with various theories of Russian experts. We did not think of, nor did we want, any academic contention. Now the situation has changed. Even students are not satisfied with the introduction of books, or doctrinaire arguments without any substance. . . ."

[*Kuang Ming Daily. May 1*

* * *

The dangers of independent thinking

WUHAN: *Kuang Ming Daily*

Chou Yu-teh [Professor, Wuhan Medical College; CSS]:

"Whenever people outside the Party hold views on work at variance with those of the responsible cadres of the Party and which result in controversy, they are branded as dangers, and are said to be trying to wrest the leadership from the Party." . . . When they (Party cadres) received any requests for support and aid appertaining to professorial duties, they would brush them aside with the excuse that they did not understand them. If one were to take the responsibility on one's own shoulders independently, then one was afraid of being branded as a danger and of trying to wrest the leadership from the Party. If one did not take the responsibility on one's own shoulders, and tried to muddle through, then one would feel that one was letting down the Party and the country. One simply did not know how to please these Party cadres. . . .

[*Kuang Ming Daily. May 10*

Ch'eng Ch'ien-fan [Professor, Wuhan Un.]:

"Gross inequality exists in the political treatment of Party members and the masses. . . . Party members enjoy many privileges which make them a race apart. . . . Some of the theories that have been advanced are rather obnoxious. For instance, 'Communist Party members are of special material.' The truth of this depends upon the degree of the member's understanding of Communism and his stamina, as well as the contributions he can make. Party membership is no absolute criterion. . . . Take 'Red Specialists,' for instance. Here, 'Red' as we all know is used in a political rather than in an aesthetic sense. The so-called 'Red Specialists' refer to those specialists who have joined the Party. Does that imply that we, the specialists who have not joined the Party, are pink, white, black, yellow or transparent specialists? The point is that we have no desire to be the above-mentioned specialists. . . ."

Yuan Ch'ang-ying [Professor, Wuhan Un.]:

"At Wuhan University the privileged-class style of work of the Party members is seen everywhere. For example, a families committee investigating the measures adopted to prevent fires visited a house belonging to a Party member who was also a Personnel worker. The committee was so loudly abused by him that the lady comrade in charge of the investigations was reduced to tears and had to leave the house. . . . No wonder that people regard Party members as belonging to a privileged class. . . ."

Han Teh-pei [Head of the Department of Law, and Deputy Dean, Wuhan Un.]:

"Although I am Deputy Dean of this University, I am unable to direct the actions of a porter merely because he is a Party member. . . ."

[*Kuang Ming Daily*. *May 17*

Several professors dealt with the problem of selecting students for advanced studies abroad, selecting research students and graduate assistants. Special attention was paid to the selection of students for going abroad; it was thought that the whole field was monopolised by Party and Youth League members. . . .

[*Forums on May 4 and 7*. *Kuang Ming Daily*. *May 19*

"Born Saints"

Professor Ma Tse-min [Principal, Central South College of Finance and Economics; Senior Member, Hupeh Provincial Committee, CDL] [said]: . . . "Some Party comrades are so self-righteous that they regard whatever they say and do as representative of the Party as a whole and

100 per cent. correct—indeed as truth itself, they themselves being the personification of truth. Whilst they do not listen to other people's views, they insist on other people listening to theirs. When they want a thing done this way, you just can't do it that way; there is no room at all for consultation. If you happen to have different views and ways, then such caps as 'you have ideological problems,' 'insubordinate to the leadership of the Party,' will soon fall on your head. The reform by education they speak of refers only to reforming others by education; when they speak of submitting views and making criticisms, they are also referring to other people; they regard themselves as completely correct, progressive and in need of no more education, reform or criticism. These people create the impression that they are 'born saints' in the true sense of the term. This is like a Christian believer saying 'I represent God.' . . ."

[*Interviewed by Kuang Ming Daily*. *May 8*

*

A 10,000-word letter to Chairman Mao

Our Constitution provides that citizens "enjoy freedom of residence and freedom to change residence." In fact, we have not given any of the 500 million peasants the freedom to change their residence to a city. . . .

Again, our Constitution provides that "freedom of the person of citizens is inviolable." During the campaign for the suppression of counter-revolutionaries in 1955, an untold number of citizens throughout the country were detained by the units where they were working (this did not happen to myself). A great many of them died because they could not endure the struggle. No matter how strong the "reasons" were for detaining these citizens to conduct struggles against them, this was, after all, a serious violation of human rights. . . .

This is tyranny! This is malevolence!

Possibly, these acts were considered "necessary" at a certain time and in a certain place, but just because of this alleged "necessity," the articles of the Constitution on human rights have become a sort of window-dressing to deceive the people. . . . Today, we do not even know the height or size of a person we elect, let alone his character or ability. We have simply become ballot-casting machines. . . .

The eight-hour working system was one of the objectives of the workers' movement before liberation. However, it has ceased to be a topic of discussion since this movement scored a complete victory in

China. . . . Of course, we have our reasons: "The present cannot be compared with the past as the situation is different." However, more important is the contention of the people: "When the present is compared with the past, our hardships remain the same! . . ."

I admit that in the seven years of our Party's rule our achievements are predominant. However, if, on the particular question of our policy towards intellectuals, I should speak not according to the accepted formula [Translator's note: This formula is, "Achievements are predominant and shortcomings are but particular instances"], I cannot help saying that shortcomings are predominant. More exactly, I should say that this policy has been a failure. . . .

At different times, intellectuals may be thrown into the fire or pushed into the water, sent down to hell, or lifted up to heaven. Going down to hell, intellectuals have a great many grievances and regret that considering themselves wise at the time of the liberation, they "did not listen to their friends' advice to go abroad to observe the conditions there." (*Ch'ang Chiang Daily* Editor's note: "To go abroad to observe the conditions there" was "go to Formosa" in the original text, and the change was made by the writer himself.) . . . In the last seven years, they have lived like a girl being brought up under her future mother-in-law in the home of her fiancé, constantly trembling with fear. . . .

We have applied to intellectuals methods of punishment which peasants would not apply to landlords and workers would not apply to capitalists. During the social reform campaigns, unable to endure the spiritual torture and humiliation imposed by the struggle . . . the intellectuals who chose to die by jumping from tall buildings, drowning in rivers, swallowing poison, cutting their throats or by other methods, were innumerable. The aged had no escape, and pregnant women were given no pardon. . . . Comparing our method of massacre with that adopted by the fascists at Auschwitz, the latter appeared more clumsy and childish (at any rate, they hired executioners), but more prompt and "benevolent." If we say that Comrade Stalin has not escaped from condemnation in history for his cruel massacre of comrades, then our Party, in my opinion, will also be condemned for our massacre of intellectuals who had already "surrendered" themselves to us. Our Party's massacre of intellectuals and the mass burying alive of the *literati* by the tyrant, Ch'in Shih-huang, will go down in China's history as two ineradicable stigma. This cannot but make us feel utterly heartbroken! (At this juncture, we can hear the warm applause in Formosa! —*Ch'ang Chiang Daily* Editor's note.)

However, we remain happy and complacent, saying: " achievements are predominant."

Where are our achievements?

Yang Shih-chan

May 17, 1957. *[Professor of Accountancy, Central-South Institute of Finance and Economics]*

[Hankow Ch'ang Chiang Daily. July 13

*

" Teachers have no say "

WUHAN: *CDL* **May 26**

Chu Ming-pi [Principal, Hupeh Medical College]:

" Many problems that exist in the institutions of higher learning today are attributable to the inappropriateness of the Party committee system. The Party committee monopolises everything, insisting on having a finger in every pie and yet knows very little about the business of teaching. . . ."

Hsu Ching-ch'ien [Chief Librarian, Wuhan Un.]:

" People say the problem of the Party committee system is that the Party is substituted for the government. If this were really so, it wouldn't be so bad, because we would at least know where we were going. The trouble is that many Party members nowadays set themselves up to supersede both Party and government. An individual Party member could lord it over his fellow men on the false pretence that he has *carte blanche* from the authorities. . . ."

[Kuang Ming Daily. June 2

*

" This is a yamen "

WUHAN: *Central China Engineering Institute* **June 12**

Professor Lu Ya-heng:

" The tendency towards Yamenisation or bureaucratisation can even be detected in such a trivial matter as distributing chairs. For the Principal of the College, there are sofas; for the Departmental heads, there are cane chairs; when it comes to the heads of the Pedagogic Rooms, there are only wooden benches. Even the calendars placed in different offices vary; the Principal has the largest ones, next come the Directors, next come the Departmental heads, and the heads of the Pedagogic

Rooms have the smallest ones. About such rigorous hierarchical distinctions, the teachers say in indignation: 'Is this anything resembling a school? This is a Yamen. Small wonder the school is in a bad way!' . . ."

[*Kuang Ming Daily report. June 12*

* * *

Debit accounts

SIAN: *Kuang Ming Daily* May 4

Chang Hsi-hua [Chief Ophthalmologist, No. 4 Hospital, Sian; CSS]:

"The memories of past campaigns are still fresh in all our minds; those who had the habit of speaking up frankly had their remarks recorded word by word, and when the time of reckoning came, it was as if these had been deposited in small amounts in a bank account which had, in the end, reached quite a tidy total. Although each year we talk of anti-bureaucratism, the more we do so the worse it becomes, because those who dare to speak out are becoming fewer and fewer. Some of the Party members who have committed errors are not only not dealt with, but have got promotion, owing to the higher-ups shielding them—which of course leads people to feel that it is useless to submit views. . . ."

Liu Pu-t'ung [Professor, North-West Un.] thought that human relations in the university were ice-cold and people were reserved rather than lively and warm-hearted. . . . He said: "The existence of dogmatism nowadays has made teaching a very convenient profession. There was a time when the 'Three-Copy' teaching method was in vogue, in North-West University: the teachers' lecture notes were copied from Soviet teaching materials, which were, without alteration of a single word, copied out on the blackboard by teachers at classes, and then duly copied into their notebooks by the students. In the case of the student not understanding a point, the teacher would confront him with the stick, with the remark 'This teaching material originates from the Soviet Union.' . . ."

[*Kuang Ming Daily. May 6*

Wang Chien-san [Professor, Sian Normal College; Shensi Province, Standing Committee, KMTRC]:

"In the dramatic circles, doctrinairism is also very serious. . . . They once regarded mythical plays as superstitions; later when they heard that Gorky had said that mythology was not superstition, they all rushed to produce plays such as *Chang Yu Boils the Sea, Splitting Open the Mountain to Save Mother*, etc. They obstinately set out to overthrow old traditions with new doctrines, and to negate our national form by applying Western rules, hence they 'condemn to death with one word' all the plays which used to delight and entertain the people. Although the situation is being improved at present, I hear that the old artists are still not allowed to undertake the actual work of directing plays. . . ."

Li Shu-li [Professor, North-West Un.; Vice Chairman, Shensi Province, CAPD]:

"To be quite honest, old teachers like us are today scared stiff, due to the accumulated experiences of the past few years. . . .

"The remarks I have had the courage to make at this forum I would not dare to make when I am back at North-West University. There seems to be an invisible pressure which compels people to say nothing. Among the democratic parties, so far as I know, it has become very difficult to understand what the masses really think. Whenever we are out to gather people's reactions, the interviewee will either nod his head saying 'Good! Good! Good!' or shake his head saying nothing. . . .

"In our University there is a batch of so-called positive elements who make a point of eavesdropping on other people's conversations and jotting down points in their small notebooks, which will be used as evidence to 'rectify' people in the future. The secretary of the Department of Economics is one of those men. Snooping around, he overheard a remark made by a certain professor. 'One can't be too careful about what one says these days.' During a campaign he seized upon this remark and made much of it. Was the professor wanting to stage a revolt, he asked. Some of the people in our University in their pursuit of Communist membership, for the sake of demonstrating their 'Party' aptitude, toady to the Party and are full of adulation. They also make it their business to deal blows to the 'backward' elements so as to create opportunities of showing their own 'party' aptitude. . . .

". . . The attitude of certain leaders on the Party committee of North-West University towards the professors is extremely crude. For instance, attendance at the extra-curricular political school should be voluntary, but the Party committee member will insist on personally taking the roll-call and pointing out who have failed to turn up. . . ."

[*Kuang Ming Daily. May 11*

Ch'ien Chu-chun [Assistant Professor, North-West Un.; CSS]:

" I am a member of the Chiu San Society and am more familiar with the position there. The meetings called by the Society are not well attended and my calculation is that only 60 per cent. of our members normally attend meetings.

" One thing I am definite about is that a section of the comrades never take part in organisational life. Organisational life is devoid of substance and it can be summed up in three sentences: (1) talking about plans; (2) talking about summing up; (3) responding to the summons.

" Therefore it only makes people feel futile and dull and thus it can neither uplift people's thoughts nor is it of any help to the business in hand. . . .

" There is a lack of concord between the Communist Party and the democratic parties in their work: (a) The Communist organisation in North-West University is 'monopolising' and 'embracing' everything and democratic parties have no room for manoeuvre . . . according to a responsible member of a democratic party when it comes to listening to major reports, he is left out; when it comes to a goodwill tour to Paochi, he is left out; when it comes to theatre tickets, he is left out; but when it comes to criticism he is in. . . ."

Liu Wei-t'ung [Professor, Sian Medical College, CDL]:

" Premier Chou once said that we should guarantee that 5/6th of the intellectuals' working time should be devoted to their profession. Sian Medical College during the year 1956 held more meetings than in the year 1955. . . ."

[*Kuang Ming Daily forum. May 12*

*

A distrust of ideas and talent

SIAN May 7

Professor Chang T'ung-ho [Director, Surgery Department, Sian Medical College] said . . . that he had recently heard a certain teacher boldly put forward the view at a forum: " I feel that the Party Organisation, in absorbing Party members seems to have a preference for those yes-men, sycophants and people who offer top hats to the Party members and leading cadres. . . ."

An old professor of Chinese traditional painting of the Fine Arts Department of the North-West Special Course School of Arts said gravely: " We here have in the past only been able to make use of slaves, not of real talent. Not only have we had no use for people with ideas but we have dealt them blows until they have submitted. . . ."

The above-mentioned old professor of Chinese traditional painting said that . . . once he painted a picture which had not displayed collectivisation; he had not accepted the leadership's criticism. Consequently for two days and nights, meetings were held at which it was demanded that he admit his mistake. . . .

[*Kuang Ming Daily report. May 7*

* * *

"Harmonious in appearance, discordant in spirit"

LANCHOW: *Kuang Ming Daily* **May 16**

Shui Tzu [Vice Chairman, Kansu Province, KMTRC]:

"Finally, I wish to talk about the problem of the style of work of the Party cadres at the basic levels. These cadres in different localities suffer from the three bad 'isms' to a serious degree; not only do they ignore people of account in society, but also they only listen to the so-called positive elements; the quality of some of these so-called positive elements is very bad and they are normally despised by people, but once they have power in their hands they abuse it and exploit it at will; this makes people look askance at them and affects the Party's prestige. The Party's central committee's policy is a good scripture, but when recited by a crooked-mouthed monk it becomes crooked too. . . ."

Yang Shih-hsing [Professor, North-West Institute of Animal Husbandry and Veterinary Science; Kansu Provincial Committee, CDL]:

"The Party and Youth League members have not exercised leadership properly in the schools; they are unwilling to undertake jobs which do not bring them fame or profit. It is these people who get promotions. No wonder the masses and the Party have become 'harmonious in appearance but discordant in spirit.' . . ."

Wang Ching-tsun [Professor, Geography Department, Lanchow Un.; Standing Committee Kansu Province, CDL]:

"The teachers in the schools are ill at ease; they generally are chary of associating with the Party and Youth League members because the Party organisation distrusts the teachers, feeling that they are unclean and impure, and treats them as outsiders. They even get the young cadres among the Party and Youth League members to check up on the teachers publicly or in secret and to report back on their problems. They almost seem to display special interest in teachers' weaknesses. In appraising teachers' teaching ability they appoint student officials such as 'course representatives' and 'class representatives,' and rely on the views passed on by them to make their judgments. Is every report correct? Can the student judge the masters? What kind of fashion is this? Some Party members even reprimand the old professors to their faces, deriding them that the education they have received is corrupt and capitalist class education. Since the old teachers are wounded at heart, the relations between old and new teachers are particularly bad. . . ."

Lin Chung-yu [Assistant Professor; Deputy Director Geography Department, North-West Normal College; Standing Committee Kansu Province, CDL]:

"In the work of allocating jobs for graduates, sectarianism is apparent. Party and Youth League members are assigned to work in the large towns and cities and the non-Party and non-Youth League members are assigned to the medium and small towns and cities. Why not let the Party and Youth League members be the first to face hardships? . . ."

[*Kuang Ming Daily*. *May 26*

*

A professor lights a "bonfire"

LANCHOW: *Lanchow University*

Ch'en Shih-wei, member of the Central Committee of the Chiu San Society and Second Vice President of Lanchow University. . . .

On June 5 . . . this Ch'en Shih-wei, who was also the chairman of the Lanchow Branch Committee of Chiu San Society, in the course of a forum called by the local branch of the Chiu San Society to discuss the subject, "Colleges Do Not Need the Leadership of the Communist Party Committee," announced the plan of "Government of the University by Professors," designed with much care and trouble, as follows:

(1) Purpose: "To correct the following defects in the existing higher institution system: chaos, indistinct division of labour, thin scholastic

atmosphere, inability of school administration to satisfy educational demands."

(2) The supreme authority in the school: To establish a school committee comprising from twenty to forty persons, mainly professors.

(3) Duties and rights: Inspection of the education plan, the posting of personnel, the drafting and approval of the budget, the election of the president and vice presidents, and other important matters.

(4) Remarks: The Party shall be responsible for guidance in policy matters. . . .

During a radio broadcast, he rumoured that in Lanchow University "vitality was low and the heart of man dissolute." He also said irresponsibly: "President Lin Ti-shen, the senior Party member in charge of the administration, is rich in peasant revolution ideology. He decides arbitrarily and acts tyrannically. He does not understand the function of specialised teachers. He is not active in securing teachers. Lu Yun-lin, another man in charge of Party members' education and Vice Registrar, has always been extending his personal influence in the school and ousting learned professors." At that moment students and young assistants to professors were in an excited mood over the shortage of teachers. Having listened to this striking piece of propaganda, they visit him in groups. Ch'en Shih-wei saw in this an opportunity for provocation and told them: "President Lin does not want good professors, claiming that good professors are not easy to lead. . . ." In this manner Ch'en Shih-wei lit a bonfire in the minds of young men who did not know the truth. . . .

In the middle of June, on the issue of the teachers problem and merger of Departments, a Contending and Blooming Committee of Lanchow University organised a students' delegation to go to Peking with a petition. At that moment Liu Ai-feng, Vice Minister of Higher Education, was in Sian. He telegraphed some of the presidents asking them to come to Sian and discuss with him the problem of Lanchow University. But the students' delegation, supported by Ch'en Shih-wei, also wanted to go. It refused to take the advice of the Kansu Provincial Committee of the Communist Party and sent double the number of delegates indicated. In Sian, Liu Ai-feng granted three audiences to the students and answered their questions sincerely and satisfactorily. But the students still insisted on going to Peking. After explaining and dissuading patiently but in vain, President Lin Ti-shen, on behalf of the University, had to dissolve the students' delegation. At that moment the students had the audacity to tell Lin Ti-shen, " You cannot dissolve us. We are appointed by the Contending and Blooming Committee! " Ch'en Shih-wei, who was himself the chairman of the Contending and Blooming Committee, remained a mute spectator to all this, never uttering one single syllable to the students from beginning to end. Things having thus reached a stalemate, the students asked for the travelling expenses to Peking, and said that without the travelling expenses, they would " beg their way back." At this instant Ch'en Shih-wei suddenly interposed with reassurance, saying: " This will not happen. This will not happen! " And thus he brought ten students and two lecturers to Peking. . . .

When the " time was ripe," the final " design," prepared long in advance, was unfolded. On the wall of Lanchow University appeared a list of the names of the new Lanchow University leaders. Among the six responsible cadres only the Party Committee secretary appeared from among the Party member cadres. . . .

Ch'en Shih-wei became practically the chief responsible person for the whole university. At the bottom of the list was the signature " Five Idealists. . . ." The names of President Lin Ti-shen and Assistant Dean Lu Yun-lin, both of them senior Party members and responsible cadres, appeared in separate postings at the side, on which were written, " President Lin should resign of his own accord! " and " Dismiss Assistant Dean Lu from all his offices! . . ."

[*NCNA. July 15*

* * *

Attacks on University Party committees

CHUNGKING

The rightist clique in South-West Normal College, composed of Professors Lo Jung-tzu and Chen Tung-yuan and Lecturer Tung Shih-kuang and the clique in Chungking Building Construction College headed by Chao Chang-keng who was in charge of the Designing Seminar . . . frantically clamoured for the " evacuation from the schools " of the Party committees, and proposed slogans such as " government of schools by professors " and " democratically running the schools," in an attempt to usurp the leadership of the schools. . . .

The rightist clique in Chungking Building Construction College, headed by Chao Chang-keng, once instigated part of the students to stage troubles and strikes.

[*NCNA. August 4*

* * *

Professors attack Party leadership

TIENTSIN

Rightist Li Pao-chen [Professor, Department of Economics] . . . held meetings together with those of the Chiu San Society who were discontented with the Communist Party and those who were discontented with the rearrangement of colleges and departments, and with the "three-anti," "five-anti" and similar movements. . . . They proposed the downfall of Teng Wei-chao, and the ousting of Li Tao-ta, head of the department, so that they might control the Department of Economics and safeguard the study of capitalist economics.

Rightist Chao Yun-shan [Professor, Department of Mechanics] . . . slanderously described the university as "a dungeon without daylight, . . ." spread among the teachers such anti-socialist views as "The intellectuals are entirely at the disposal and mercy of the Communist Party," "The lay Communist Party cannot lead in technical things" and "It is basically impossible for the Party committees to lead universities."

Rightist Hsiang Tzu-kang [Professor, Department of Chemical Engineering] . . . slanderously described the movement for the suppression of counter-revolutionaries as "a struggle against those who had offended individual Party members, League members or activists," and inveighed against the activists of the movement "whose tongues were reeking with fresh blood."

[*NCNA*. *August 4*

Nepotism

SHENYANG: *Kuang Ming Daily* May 8

Li Hsien-yuan [Lecturer, North-East College of Finance and Economics] said: . . . during past campaigns in criticising a certain man's thoughts it was often pointed out that that man had made a certain remark in a certain month of a certain year; while, in actual fact, that man had made three remarks and not one. The way that people's remarks are taken out of their contexts to be criticised during struggles will not win people's confidence. . . .

Hsu Kung-chen [Lecturer, Shenyang Normal College; CDL] said that their college showed grave sectarianism in its personnel arrangements.

For instance, the head of the Russian Language Department did not know a single Russian letter, but he was able to become head of the Department simply because he was a Party member. The head of the Department of History had never previously studied history; it was only because she was the wife of the Principal of the College. . . .

[*Kuang Ming Daily*. *May 11*

*

Two professors denounce the Party and its leaders

SHENYANG: *Normal College* **June 10**

Chang Po-sheng and Huang Chen-lu at a "contention" meeting of the faculty members of the Shenyang Normal College on June 10, jointly made a long speech lasting about three hours. . . . Chang Po-sheng is head of the propaganda department of the Communist Youth League in the Normal College and Huang Chen-lu is editor of the school paper. . . .

They said: "The suppression of counter-revolutionaries was necessary and timely but too many persons were put to death. . . . Many among the executed were formerly military and political personnel of the so-called Manchukuo and the Kuomintang and landlords, but they were not guilty of heinous crimes, still less were they flagrant counter-revolutionaries; they were the product of history. . . . It is inhumane to put all of them to death. . . ."

They said: "If the cause behind the mistakes of the campaign for rounding up counter-revolutionaries is traced, it will be traced to the Party centre. The 5 per cent.—Party centre's estimate of the percentage of counter-revolutionaries in the population—is a gross manifestation of subjectivism and bureaucratism. The idea is influenced by Stalin's erroneous theory 'the more developed the socialist cause, the more the enemy.' . . ."

Huang Chen-lu went on: "Socialist transformation is over-hasty all round. It is not a question of whether co-operativisation is called for but a question of how to do it. To this question no answer was given by Chairman Mao in his report to the Supreme State Conference. . . . Outwardly the movement was launched with a fanfare; actually, it was too early. It is not true that all the peasants consciously want to join the co-operatives; as a matter of fact, the majority of them are forced to join. That is why Agricultural Producer Co-operative cadres are short, their quality is not high, work is chaotic, non-productive personnel are too large in number and production enthusiasm is low." Huang Chen-lu proposed that, where conditions were not appropriate, co-operatives should be allowed to disband themselves and the state should concentrate on the state farms and permit purchase and sale of small holdings. . . . With the private industrial and commercial establishments coming under state-private ownership, large numbers of directors, accountants and cashiers—" leading personnel "—had appeared, and money had flowed into their pockets. Moreover, there had been more trouble for consumers. " Can there be any disturbance if they are allowed to run their businesses independently under the leadership of a powerful state economy? "

The central problem brought up in the joint speech by these two men was " doing away with the absolute leadership of the Party."

" Doing away with the absolute leadership of the Party," said Huang Chen-lu, " is aimed at strengthening the Party leadership and making the Party a vanguard. . . ."

Huang Chen-lu said: " Before the liberation the Party enjoyed high prestige, maintaining intimate connections with the people and uniting with the people, and there were no such contradictions as exist today. Since the founding of the Republic, particularly in the last one or two years, the Party has become superior to the people and has assumed privileges, praising itself for its ' greatness, glory and correctness ' and placing itself above the state, above the people. For this reason, Party prestige is falling day by day. More and more persons with impure motives join the Party. They join the Party because they can win glory and acquire power, influence and money. Imbued with despicable individualism, they insinuate themselves into the favour of the Party, flatter the Party, bow to the Party and obey the Party on everything. . . . The Communist Party has 12,000,000 members, less than 2 per cent. of the total population. The 600 million people are to become the obedient subjects of these 2 per cent. of people. What sort of principle is this! The absolute leadership of the Party must be done away with. The privilege of Party members must be done away with! "

Supplementing this point, Chang Po-sheng said in his speech: " Now that the Party is in a privileged position, Party members of mediocre talent are found everywhere occupying high positions. Old Party members, forgetting the tradition of working for the nation and the people, are fond of flattery and loath to accept criticism. The Party centre takes the lead, ' setting a bad example to those in low places.' The Press unanimously sings the praises to its meritorious service and virtue.

. . . We warn the Party; beware of organisational and ideological ossification!"

Huang Chen-lu said: "It was logical that the Party should exercise absolute rights of leadership and that Party members were put into important positions before and at the beginning of the founding of the Republic. Conditions have changed today and history demands the liquidation of the absolute right of leadership of the Party and the privileges of the Party. Otherwise, the course of history will be obstructed." In their opinion, only when the privileges of Party members were done away with would genuine Communists join the Party and only such Party organisations could preserve their purity and lead the state with a correct policy; otherwise, the Party and socialism would be buried.

"There has been no socialist democracy in the years since the liberation, and what democracy there is is only in form and there is not even the pseudo-democracy of capitalist countries," Chang Po-sheng said. "The Constitution is a scrap of paper and the Party has no need to observe it. Outwardly we have democratic elections, a united front policy and non-Party people exercising leadership; actually, the Party exercises dictatorship and a few persons of the Political Bureau of the Party centre exercise absolute power. Since the election of people's deputies is not democratic, elections are actually a variety of appointment. Although some non-Party people occupy leading posts, they perform duties but have no power. . . . Nor is there democracy within the Party. The convening of the 8th National Congress, for instance, was a great event, but which Party member could put his views to the congress? . . . As to freedom of assembly, association and publication, that is just something written in the Constitution; actually, citizens can only become obedient subjects or, to use a harsh word, slaves. The Party is the emperor and an august and sacred body. Who dares to oppose it when it holds the bible of Marxism-Leninism in the one hand and the sword of state power in the other? You would either be labelled an anti-Marxist-Leninist or handcuffed with 'unfounded charges.'"

"If this state of affairs is to be changed, a system of general election campaigns should be put into effect alongside the abolition of the absolute leadership of the Party. The people should be allowed freely to organise new political parties and social bodies, and to put out publications so as to open the channels of public opinion, supervise the government, combat cheap praises and encourage them to oppose an undesirable *status quo* even if it meant opposition to the Communist Party, provided they do not stand against the people and socialism. The

Communist Party, if it really represents the people, will not be kicked out; if the Communist Party is kicked out, it means it no longer represents the people. Is it pitiable to have such a Party kicked out? "

Chang Po-sheng went on: "Whose words count in connection with state affairs? The Constitution lays down that the words of the National People's Congress and its Standing Committee count, but actually the National People's Congress is nothing but a mud idol while all power is in the hands of the Party centre. The National People's Congress merely carries out the formality of raising hands and passing resolutions. In all these years, one has seldom seen a Standing Committee member putting forward an important motion, though occasionally one has seen some of them publishing unimportant notes on inspection tours in the Press. Is this not laughable? Why did the National People's Congress deputies see no contradictions among the people during their inspection tours? They saw only what the Party said and saw nothing when the Party did not say anything. They did not see or they dared not say? Even more laughable is that the 'Chinese People's Political Consultative Conference,' which is said to be representing the united front, spends most of its energy on work connected with organisation of studies. . . . Like two paper flowers the National People's Congress and the People's Political Consultative Conference decorate the façade of democracy. . . . All kinds of important questions are decided upon by six persons—Chairman Mao, Liu Shao-ch'i, Premier Chou En-lai and those above the rank of the secretary general of the Party centre—at their table [the others—Chu Teh, then Vice Chairman of the Republic; Ch'en Yun, a Deputy Premier; Teng Hsiao-p'ing, Party Secretary General; the six composed the Politburo's Standing Committee—*Ed.*]. The destiny of 600 million people is dictated by the pen of these six persons. And how can they know the actual situation? At best they can make an inspection tour of the Yellow River and swim in the Yangtze. [A reference to Mao Tse-tung's much-publicised swim across the Yangtze in May 1956.] Even if they talked with the peasants, the peasants would not tell the truth and could only say: 'Chairman Mao is great.' How can mistakes be avoided when such a small number of people take arbitrary action and recklessly issue orders? The Party centre has never criticised itself publicly since the founding of the Republic. If this dictatorial obstruction to national affairs is to be changed, the Party must be removed from its position of superiority to the National People's Congress and the government, the government must be placed below the National People's Congress and the National People's Congress must be made an organ exercising genuine power. . . ."

Chang Po-sheng said: "Personnel work is in a complete mess. Incompetent persons become leaders and competent ones become men without official standing. . . . Full-time Party cadres should be drastically reduced. . . . One hears that the Young Communist League of Yugoslavia has only some 170 full-time cadres throughout the country, whereas our First Motor Car Plant alone has more than 100 full-time League cadres. This is indeed a laughing matter, a big laughing matter! . . . If a person is a Party member, he is made a leading cadre; if he is not a Party member, he is placed at a lower level. . . ."

"Whether a post should be high or low should be determined by whether the person is equal to the post. How about the veteran revolutionary cadres who have worked for the revolution for several decades but whose cultural level is very low? They may be employed as grooms but, since they have rendered meritorious service to the revolution, we should respect them and grant them a service allowance. . . ."

In conclusion, Chang Po-sheng explained that the views as expressed in their speeches were at the stage of fermentation in December 1956 and were only written down yesterday.

[*Shenyang Daily*. *June 11*

* * *

"Feudal princes and stinking charlatans"

CHANGCHUN: *Kuang Ming Daily* **May 20**

Kuang Wen-ying [Associate Professor, North-East Normal College; KMTRC] said:

"My university, for one, is overwhelmed by officialdom, where the Mandarin's way of life has superseded that of the scholar's. The heads of departments and sections run into alarming figures. Take the Department of History, for instance, there are twenty-three heads under that department alone—namely, one head of the department, two assistant-heads of the department, one assistant-head in charge of the Correspondence Course, one assistant to the head of the department, ten heads (including assistant heads) of Pedagogic sections, five heads of reference libraries, one head of the departmental office, two heads (including one assistant head) of the Translation Section. The place is absolutely littered with feudal princes and stinking charlatans. . . ."

Yang Ch'ing [Head, Department of Education, North-East Normal Un.; Kirin Provincial Committee, CDL]:

" With regard to promotion, assignments, the allocation of duties and powers, Party members also enjoy a distinctive advantage as 'political aristocrats.' All departments without exception tend to shower favours upon Party members, as if a man would all of a sudden become omniscient as soon as he acquires a Party card and he could henceforward be regarded as an eligible candidate for all sorts of positions of leadership which happen to be going. . . .

" Nowadays, some Party members, especially those in leading positions, habitually flout the Constitution. . . . I propose: From now on the Party committee should act in accordance with the Constitution in every case; they should not take the place either of the administration or—more important—of the judiciary. The judicial bodies must not pass sentences without having ascertained and studied the relevant facts. In the past, making false charges was an indictable crime, but this does not seem to be the case today. I suggest that henceforward those found to be informing against innocent people or trumping up malicious charges should receive due punishment. . . ."

Wu Li-min [Professor, North-East Normal Un.; Changchun Committee, CSS]:

" I am told that a porter [Party member], after a succession of promotions, has now actually become a Secretary of a Personnel Department. The other day he even led a party of teachers and students on a tour of inspection in the capacity of group leader and was called upon to make a speech on behalf of the University. The pity is that his cultural standard was so low that he was hardly coherent. . . ."

[*Kuang Ming Daily*. *June 3*

* * *

Department stores wanted, not universities

CANTON: *Kuang Ming Daily*

Lin K'ung-hsiang [Professor, South China Agricultural Institute]:

" I think the Personnel Department has outlived its usefulness. Its duties and powers should now be drastically curtailed, confining itself to the supervision of the administrative staff. A Personnel Committee should be set up to deal with problems concerning the teaching and technical staffs. This Committee should be composed of the Principal, the Dean and a few highly respected professors. . . .

" Having made lengthy investigations into the problem of fruit falling from the trees in many districts of south China, I diagnosed this as a disease and suggested methods of prevention. In 1951, at the South China Agricultural Science Technical Conference, I made a report on my inquiry into this problem and in the course of my report I had occasion to cite some American literature on the subject. I had the Secretary General of the Conference, Chang Yi, very worried, and he tossed me a note asking me to stop then and there. While the results of my research were brushed aside, the opinions of a Soviet specialist on the other hand received a fanatically enthusiastic ovation—in spite of the fact that the specialist in question was no specialist in plant pathology, and had only made a casual five-minute investigation into the problem. However, facts were able to prove my conclusion to be unassailable, even though I did have to use American sources. . . ."

Feng Ping-ch'uan [Dean, South China Engineering Institute]:

" [Party cadres] do not understand the characteristics of higher education and higher intellectuals. They even lack common sense in this direction. Whilst we want to set up an institution of higher learning, they on the other hand want to run a department store. These two are entirely different things. How can we listen to them in everything? . . ."

[*Kuang Ming Daily. May 19*

Chung I-chun [Professor, Chungshan Un.]:

" The trouble is that many an innocent man was wrongly convicted during the movement [against counter-revolutionaries]. The Constitution stipulates that where there is infringement of people's rights, redress should be offered. But there has never been any redress for those wronged apart from the usual apologies; even then they are often offered halfheartedly followed by some such lame explanation as ' the authorities have changed their line of approach ' and so on. . . .

" We often read in the newspapers that quite a number of cases involving breaches of law and order had to await the intervention of some Party members before they could be brought into the open and dealt with justly. The court either would not or did not dare interfere.

We must point out that this is rather an extraordinary state of affairs. . . ."

[*Kuang Ming Daily. June 1*

* * *

The Democratic League's academic programme

(i) *The problem of the schedule of scientific*[3] *workers*—We propose (a) that with few exceptions, scientists with the ability to lead scientific research should as far as possible avoid administrative work, especially those older scientists over sixty who are needed to pass on their knowledge to the next generation. We should reserve to each scientist a definite period in every year when he is completely free to do research work; (b) we should like the Government to consider regulating the system of holidays and advanced studies for professors and research workers; (c) with a few exceptions, those scientists who are at the same time Peoples' Representatives or Members of the Political Consultative Conference, etc., should not normally occupy more than one outside position . . . ; (d) due to the necessity of developing scientific research work, scientists should be granted a permanent holiday from social activities and administrative work; (e) we realise that the entertainment of foreign guests is not unnecessary but this need not fall upon the scientists.

(ii) *The problem of assistants*—There are still scientists who are short of the necessary research assistants or administrative staff and this state of affairs affects the efficiency of their work. We propose that those scientists with the ability to lead scientific research (for instance, members of research departments under the Academy of Sciences) should be provided with suitable assistants of their own choosing.

(iii) *The problem of equipment*—At present the problem of housing, reference libraries, scientific apparatus, general equipment, chemicals for experiments, materials for tests and specimens for scientific research, etc., has not been properly solved. . . . In the institutions of higher education all over the country, equipment is still very primitive. . . . We propose that this gap should be filled as soon as possible.

(iv) *The problem of reference materials*—The severity and rigidity of the security system that has now become one of the main stumbling-blocks to scientific research. . . . We propose that, military and diplomatic spheres and new discoveries apart, there should be no secrecy surrounding professors' expertise.

[3] " Science " includes social sciences

(v) *The problem of funds*—As regards the problem of funds for scientific research, at present there still exist cases of personnel without money, or money without personnel. . . . We propose that we should establish special funds in the institutions of higher education so that the research plans will not fall by the wayside due to lack of money, and also to establish a scientific foundation to strengthen financial backing. . . .

(vi) *The problem of " recall to the colours "*—Help should be available to scientists who have not yet been employed or who have been misdirected to the wrong professions to facilitate their " recall to the colours " . . .

Regarding the problem of the social sciences

Certain subjects have actually been dispensed with since the liberation, or have ceased to be independent subjects; and a number of people, who in the past specialised in sociology, political science and law, have now changed their profession. A number of subjects have been dispensed with just because they do not appear in Soviet Russia's syllabuses. Certain subjects such as the political conditions in capitalist countries, political systems, international relations, international law, etc., which in the past were all essential, are no longer receiving due emphasis. We regard this line of approach as being inappropriate. Our attitude towards the traditional social sciences should be one of reform rather than abolition. Therefore we should take appropriate steps to reinstate these subjects where circumstances warrant it and lay emphasis where emphasis is due. . . .

In the field of finance and economics, once the people in charge of government departments have made their declarations of policy, all the scholars do is to follow suit, publicising them and elaborating on them. This is not good enough. . . . We deem it necessary to encourage social science research workers to lay stress upon investigation and research work and to submit proposals concerning the government's policies and statutes to further the search for truth. . . .

Regarding the problem of fostering new blood

In the past in promoting, both to higher schools and higher grades, and in selecting research students and students going abroad, there was a bias in favour of stressing political qualifications. We think that from now on as much importance should be laid on specialised subjects as on politics. . . . We support and uphold the State Council's decision concerning the examination and selection of students going abroad for advanced studies. . . .

[*Kuang Ming Daily*. *June 9*

Lawyers and Economists

THE criticisms proffered by lawyers and economists are worth particular attention. Those of the lawyers indicated clearly that the Party members had little respect even for such laws as had been enacted; they considered the Party—and themselves, as its representatives—as a law unto itself. It is doubtful if the lawyers, in view of their past experiences, could have hoped for much amelioration from the enactment of the missing codes.

The record indicates that the economists were beginning to exercise a little freedom in their own field as a result of the hundred flowers policy. It is here, probably, that the régime would have most welcomed the assistance of non-Communist intellectuals. The manifesto of the economists—published long after criticism had been halted, as evidence against its signatories—shows that the Five-Year Plan had been proceeding on very shaky foundations. But in the atmosphere of the anti-rightist campaign, such trenchant criticism of the relevance of the Marxist classics and the effectiveness of current economic policies could not be tolerated.

" Golden rules and jade laws"

PEKING: *For lawyers* **May 26**

Wu Wen-han [Assistant Professor, Lanchow Un.] . . . said:

" Although the constitution has come into force yet there are still a section of the leaders who take a nihilist standpoint towards law, maintaining that it is only natural for the Party to take the place of the Government, that the Party's orders are above the law; the words of Party members are regarded, by themselves, as 'Golden rules and jade laws.' This is in contravention of the legal system. . . ."

A movement " to alight from sedan chairs "

PEKING: *For lawyers* **May 31**

Yang Yu-ch'ing [Assistant Editor-in-Chief, *Fa-cheng Yen-chiu* (*Research in Political Science and Law*)] referred to the current rectification movement as the movement " to alight from sedan chairs." Some Party members had been sitting in sedan chairs and keeping themselves aloof from the masses. What sort of people had been trained in the past eight years? They were nothing but chair bearers. Even at the present moment, many of the Party members sitting in sedan chairs were still unwilling to alight, and many of the chair bearers were reluctant to lay down the sedan chair poles. . . . Some top-ranking cadres in Peking should alight from their sedan chairs, and some should even be removed from office. . . .

Another category of people should also be removed from office, and one of them was the Editor-in-Chief of the *People's Daily*. For the Editor-in-Chief of the *People's Daily* had done nothing but sing praises during the past several years; he had even tried to " restrain " rather than " expand " the present campaign. . . .

[*People's Daily. June 5*

The Criminal Code

PEKING: *For lawyers*

Chi Ch'ing-yi [Editor, Legal Publishing House]:

" We are told that the work of drafting the criminal law has been under way for a long time. But ' one hears the sound of footsteps on the stairs without seeing anyone coming down '; the criminal law remains unpromulgated. This, it is said, is to make life easier for the legislators by lessening their professional hazard of making mistakes; but the consequence is that miscarriages of justice become unavoidable, because the judiciary having ' no law to rely upon,' are left with too much latitude in passing sentences. . . ."

[*Kuang Ming Daily. June 1*

The laws receive scant respect

PEKING: *For lawyers*

Ch'en T'i-ch'iang [Member, International Relations Research Group]:

" The work of legislation is at present proceeding at a very slow pace, and current laws receive scant respect. Take the marriage law, for instance; a large number of cadres—including old cadres—resort to so-called 'negotiations' to solve their marital controversies, rather than observe the due process of the marriage law. During the campaign against counter-revolutionaries, all sorts of illegal acts were committed. All these call for rectification."

Professor Wang Tieh-yeh [Peking Un.]:

"The study of international law and the training of international lawyers has been suspended for seven years due to the fact that traditional legal science has been completely written off as of no practical use. . . ."

Yu Chung-lu [Adviser, Supreme People's Court]:

". . . Some of the judicial personnel are unable to draw the line between internal and external contradictions, between crimes and non-crimes. Also the punishments meted out are subject to the whims and fancies of the court. . . . In assessing judicial work, we are often inclined to say that the successes are the main thing and that mistakes are relatively few and isolated. This is all very well, but some judicial workers today when reviewing the merits and demerits of past cases are often content with a certain percentage of justice. We must realise that 1 per cent. miscarriage of justice on the part of the judicial workers means 100 per cent. suffering to the victim. . . ." Yu Chung-lu objected to the fact that the majority of the appeal courts had adopted the system of dealing with cases in writing. He said: "The appeal courts should hold 'factual trials' based on the principle of direct hearings as in public debates. . . ."

[*Kuang Ming Daily*. *May 29 and June 10*
[*Forums held by Chinese Society for Political Science and Law.*

*

The teaching of law

PEKING: *Lawyers*

But under the present circumstances, data concerning the actual trials taking place in different grades of court up and down the country are barely accessible to people like us engaged in legal education. Therefore, we are hardly in a position to make full use of this data. The result is, theories inevitably become divorced from reality in teaching. It is the same with research. . . .

[*Han Teh-p'ei (Head of Department of Law, Wuhan Un.).*
Kuang Ming Daily. *June 12*

* * *

A new approach to American capitalism?

PEKING: *Economists*

Since February of this year, the Institute of International Relations of the Chinese Academy of Sciences has five times invited teachers and research workers of various economic institutes and colleges to meet for intensive discussions on the problem of the American economic cycle since the war. . . . One school believes that the world has now reached the stage of a new industrial revolution, presenting a wider prospect for fixed capital investments. . . . Therefore the American economy is likely to maintain its prosperity for some time. Another school is of the opinion that it is worth considering whether the "production relations" of American capitalism and its upper-layer structure would permit the productive power of the new industrial revolution to continue to expand. Therefore, it is doubtful whether the things produced will find markets and be fully utilised. . . .

At the meetings, many others pointed out that there were many shortcomings in our study of American economic problems in the past. Some were of the opinion that since the war, Marxists had failed to subject the capitalist economic crisis to concrete analysis in the light of the new conditions, and had shown a serious tendency towards doctrinairism. Therefore, some of the arguments presented in a number of theses were not entirely convincing. . . .

[*Report in Kuang Ming Daily. June 12*

*

PEKING: *Economists*

At a forum in Peking on June 12, economists debated whether there were any useful elements in Keynes' theories. They were unanimous that his system of economics as a whole was reactionary, but a majority of the forty or so present believed that his theory of the "multiplier" could not be ignored; others denied its validity and said that it was part of the whole structure. . . .

[*NCNA. June 12*

*

The manifesto of the economists

(1) *Work in the science of economics and the socialist economic development of our country*—In view of the fact that the classical Marxist-Leninist writers were not able to draw up a set of universally applicable formulae for socialist economic development in each country, and that during the last eight years since the liberation, in our advance

towards the rejuvenation of the national economy and in the work of socialist economic construction, we have been largely groping in the dark as it were, it has become all the more urgent for us to speed up the development of our work in the science of economics. Our concrete work . . . to be quite frank, has been largely proceeding in an exploratory manner. Our financial and economic policies and measures have either been borrowed blindly from Soviet Russia's precedents or have been sheer trial and error, subjectivism and recklessness personified, based on no objective economic laws whatsoever and in any case we do not know what laws there are worth following. That is why we have not been free from mistakes and deviations in our work, and at times serious mistakes and deviations at that. . . .

Actually, our science of economics as it stands at present is still retarded at a rather infantile stage; apart from transplanting in a doctrinaire manner Soviet Russia's textbooks and the like, we have nothing to show beyond descriptions of the existing system. . . .

(2) *The problems besetting current economic science work in our country*—Among the factors contributing to the present state of affairs we consider the scornful attitude towards the science of economics taken by personnel working on economic affairs to be the primary one. . . .

Just after the liberation, teachers of economics in the institutions of higher education in Peking still had the opportunity of listening to the reports on financial and economic measures and policies by leaders of our Government. Since the establishment of the People's Government [presumably refers to the reorganisation of the Government in 1954 after the adoption of the Constitution—*Ed.*], with the exception of the fact that recently there have been isolated cases of administrative departments or industrial establishments inviting one or two teachers at higher educational institutions or research workers to discuss a few concrete and technical problems, we do not know whether or not anyone has ever had the opportunity of coming into contact with other problems of the national economy. . . . It may be that the administrative departments do not think that these so-called specialists can be of any use. . . . They know nothing of Marxism-Leninism, and their knowledge of practical affairs, such as it is, is anyway ascertained from the administrative departments concerned. At best they know something of capitalist theories, or the systems and methods of the capitalist countries. . . .

With regard to the serious extent to which doctrinairism has inundated economic circles, Comrade Yu Kuan-yuan sounded the first warning bell as early as 1954. He said: 50 per cent. of our articles nowadays consists of quotations in inverted commas, and 40 per cent. consists of indirect quotations. The author can claim only the remaining 10 per cent. as his own words—which should be treasured highly if only because of their rarity value, even though they are ridden with fallacies.

Things have taken a turn for the better since the " Let 100 schools contend " policy has become operative but we feel that at least the following problems still exist:

(i) The problem of accepting the criticisms of capitalist economics. . . . In economic circles we have also started work on introducing important capitalist economic theories such as Keynes' economic theories and the like, with the sole intention of enhancing our understanding so as to impose criticisms; however, no one has ever raised the point of whether or not we can derive any useful ideas or any analytical methods from them. . . . We feel that many concepts in capitalist statistics such as the theory of sampling, normal curves, time-series and coefficient, etc., can be similarly used to analyse our socio-economic phenomena, but these have all been thrown out of the field of statistics, without discrimination. What remains of statistics today amounts to precious little apart from addition, subtraction, multiplication, division and simple averaging, with the result that it has become absolutely dull, simple and anaemic. Are we over-exaggerating the class nature of certain branches of learning? . . .

(ii) The problem of how to treat classical works: There is quite a vogue amongst us nowadays of regarding every word or sentence from the classical works as worth its weight in gold, and contenting ourselves with merely juggling with quotations and commentaries, word-by-word reiterations and recitations, or putting footnotes to classical teachings, sometimes even endeavouring to get a good grasp of " the spirit and essence " of misprints or mis-translations or indigestible translations. . . . The trouble is that many a classic work was written a hundred years ago and it could only prophesy the rough outline of the state of affairs a hundred years hence, and not the minute details, and could only foresee the general tendencies, not the actual time and place for things to take place. Isn't the October Revolution which broke out in an industrially backward Russia a glaring example? That the works of Marx and Lenin are impressive in number is a fact that no one will dispute. But most of Marx's works were published posthumously; how then could we expect every word from them to be of pearl or jade, and yet who amongst us during all these years has had the courage to voice in public his doubts as regards " the theory of absolute impoverishment? . . ."

(iii) The problem of creatively drawing a line of demarcation between Marxism-Leninism and Revisionism! Due to our treating the classical Marxist-Leninist works as mere mummified words, we are in the habit of putting the cap of Revisionism on whatever school of thought which happens to differ from the stand taken by the classical works. . . . The result is: for the sake of avoiding trouble, for the sake of peace, for the sake of avoiding the terrible notoriety of revisionism, everybody wants to avoid stirring up the hornet's nest. This, in turn, blocks whatever possibilities there are for creative development of the science of economics, and fans the flame of doctrinairism.

(3) *The problem of the supply of reference material also constitutes an important factor affecting the development of the science of economics*—In the past, to find some practical reference material to meet the needs of scientific research or tuition has been as difficult as endeavouring to enter heaven. One of the reasons for this is that the administrative departments do not have a high opinion of research work in economics. Another reason is the undue emphasis laid upon security, which provides a pretext for those who do not hold scientific work in esteem to lock up reference materials . . . sometimes even figures concerning national finance, which can easily be ascertained from the public reports of leaders of the Government, become something nobody dares to divulge. Hence, we often find ourselves completely in the dark about things which have become common knowledge in capitalist countries. . . .

["Some of our views on current work in the science of economics." By Ch'en Cheng-han, Hsu Yueh-t'an, Lo Chih-ju, Ku Ch'un-fan, Wu Pao-san, Ning Chia-feng. Published as an Appendix to Ching-chin Yen-chiu (Economic Research) No. 5, October 17, 1957.

School Teachers

THE brief extracts from a Peking forum illustrate the situation of non-Party school teachers. Subsequent revelations show that the teachers were even more forthright.

School teachers speak up

PEKING: *CAPD*

Liu Wei-kuang [Teacher, Peking Third Middle School]:

"In our school in the past, a wide gap existed between the Party fraction and the masses, and people generally dared not say anything.

There was one teacher who often accused the school of being undemocratic and unconcerned with the masses; he was made a target during the movement against counter-revolutionaries and subjected to repeated struggles. Finally it was found that there was nothing wrong. Although the district Party committee and the Party fraction did apologise to him, yet it was explained that the whole thing was not started without reasons. Has this man still courage to bloom now? I ask you. . . ."

Teng Tzu-yen [Teacher, Peking Eleventh Girls' Middle School]:

"The contradictions in Party-masses relations in our school—the Eleventh Girls' Middle School—mainly express themselves in the fact that the recruitment of new Party members is confined to young teachers; the young teachers, on joining the Party, cannot take the initiative in uniting with the old teachers; the old teachers consequently, feeling that they are getting on in years and that they will not be able to join the Party no matter how well they do their jobs, lack political enthusiasm and treat the young Party and Youth League members 'like the spirits, to be respected but kept at a distance.' . . ."

Wang Mu [Teacher, Peking Twenty-second Middle School]:

"There exists a chasm between the members of the Party and Youth League and the masses in our school. Among the Party members themselves, everyone is full of solicitude for the other. Among the Youth League members themselves, the atmosphere is full of *bonhomie* and full of singing and dancing. But as soon as an ordinary teacher appears on the scene, the Party members stop their conversation, and the Youth League members stop their fun. The two groups are as cold as ice to each other, and there is no conversation between them apart from liaison at work. . . ."

[*Forums, May 6 and 13. Kuang Ming Daily. May 16*

* * *

Rightist secondary school teachers

SHANGHAI

Lo Hai-sha [Teacher at Hsinhu Middle School, Vice Chairman, Hongkew ch'u Preparatory Committee, KMTRC] engaged in behind-the-scene activities and fomented troubles. At his instigation, responsible persons of the Democratic League and the Association for Promoting Democracy called joint meetings of democratic parties and groups. The organisation of the *Trouble-agitating Conning-tower* was moved and carried out. They won over Tseng Pao-ting, member of the Democratic League, and, jointly with him, drafted "Ten major accusations, ten suggestions and three attitudes." They instructed Tseng to raise the following at the general meeting: "Replace the Party branch committee, expel the bad Party member [secretary of the branch] and dismiss Principal Lu from office. . . ."

During the period of contending and blooming, the branch of the Association for Promoting Democracy in Tsaoyang Middle School was in the hands of Huang Chun-shih and opposed the Party branch in every respect. . . . Huang Chun-shih also said: "Against the Party members, we can only resort to tempests and storms." He advocated the setting up in the school of a so-called joint meeting of the two parties, with a view to leading the school in rotation with the Communist Party.

Liu Fei [rightist of the Second Normal School, Shanghai] once frantically demanded that the counter-revolutionaries should be "cleared." In order to hoard up anti-Party and anti-socialist material, he visited many schools to collect facts, falsely claiming that he did so by order of the Director of Education in Shanghai. . . .

Rotate the parties

CHANGSHA

Third Middle School in Changsha, Hunan. . . . At the beginning of the rectification movement, Yang Chi-hua [a teacher of languages] published in the *Hsin Hunan Pao* and the *Changsha Daily* a reactionary article entitled "My Humble Views and My Good Advice," in which he said that . . . it would be better to call elections appointments, and that sectarianism had become a nation-wide calamitous flood. . . .

[*NCNA. July 26*

CANTON

Recently several middle schools in Canton have one after another discovered rightists who, upon the occasion presented by this year's comparatively tense problem of going on for higher studies, distributed reactionary pamphlets and agitated students' troubles. . . .

[*NCNA. July 26*

TIENTSIN

Rightist Huang Hsin-ping [Teacher at the Third Girls' Middle School, Tientsin] . . . once frantically demanded government by various democratic parties in rotation with the Communist Party. . . . He confessed that after the unleashing of certain " international storms " such as the Beria incident and the Hungarian incident, he was " influenced " and " conceived certain doubts regarding the one-Party dictatorship. . . ." He suggested that " the three major ' isms ' have their root in the one-Party dictatorship. . . ."

[*NCNA. July 26*

Earlier when, upon the occasion presented by the Party's rectification movement, rightists in society were attacking the Party, a few rightists in middle schools also rose in response. They " lit fires " here and there among teachers and students. They and the rightists outside were at one another's beck and call. Inside the schools they concentrated fire on Communist Party leadership, the socialist system and the like. They " demanded the evacuation from schools of the Party and the League in favour of various democratic parties and groups which would organise School Management Committees to govern the schools." They inveighed against Party and League members for " their lack of human nature," for " being special agents." They described the system of our state as something in which " there were only dictatorship and centralisation, while the people had not any democratic rights." They slanderously described the Party's policy towards the intellectuals as " suppression," " regarding intellectuals as draft animals " and so on. What was even wilder, a few reactionaries " demanded the killing of all Communist members " and declared, " If only we could overthrow the Communist Party, we would not mind personal sacrifice." Some among them maintained close contact with rightists such as Lo Lung-chi, Fei Hsiao-t'ung and P'an Kuang-tan. . . .

Sung Jung-tao [rightist in Tientsin Seventh Middle School, CAPD] . . . spread far and wide such absurd views as " the movement for suppression of counter-revolutionaries was a mess." He urged everybody to " air unjust convictions " and to " rehabilitate. . . ."

During contending and blooming, one rightist in Tientsin Normal School offered money and ideas to urge students of uncertain views to print a publication for disseminating absurd anti-Party and anti-socialist views. Whenever the principal made any arrangement for work, this publication brought forward a series of destructive views directed against the principal's decisions. This prevented smooth working and created great confusion in the ideology of the students. . . .

Several young teachers of Tientsin Girls' Fourth Middle School and Tientsin Thirty-eighth Middle School, who were once won over by rightists, exposed in forums many of the rightist conspiratorial activities. With profound sorrow they resolved that as they were still young, they would never allow the rightists to destroy their future.

[*NCNA. July 29*

7

DOCTORS

THE evidence of visitors to China indicates that the régime has achieved significant results through vigorous health measures such as mass sanitation campaigns. But the story of the "painless" childbirth experiment shows that careful assessment of all claims made is still necessary. It is clear, too, that while mass campaigns may have brought results in this field, there has been a dangerous neglect of vital aspects of the task of laying the foundations of a sound, modern medical service.

Traditional medical techniques have been held up as worthy of study and employment by the régime, largely because of the shortage of orthodox doctors. But the lack of respect accorded to traditional doctors and their research [forum on May 20] indicates that this sensible policy has not been as successful and thorough as claimed.

"Painless" childbirth

PEKING: *CSS* April 29

Tsui Ku-ch'en [Superintendent, Peking Tuberculosis Hospital]:

"In the past, there have been many problems in our medical circles which we dared not speak of openly, but only in private because we were afraid of being accused of 'infringing policy.' When the method of painless childbirth was being introduced, the rate of success was said to be above 90 per cent., and even the Soviet specialists began to be a little incredulous; . . . in fact the pain felt by some women during conception was referred to by the doctors as merely 'soreness' not 'pain,' therefore the medical circles at that time termed it 'the method of painless but sore conception.' Why is it like this? Because in using administrative orders to carry out progressive experiments, the leadership likes subordinates to report good news instead of bad. . . ."

[*Kuang Ming Daily. May 3*

*

Deficiencies in medical education

The professors thought that at present the central problem of medical education was the contradiction between quantity and quality. There were insufficient qualified teachers at many medical colleges and the quality of teachers was not high, which made the raising of the quality of teaching and studying difficult. The students, due to the low education standards in the Middle Schools, had a very poor foundation in foreign languages; their knowledge of biology, chemistry and physics was also extremely deficient, which created many difficulties in teaching and learning. . . .

[*Forums held by Peking Union Medical College on March 29 and April 30. Kuang Ming Daily. May 7*

PEKING: *Chinese Medical Association* **May 5**

Wu Ying-k'ai [Chest Specialist] held that the programme of work of the Chinese Medical Association was very vague. . . . He expressed doubts as to what function the Chinese Medical Association had performed in promoting the development of medical science. He thought that although in name the Chinese Medical Association had various specialised associations, in actual fact these specialised associations were without substance. . . . Lin Ch'iao-chih, Chin Pao-shan, Lin Tsung-yang all expressed agreement with his views. . . .

The specialists had much to say about the Ministry of Health—in particular they were extremely dissatisfied with the way in which the Ministry of Health for the last few years had only laid emphasis upon the development of medical establishments whilst ignoring the work of medical education.

Hu Ch'uan-k'uei [Principal, Peking Medical College] said:

"Medical education is the heavy industry of the Ministry of Health. But the Ministry of Health does not lay stress upon medical education. Since the liberation, the students of Peking Medical College have increased from 400 to 3,000, but there are only 700 beds in the attached hospital, which does not provide sufficient ground for practice and seriously affects the quality of teaching and learning. . . ."

[*Kuang Ming Daily. May 7*

PEKING: *Union Medical College* **May 20**

Many comrades say that the Union Medical College, in spite of frantic efforts in the last few years, shows very few results. What is the reason? Dr. Wu Wei-jan says that this is mainly due to leading comrades of the college failing to understand the feelings of the intellectuals, and failing to come to grips with their work. Whilst the Party committee members cannot cope with technical work, they refuse to learn or rely upon specialist advice. . . . The Principal of the College, Li Tsung-en, says that in the last few years the Union Medical College has been frantically busy, yet there is no system in its work and it had failed to come to grips with the main problems. They all said that the Union Medical College was led by the Party committee but up to the present time he still did not know who the Party committee secretary was. It was only on occasions when they worked at a united front office that the principal of the college had the opportunity to meet and chat with the members of the Political Committees. . . .

[*Kuang Ming Daily. May 20*

Li Tsung-en

In opposing the leadership of the Communist Party in medical and the public health enterprises, Li Tsung-en composed the " trilogy " of: exaggerating and distorting the mistakes and the shortcomings in the work of Union Medical College, obliterating the achievements during the past few years, and attributing these mistakes and shortcomings to the leadership of the Party. . . . In a prospectus Li-Tsung-en wrote: " The quality of the work of Union College has deteriorated. It will take Union College a certain period of time to repair the damage done in the past few years. . . ." He also cried aloud: " The whole of Union College is in chaos; the Party committees are simply hopeless. . . ."

[*People's Daily. October 6*

*

Neglect of preventive medicine

PEKING: *Ministry of Health* **May 4**

Several experts criticised the Ministry for not seriously carrying out the principle of " prevention first." Public hygiene expert Chin Pao-shen said that for the past several years the Ministry had laid too much emphasis on medical treatment at the expense of preventative work which ensured the overall protection of the health of the people and prevented the spread of diseases. The same situation existed in medical training. . . [*Kuang Ming Daily*. *May 5*

✱

Accepting Soviet experiences

PEKING: *Chinese Academy of Medical Science*

Many people also criticised doctrinairism in learning from the advanced experiences of the Soviet Union. For example, in 1952 a Peking newspaper published a report from Russia saying that Soviet scientist Po-Shi-Yang believed that cultivated bacteria might crystallise into disease-causing poisonous substance. At that time no second person in the world could confirm this theory. But at a meeting called by the Chinese Medical Association to study Po-Shi-Yang's theory, when some people expressed doubts about it they were accused by a Department Director of the Ministry of Health of "unwillingness to accept new things." Now the Soviet Union had already denounced Po-Shi-Yang's theory as idealistic, and contrary to Marxism and Leninism. . . .

[*Kuang Ming Daily*. *May 6*

✱

Traditional Chinese medicine

PEKING: *CPWDP* **May 20**

Wang Po-yueh [Secretary, Academic Secretariat, Institute for Research into Chinese Medicine]:

"The doctors seldom have the time to engage in research work, their main duty being attending the senior cadres. . . ."

Luan Chih-jen [Professor, Institute of Chinese Medicine] said:

"Work in Chinese traditional medicine during the last few years has actually shown no development. Traditional doctors have neither positions nor power. The highest post held by a traditional doctor in Peking is no more than a deputy section chief. . . . The Society for Chinese Medicine is only an empty vessel; the Ministry of Health has not emphasised the development of its work."

Wang Lo-t'ing [Acupuncture Section, Institute of Chinese Medicine] said:

"There is not a single principal of any college of traditional medicine who is himself a traditional doctor. . . ." [*Kuang Ming Daily*. *May 24*

✱

Medicines

PEKING: *Chinese Pharmacological Society* **May 22**

Hsieh Ch'ung-chang [pharmacologist] . . . said that among the cadres of the Ministry of Health there was not a single one who had seven years of pharmacological experience. . . . Someone in his report to an Assistant to the Minister had said it was difficult to carry on work as there was no code or system in pharmacological administration. Instead of listening to his view, the Assistant to the Minister replied: "We have got along without criminal and civil law since the founding of the Republic. So what! . . ."

[*Kuang Ming Daily. May 25*

*

Deficiencies in physical culture

PEKING: *CDL* **May 24**

Li Ho-ting [Professor, Peking Institute of Physical Culture] . . . criticised the National Physical Culture Committee for failing to take the health of 600 million people as its starting point, and ignoring the development of physical training for the masses. He said: "To lay stress only upon a minority, while disregarding the majority, is the wrong way of doing things. To put it in stronger terms, we may say that New China's approach to physical training is the same as that of the capitalist countries. . . ."

Hsu Pao-ch'en [Lecturer, Peking Institute of Physical Culture]:

"The best sportsmen today are being pampered like the 'little masters' of old days. Some of the sportsmen have to rely on stimulating drugs to see them through contests. . . ."

Liu Yueh-lin [Professor, Sian Institute of Physical Culture]:

"Among the first list of National Referees published by the National Physical Culture Committee, there are a minority of unqualified ones, who became national umpires on the strength of their being Party members; whereas a number of qualified people have not been appointed. . . ."

[*Forum held by CDL. Kuang Ming Daily. May 27*

8

STUDENTS

STUDENT demonstrations have played an important role in modern Chinese history ever since Peking undergraduates started their country's first nationalist demonstration on May 4, 1919. On that day, some three to five thousand students demonstrated against the decision made at the Paris Peace Conference to award the former German concessions in Shantung Province to Japan. They burnt the house of the pro-Japanese Minister of Communications, and as a result of clashes with the police, some of their number were killed and others imprisoned. Calling a student strike, the Peking demonstrators spread patriotic leaflets and harangued the townspeople. They sent telegrams to fellow students throughout the country, which resulted in similar demonstrations in half a dozen other major cities. The response of the urban population to the students was striking. Merchants shut their shops and laid a boycott on Japanese goods with considerable effect on Japanese trade in China. Workers also came out on strike.

This "May 4th movement" and the many subsequent political demonstrations in which students participated during the twenties and thirties are highly relevant to the events of the summer of 1957. They provided both students and their elders with a yardstick with which to gauge the power of student agitation. Mao Tse-tung and his colleagues, who were themselves rioting students during the May 4th period, must have been alarmed to learn students were attempting to rekindle the spirit of those times against themselves. And there seems to have been little doubt in the minds of a number of prominent non-Communist university teachers that the situation was as serious as in 1919.[1] The fact that reports on unrest in the universities and the schools were largely suppressed until the

[1] See "An emergency conference convened by Chang Po-chun," p. 167.

situation was again under control [2] is certainly indicative of official concern.

Because of this Press blackout, it is difficult to trace the spread of student agitation with any accuracy. Student " blooming and contending " started spontaneously some time after the Party had begun asking non-Communist politicians and intellectuals for their views. The first posters did not go up at Peking University till May 19 and the immediate reaction of the Party committee was to frown on such activities. But a flood of posters denounced this attempt to hinder free expression of views and on the evening of May 20, the first secretary of the Party committee told a general meeting of staff and students that the committee was prepared to give full support to this method of student criticism.

From then on, the situation developed rapidly. The news of the activities of the Peking University students was spread to other colleges by means of two newspaper articles, letters, special student magazines and even visits by student delegations. Some student leaders like Miss Lin Hsi-ling became nationally known despite the lack of publicity given to their activities in the Press. The seriousness of the student situation from the official point of view lay in the fact that student leaders were not content merely with the idea of rectifying abuses in education, but were concerned to alter the system of Party dictatorship because of the injustices flowing from it. The official reports indicate that they had a considerable following, though they attempt to soften this alarming fact by suggesting that the followers were sound at heart but had been led astray.

Could " the storm " in the universities (as it was later officially described) have led to wider unrest if it had gone unchecked? Certainly there is some evidence of peasant and worker discontent at this time; and the official line that workers and peasants " spontaneously " protested at student demonstrations and riots can be treated with the same scepticism as the students themselves felt. Perhaps the most telling evidence is the suppression of the Press reports which certainly shows that the spread of student unrest was considered a serious possibility.[3] And we can conclude from that

[2] See the introduction to the section on The Press, p. 59.
[3] This question is considered again in the section on The Peasants.

action and from a comparison of the violence of student criticism and activity with the more restrained behaviour of their elders that it was the student situation that was the most important factor in deciding the Communist Party to halt the rectification movement.

N.B.—Some of the reports included here are unbelievably fully detailed. One can assume, however, that the general picture is accurate.

PEKING

Peking University—The "Democratic Wall"

Peking University has all along been ahead of the other institutions of higher education in the capital in "blooming and contending." Before May 19 the blooming and contending was confined to the teachers, but since then the students also have joined in. They have started a "Democratic Wall" on the campus in front of the dining hall and through the medium of large-character newspapers many views have been put forward directed against the "three evils." Up to the present moment, apart from there being a "tinkling of gems" on the campus in front of the dining hall, the dormitories of the different departments are also pasted with many large-character newspapers.

On May 19 a large-character newspaper appeared on a wall in front of the main dining hall put out by students of the Department of History of Peking University, under the pen-name of "A group of Youth League members and young people," which, in essence, submitted views to Peking University's Youth League committee requesting to know whether Peking University had sent representatives to the third National Congress of the Youth League and, if so, how were they produced. They hoped for a reply from the Youth League Committee. Soon a second large-character newspaper appeared demanding to open up a democratic garden to enable people to submit views to the leadership of the university and to help in rectification. From then onwards large-character newspapers appeared one after another on the walls around the main dining hall. These large-character newspapers were mainly devoted to making criticisms and suggestions with reference to the failings in the work of the leadership of Peking University and the Ministry of Higher Education, and how to make improvements.

At the beginning some of the students made the suggestion that they hoped that classes would cease so that they could help the school in its rectification. After the appearance of this large-character newspaper, the large majority of students expressed disagreement as they thought that the cessation of classes in order to take part in rectification was not in conformity with the spirit contained in the directive on rectification, issued by the Communist Party's central committee. The students who made the suggestion then withdrew it.

During the week the students were as usual studying very hard But after the end of each class there was an unending stream of student outside the main dining hall, either putting up or reading the large-character newspapers. Some of the Departments even published ink-duplicated special editions of periodicals devoted to the removal of the three evils. . . . Some of the large-character newspapers point out the fact that the selection of students going abroad has been monopolised by the Party and Youth League members and that people outside the Party and Youth League have no chance of being selected is an expression of sectarianism. . . . Some . . . point out that in the allocation of work for the graduates, Party members get better posts and non-Party members are assigned posts in remote areas . . . some advocate changing the political course into an optional subject. . . . Some suggest liberalising the responsible Party committee system and strengthening the School Affairs Committee to lead school work. Some advocate that the students should have freedom as regards attendance at lectures and suggest the adoption of a credit system in the schools; . . .

The large-character newspapers of the students of Peking University make a tremendous display, and are full of variety. Amongst them are long-winded articles, short essays, miscellaneous prose items, poetry, cartoons and serialised novels. Some of the large-character newspapers after their emergence repeatedly put out views representing pros and cons, and developed debates; some of them also stated that arrangements could be made with a view to carrying on the debates "in person." Some of the problems, due to the divergent ways of looking at them, have led to the organising of debates after supper. Such debates have already occurred many times, and normally there are a few students standing round listening. . . .

The students themselves considered that in opening up the "Democratic Wall" and publishing large-character newspapers they were not hindering their studies, but they thought that this was carrying on the democratic traditions of Peking University at the time of the May 4th Movement. . . .

[*Kuang Ming Daily. May 26*

Some bulletins pointed out that the absolute majority of the publications carried sincere statements and were of great help to the rectification movement. But there were also some which exploited the occasion to give vent to their personal grievances. Some bulletins even stated that there were poisonous weeds and demanded that these must be uprooted. But there were also people who said that there was no need to fear the weeds, for in the process of uprooting them the fragrant flowers might also suffer alongside. The arguments were couched in very sharp terms, naming the persons attacked without the least consideration for personal feelings. Some even feared that the students might have carried the matter to excess. Your correspondent interviewed many students and teachers, including a few members of the Communist Party, and the absolute majority of them considered such fears groundless. . . . Old President Ma Yin-ch'u also considered that it was a good sign for all to speak their minds fully in the bulletins. . . .

On the square in front of the Mess Hall, like in Hyde Park, thousands of students were listening to one heated debate after another. The Student Association announced that the period from 5 p.m. to 10 p.m. would be given to debates, and two classrooms were allotted for the purpose, while platforms were also erected and loudspeakers installed on the square to facilitate the holding of debates. The university magazine, the broadcasting station, and the Blackboard Bulletin all carried reports on the viewpoints expressed by the students in the course of their contention. . . .

In Peking University with its glorious revolutionary tradition, more than 8,000 young people had become inflamed with enthusiasm. . . .

[*Wen Hui Pao*. *May 27*

Khrushchev's secret speech appears

Parts of Russian leader Nikita Khrushchev's denunciation of Stalin at the Soviet 20th Party congress last year have appeared on notice boards in Peking University. These extracts represent the first time as far as is known that any part of the speech has been published in China. They appeared following an earlier notice complaining that "We want to know about Khrushchev's report. The United States knows it in an English version and why shouldn't we."

It was not known who posted the extracts which were not visible tonight, but many students who said they'd seen it said it was "extracts translated from the English. . . ."

One notice asks why writer Hu Feng, who was arrested in 1955, has not been brought to trial according to law. [Hu Feng's arrest was the high point of a campaign against "counter-revolutionaries" which effectively brought work to a stop, see p. 174.] But critics don't have it all their own way and there are vigorous replies—for instance, enumerating evidence of Hu Feng's counter-revolutionary activities—to many of the posters. . . .

Thousands of posters have been stuck during the past ten days, but students are reminded by a huge white slogan painted on the side of a building that "all arguments and actions which ignore socialism are wrong."

[*David Chipp. Reuter. Peking. May 27*

The "100 Flowers Society"

Not long after the launching of the rectification campaign, a small reactionary group, known under the name of the "100 Flowers Society," made its appearance in Peking University. The key members of the society have openly declared that their purpose was not to help the Party in its rectification campaign, but to initiate a "movement for freedom and democracy," a "movement for the thorough reform of the political system." They cry, "Marxism is out of date," and "the dictatorship of the proletariat is out of date, and unless a change is made there will be danger of being detached from the masses." They suggest "learning from the democracy and freedom of the capitalist countries" and want a "new interpretation of capitalism. . . ."

The "100 Flowers Society" . . . was the first reactionary group of the right-wing bourgeoisie among the students in the institutions of higher learning in Peking to attack the Party and socialism. Inside and outside the university they cried: "The time has come! Hold high the torches and dispel the darkness!" and "The tide of freedom, democracy and reason is rising all over the world, and once more the dim fire of life will blaze!" Even more militantly, T'an T'ien-jung has cried: "The sword is shining white, the fire is burning red! This is the last life-and-death struggle!" Condemning the Communist Party as a "selfish party," Ch'en Feng-hsiao shouts: "Youths, unite and do things ourselves!" He also incited those counter-revolutionaries who had been accused during the campaign for the suppression of counter-revolutionaries to come forward to voice their counter-accusations. One of these counter-revolutionaries, Liu Ch'i-ti, who was dealt with leniently during that campaign, did come forward to demand justice, crying: "The world is on the verge of total darkness." He was immediately invited to join the leadership of the "100 Flowers Society" by T'an T'ien-jung and Ch'en Feng-hsiao. They also proposed to organise a political party. Some of the members of the group ran such publications as the *Public Square* and *The relay baton of Peking University* to publicise their reactionary programme in the institutions of higher learning in Peking and Tientsin, and organised activities and tried to enrol members in the group. They manufactured and circulated rumours designed to confuse the minds of the students. They went to the factories to "kindle fires" and called upon the workers to rise "to overthrow the new oppression and new injustice." They also joined hands with Lin Hsi-ling, a rightist in the China People's University. . . .

The key elements of this reactionary group have not yet completely given up their reactionary ideas and activities. Let us read this latest "declaration" by one of the leaders of this reactionary group, Yang Lu:

> "I have never loved this world, nor has the world loved me;
> Its filthy and foul breath I have never praised;
> I have never knelt to its idolatrous dogmas,
> Or smiling, obsequiously against my will, sung their praises parrot fashion.
> Therefore the world cannot regard me as a fellow being.
> I am not one of them, and although I am among them,
> My thoughts are entirely different from theirs. . . ."

All these key members of the reactionary group are youths in their early twenties and they have spent about one-third of their life in the new society, but it can be clearly seen from the facts described above how these rightists are still refusing to relinquish the interests of the dying class of exploiters. . . .

[*NCNA. July 12*

" What terrible voids and confusion . . ."

T'an T'ien-jung, chieftain of rightist students in Peking University once said: "What terrible voids and confusion exist in such noted scholars as Chou Pei-yuan [Vice President, Peking Un.], Ch'ien Hsueh-shen, Hua Lo-keng, Kuo Mo-jo [Chairman, All-China Federation of Literary and Art Circles] and Ai Ssu-ch'i [Deputy Chairman, Philosophical Society] in things connected with philosophy, science and general knowledge!" And again "Editors of all publications, for instance the

People's Daily, the *Chinese Youth Newspaper* and the *Journal of Physics*, are absolutely ignorant of Marxism, and are completely unfamiliar with dialectics. This ignorance, this unfamiliarity, and the infinite stupidity contained in their metaphysical brains form a great wall which shuts out the truth. . . ."

[*The Chinese Youth Newspaper. August 9*

The agitators from Peking University

As early as on May 29, before the publication of the reactionary *Public Square*, rightists Wang Kuo-hsiang, Chiu Te-fu, and some others in Peking University, jointly with rightist Lin Hsi-ling of China People's University, secretly discussed problems relating to the contents, nature and purpose of the publication in question, the estimate of current situation and so on. The exact mission which they assigned to themselves was: "We shall walk in the very forefront, we shall be the fire-lighters, we shall lead the movement properly and we shall edify the masses. . . ."

The editorial committee of the *Public Square* was a combination of the "100 Flowers Society," the "100 Flowers Tribunal" and the poetic group of Chang [Yuan-hsun] and Shen [Tse-i] from the "Free Tribunal." It was a Grand Alliance of the rightists. The fifteen members of the editorial committee were, one and all, notorious rightists in the university. Although rightists T'an T'ien-jung and Hsu Nan-ting did not nominally take part in this editorial committee, yet they did actively assist in the work of the *Public Square*.

What specimens of humanity are these core elements of the reactionary *Public Square* clique? These fifteen people included: Liu Ch'i-ti, a counter-revolutionary who had been released as a result of leniency; Li Yen-sheng, who had twice stolen his way into the ladies' lavatory and who had just served eight months' imprisonment on a charge of larceny; Lung Ying-hua, a traitor to the Communist Party; Li Ya-po, habitual stealer of books; Yeh Yu-sheng, a cowardly deserter from the resist-United States and aid-Korea front and a propagator of rumours; Chang Yuan-hsun, who had been expelled from the Youth League for hindering other people from joining military and cadre institutions and for disseminating reactionary views; Ch'en Feng-hsiao, a member of the reactionary bourgeoisie, and so on. As for the origin and family background of these self-styled "democratic warriors," eleven out of them, that is 75 per cent., came of landlord, bureaucrat and capitalist families. . . .

In the first preparatory meeting of *Public Square*, fourteen principles were decided. Throughout, these principles were anti-Party and anti-socialist. The principles behind their struggle were "gradually shift the centre of gravity to the probing for the root of the three evils, so that people may see clearly that the question at issue involves not merely the work style but also the system of the state." "Fight for the freedom of the Press, thoroughly practise the rights of freedom of speech, publication, assembly and society; the freedom of the Press allows the propounding of theories which will constitute a social pressure to force back the conservative forces," "abolish censorship of publication, allow private newspaper enterprises, for otherwise the directive for contending and blooming will have no material safeguard." They also laid down in their principles the following: "For the gradual execution of the above-mentioned schemes, we must make our society the core of the masses currently engaged in the movement. We must expand our influence

"We lacked a common language"

There was a fellow student of mine who told me about her state of mind and her romantic problems. She said that she had read many West European classical novels, and the works of Romain Rolland in particular had greatly influenced her. . . . She had the idea of getting some enlightenment and help from me. But as for myself, I have not even seen the cover of the book to which she was referring. The "Big Principles" which I would discuss, she would not be disposed to listen to; when it came to concrete analysis, what could I talk about? We lacked a common language. . . .

[Chou Chih-liang (Assistant Secretary, Communist Youth League, Peking Normal Un.). *Chinese Youth*. No. 11. June 1

Let youth read "poisonous works"

I have an idea that we should from now on deliberately unleash "poisonous articles" among the youth. I think Chinese Youth *could blaze a new trail by publishing some of the typical and representative Impressionist and Dadaist works, as well as English and American modern short stories which depict certain aspects of the reality of life. . . .*

[Fang Yu-chung (General Secretary, Communist Youth League, Hopei, Peking Middle Schools). *Chinese Youth*. No. 11. June 1 through a variety of forms. In addition, to co-ordinating debates, speeches, discussions and other forms of activities, we must spread our influence outside the university." Summing up the current situation in the university, the rightists propounded the following: "We should show our concern over the urgent questions raised by students. We should adopt an acute and stern attitude. We should turn society into a lasting organisation. . . ."

Simultaneous with the conspiratorial activities within the university, the members of the editorial Committee of *Public Square* also planned to "file a petition in June with the National People's Congress, and to incite a Hungarian incident in the streets." To execute their plan, they secretly conducted some organisational activities in addition to verbal and oral propaganda. A general alliance was formed between them and the rightists in various institutions in Peking. Ch'en Feng-hsiao, one of the major warriors of *Public Square*, went to Peking Normal University and set up connections with the two reactionary *Bitter Medicine* and *Voice of the lowest Stratum* cliques in that university. He told them that to oppose the university Party committees alone was "narrow-minded and short-sighted." He urged them "in future to expand the question and to dig out the root of bitterness." Following this, responsible members of these two societies went to Peking University to fetch reactionary pamphlets. They intended to overthrow the university magazine of Peking Normal University, to take over the broadcasting station, and to issue publications. They also instigated the rightists in Peking's Geological and Petroleum Institutes to set up an organisation known as the "100 Flowers Branch Society." Han Hung-peng, head of the rightists in the Geological Institute reared by *Public Square*, repeatedly declared an intention of killing all Communist Party members.

To enable the rightists to gain a foothold in Tientsin, T'an Tien-jung and five other people under the usurped name of "Peking University visiting group," went on June 2 to "light fires" in Nankai University, Tientsin University, Tientsin Normal College and various other colleges in Tientsin.

In addition, their excessive optimism led them to compile seven of their reactionary essays into the *Democratic Relay Baton* and to circulate it widely in all colleges in the country.

In all the actions undertaken by the rightists, the effect was diametrically opposite to their expectation. They were set back everywhere. . . .

The funds of this reactionary clique were ample. The following were seen from one of their disbursement memoranda: 100 yuan for propaganda in Tientsin, 100 yuan for printing pamphlets . . . total disbursements over 1,700 yuan. . . . As to the source of the funds, according to the preliminary account rendered by Chang Yuan-hsun, Ch'en Feng-hsiao had altogether contributed over 700 yuan which was remitted to him by registered mail from "friends outside the school." What kinds of people were these "friends outside the school"? This must be clarified thoroughly. . . .

[*People's Daily. July 24*

*

"Lin Hsi-ling, the black sheep"

Lin Hsi-ling, whose rightist utterances were for a time all the rage among young people throughout the country, particularly university students, is now no longer strange to us. . . . [*The Chinese Youth Newspaper*, July 12.]

On the evening of May 23, Lin Hsi-ling made her first public inflammatory speech at the open-air forum at Peking University. She said:

"Hu Feng's opinions were basically correct. The 'Let a 100 flowers bloom, let a 100 schools contend' policy which the Party offers us today is essentially the same as Hu Feng's proposal.[4] True socialism is highly democratic but the socialism we have here is not democratic. I call this society a socialism sprung from a basis of feudalism. We should not be satisfied with the Party's rectification and reformist methods and the slight concessions made to the people. . . ."

At this point discussion at the meeting became confused and many students angrily demanded that she stop talking and quit the platform. But at the same time there were people who supported her and wanted her to go on talking. They said: "This is a free discussion platform; those who don't want to listen can go. . . ."

In order to allow Lin Hsi-ling to explain her points, the China People's University student society organised a free discussion platform. . . .

She arranged certain phenomena in the life of our society—such as the division of officials into grades for hearing reports and seeing documents and the distribution of furniture by their offices—and called them a class system, saying that it (*i.e.*, class system) had already entered all

[4] The Hu Feng case is discussed in the section on Writers and Artists, p. 174.

aspects of life. She also said that sectarianism was clearly exhibited in the personnel system. She said that these concrete systems were organised into a general system and that now the social system itself produced the "three evils. . . ."

Because she could not theoretically explain how socialism produced the "three evils," she said with ulterior motives that the social productive forces in both the Soviet Union and China were very low and that these two countries had not yet eliminated class differences. In particular, these two countries operated a dictatorship of the proletariat. Moreover, quoting Engels' theory that one country cannot construct socialism and Lenin's dictum that socialism is the elimination of class, she arrived at the conclusion that present-day China and Russia are not socialist. She loudly demanded a search for "true socialism" and advocating using explosive measures to reform the present social system.

She maligned the members of the Chinese Communist Party as mostly being "rotten eggs," intellectually stagnant and useless, with comparatively few true Bolsheviks among them. . . . She rumoured it that the movement against counter-revolutionaries had wronged 720,000 persons. . . . Apart from this she also publicised such fallacious theories as . . . "China has no freedom of the Press. . . ."

[*People's Daily. June 30*

*

Bomb attack on Party official

PEKING: *Medical College*

At 00.10 on June 17, a bomb exploded in the home of Ch'u Cheng, Deputy Director of Peking Medical College and Secretary of the Communist Committee of the College. Only slight damage was done and there were no casualties. The Peking Security Bureau arrested a 23-year-old former student of the college, Tu Mao-chin, who is now a student teacher at the Fifty-third Peking Middle School, who admitted that he had used a home-made bomb in an attempt to kill Ch'u Cheng. . . .

[*NCNA. June 20*

* * *

TIENTSIN

Nankai University and the Peking student delegation

At the instigation of T'an T'ien-jung and Liu Ch'i-ti of a small reactionary clique in Peking University who came to Tientsin from Peking on June 2, some bourgeois rightists in Nankai University made anti-socialist and anti-Party leadership speeches a month ago in the name of helping the Communist Party rectify its working style. They posted big-character bulletins and cartoons and made slanderous charges that the "dictatorship of the proletariat is the root of the three evils," "socialism is not as democratic as capitalism," "the result of the campaign for the rounding up of counter-revolution is nil. . . ." Raising such slogans as "carry on the May 4th tradition of revolution" and "hold aloft the May 4th torch," they agitated the minds of others. The students stood against such reactionary speeches at that time; . . . But fanned up by a handful of rightists, this slight head wind for a time disturbed the atmosphere and confused right and wrong on Nankai University campus, so much so that the reactionary slogan "Exterminate the Communist bandits" appeared on June 16. . . .

The reactionary arguments put forward by the Peking University students T'an T'ien-jung and others denounced by the Nankai students, threw mud at Marxism by dividing it into five stages. They argued that Mao Tse-tung's thought was a transition from metaphysics to dialectics and a thought designed to mislead the people. They also threw mud at the existing social system. Nankai students correctly expounded the process of development of Marxism and, citing the fact that Lenin developed Marxism, overpowered the absurd view of T'an T'ien-jung and his followers that Marxism had ceased to develop since 1895. . . .

Rightists Liu Li-wen and Chang Pu-ming, anti-socialist activists in the Department of the Chinese Language, published their first big-letter bulletin calumniating the Constitution as being false. . . . Liu Li-wen . . . said that there was no freedom of speech, publication and Press. . . .

[*NCNA. June 29*

Students wanted chaos

When the Party's rectification movement first started, the rightists in the colleges of Tientsin, at the direct instigation of the rightist anti-socialist influence of Peking University and that of reactionary T'an T'ien-jung, took the opportunity to do things . . . they fabricated rumours, sowed discord, inflamed the people, and seemed bent on bringing chaos into the world. Reactionary posters, slogans and cartoons stained the beautiful campus. . . .

Tientsin Medical College. . . . With the publication of the *Peasants and Workers Tribune*, the branch of the Peasants and Workers Democratic Party in the college took the initiative in attacking the Communist

Party. On the first issue of the *Peasants and Workers Tribune* they publicly branded the Party members as uneducated and clamoured for the abolition of the Personnel Department. Next was their demand for the promotion of Lei Ai-te [Chief of Teaching Materials Section], chairman of the branch of the Peasants and Workers Democratic Party, to presidency of the college, which was published on a poster there. Also appeared a name list of proposed leadership personnel, which did not include a single Party member. . . .

In Tientsin Normal College . . . the reactionary assertions of Nieh Kuo-p'ing, comptroller and committee member of the Democratic League branch, and Liu Tseng, member of Democratic League and clerk in the Comptroller's Office, were exposed by many students and teaching members. Being a people's deputy of Tientsin municipality, Nieh Kuo-p'ing claimed, "I represent the Vatican." (Nieh is the Vice Chairman of the Tientsin Municipal Catholic Church Reform Committee.) He also accused the Catholic Church Reform Committee of having "done damage to the feelings and self-respect of many faithful Christians." In particular, Nieh Kuo-p'ing was opposed to the Party's mobilisation of the masses of the people in waging the movement for the suppression of reactionaries. Liu Tseng . . . once ferociously alleged that "the Party members are secret agents and they are worse than the Japanese agents during the occupation period." When the Party's rectification movement was started, Liu Tseng publicly suggested with inflammatory intent "now is the time for revenge. . . ."

The rightists in Tientsin University imitated T'an T'ien-jung's "100 Flowers Society" by organising eight "groups." Under such names as "Trumpet," "Wild Grass," "Spring Thunder" and others, they put up many posters slandering the socialist system and Communist Party. . . . Editor Li Ch'ao-kuei of "Spring Thunder" described the present society in a poster as a place of total darkness. . . .

Tientsin Normal College. . . . Liu Shao-yao, a student of the Chemistry Department not only poisonously denounced the Communist Party and socialism but also shamelessly said: "During the Japanese occupation period, everything was better. . . ."

[*NCNA. June 30*

WUHAN

Wuhan University—"Tempest over Mount Lochia"

Among the thirty-three students in the 3rd year, 871st class, of the Department of Chinese in Wuhan University, twenty-five came of landlord, bourgeois or exploiting families. Many of their relatives were struggled against, imprisoned, kept under surveillance or suppressed in the process of the revolutionary socialist movement, while many among themselves, because they had not changed their class stand, also underwent struggle, punishment and expulsion. . . . They were very discontented with the Party and the new society. Wu Kai-pin, Yao Chung-chi, Li-Cheng-yu and Lu Ssu-fei, who occupied room No. 209, were especially so and cherished great rancour in their heart against the Party and the new society. They shouted, "There is no democracy today, there is no freedom of speech today." Wu Kai-pin said: "What a dull thing is this socialism!" They were opposed to all political activities and attacked all political classes. They advocated "independent thinking and contemplation," alleging that it was not right to have too much faith in "dogmas. . . ."

Wu Kai-pin, Yao Chung-chi, Fang Yu-ching and Chiang Chao-hao . . . mobilised the 3rd year students to take the lead in "contending and blooming," and organised a headquarters—the *Flame Newspaper* Office—for attacking the Party. In the first issue of the *Flame Newspaper* they published a "Letter to Students" which encouraged "contending and blooming." They also sent representatives to call meetings in various departments, to make speeches, to establish connections, to encourage them to issue publications to lead "contending and blooming" and to light fires among the workers and staff. . . . In order to let all the bad elements betray themselves, the Party committee significantly adopted the attitude of indulgence and time and again called upon Party and League members to remain calm, to be patient, and not to strike back indiscreetly. For a short period, the rightist flame soared to the skies. The rightists . . . seized control over the "liaison station of students' publications" in opposition to the "contending and blooming" organisation led by the Party committee. They colluded with rightists in various departments; mobilised unlawful elements who had been struggled against, imprisoned, kept under surveillance or suppressed in the past, to "air grievances"; and published the "grievances" of the "plaintiffs" in the *Flame Newspaper* with large-character headlines. They stigmatised the personnel department as "a dark little empire" and proposed to replace the director and deputy directors of this department, to reorganise the department and to publish its archives. . . . They clamoured for the abolition of the system of leadership by the Party committee, and called for the setting up of a system whereby teachers would democratically govern the university. At the same time, they spread the movement to factories and rural areas and mobilised the masses to stand up to fight for "democracy," "human rights" and "liberty. . . ."

Cheng Chien-fan, chieftain of the rightist professors in Wuhan University and henchman of Ma Tse-min provided the principal support and guidance to this small group of rightists. . . .

Ch'u An-p'ing sent reporter Chien Tung-kang of the *Kuang Ming Daily* for incendiary activities, thus also giving great help to the rightists. . . . Lin Hsi-ling, who had close connections with T'an T'i-wu, also gave her support to these rightists. The *Accusation* and the *Public Square* magazine of rightists in Peking University, which she sent to Wu Kai-pin, strengthened the rightists in their determination to carry out incendiary activities. By means of letters Lin Hsi-ling also instructed Wu Kai-pin "not to carry out reforms bit by bit, but to revolutionise things thoroughly." Wu Kai-pin called Lin Hsi-ling a bosom friend and a heroine. . . .

[*People's Daily. August 17*

Cheng Chien-fan—"Chieftain of the rightist professors"

Cheng Chien-fan [Professor, Chinese Language Section, Wuhan Un.] . . . drew many caricatures with captions slandering and berating the Party. . . . He termed the "three-anti" and ideological reform movements as "sectarian movements," and referred to the discussions during such movements as "confessions through torture." He also spoke of the suppression of counter-revolutionaries as "individual retaliation," "betrayal schemes, . . ."

After Wu Kai-pin and their rightists had put pressure on the Party committee and urged a settlement of "basic problems," Cheng Chien-fan told them: "The most important matter is the problem of systems; the struggle is to achieve genuine democracy. . . ."

[*NCNA. July 31*

*

Students strike out

June 12

The "Hungarian Incident in miniature"—A counter-revolutionary clique led by Assistant Principal Wang Chien-kuo of the First Middle School in Hanyang hsien on June 12 and June 13 incited what it itself described as the "Hungarian Incident in miniature" at Tsaitienchen, the centre where the important local organisations of Hanyang hsien are located. The clique acted on the promptings of Ma Tse-min, responsible member of the Chang Po-chun-Lo Lung-chi alliance, stationed in Wuhan, and enlisted the support of Yang Huan-yao, member of the Democratic League and concurrently head of the joint group of democratic parties in Hanyang hsien. . . .

"*Sedition incited on question of advanced study*"—The school graduated this summer nine classes of 459 students. They were very much concerned with the question of advanced study.

At the last lesson on the morning of June 12, Chemistry Teacher Li Hui started a rumour in the fourth classroom of the third grade: "Enrolment this year is restricted; only one or two out of twenty will have an opportunity. The Merit-points of your class are low and it is possible that only two of you will succeed." There was an uproar in the classroom. The news quickly got round to the other classrooms of the grade and heated discussions ensued. At this moment, Yang Sung-tao, a member of the counter-revolutionary clique and supervisor of the school, went to the fourth, sixth and seventh classrooms and urged the students there to see the principal and to ask for the relevant documents. This they did and Principal Han Chien-hsuan [Communist Party member] told them: "I have no documents except conference minutes." These he quickly turned over to the students. But Yang Sung-tao thundered from among the students: "You have the documents but you don't want to show them to us. Isn't this an act of deception?" He attempted to get up a riot on this score. Immediately, the deputy director of culture and education of the hsien committee called up the district committee for instructions and obtained confirmation that the percentage of enrolment for the district was 26·3. He rushed to the school and explained the matter. But Deputy Director Hu Ping-hsuan of the Education Bureau for the hsien (a member of the counter-revolutionary clique) deliberately told the students: "The provincial committee has set the percentage at 30 with a minimum set at 5 per cent." When the students heard that the minimum was set at 5 per cent., they became even more enraged. Strike slogans appeared in the nine classrooms of the third grade. Some of them carried: "Down with Thief Chang! [Chang Hsi-jo, Minister of Education—*Ed.*] Capture the scoundrels of the Education Bureau alive!"

At that point, some students asked Yang Sung-tao if "we would make a mistake by handling the matter in this way." Yang answered: "No, your action is righteous." A number of teachers wrote slogans:

"We support your righteous action! Fight for the privilege of education!" This was fuel to the flames. Some students rang the school bell and started assembling, shouting that they would go to the hsien People's Council to see the relevant documents. They milled around in front of the classrooms of the first and second junior grade and threw stones into them, forcing the students there to come out. Principal Han Chien-hsuan tried to call an emergency meeting of teachers to put down the disturbance but none of them turned up. The students, in agitation and confusion, marched out of the school.

At first glance, the disturbance seemed to have arisen out of the problem of advanced study. But when the students appeared on the streets, they posted and shouted the slogans: "Welcome back to the Kuomintang! Welcome back to Chiang Kai-shek!" and "Let us go to Taiwan." A large Kuomintang party insignia was drawn on the ground at the school. The true nature of the riot began to emerge.

"*Counter-revolutionary clique betrays its designs*"—When the students reached the hsien People's Council, they first stormed into its Culture and Education Bureau, rummaging through files and records. They then raided other offices, breaking down the door of the magistrate's office. On the door of the magistrate's living quarters, they wrote: "Hypocritical magistrate, lackey of the beastly Central People's Government! Get off the stage [*i.e.*, resign], you who eats but doesn't work!"

Some students tried at the Council to telephone the Second and Third Middle Schools for sympathy strikes and, failing to get through, pounded the receiver to pieces. A number of students stole the pedicabs of the Council and rode on them to the rural areas. Yang Huan-yao, who was hiding in a nearby grocery, came out and urged the students on "To the Post Office!" Thereupon they swarmed into the Post Office only to find its workers and employees on guard around its central machine room to prevent any intrusion.

At this point, teacher Wang Hsiao-p'ing came forward and asked the office's cadres to get the magistrate to come to the office because "without the magistrate being here, the students will not leave." The students then put forward three demands: (1) that the percentage of enrolment be made public; (2) that a unified school enrolment be adopted for all areas of the nation; and (3) that enrolments in urban and rural areas be made to correspond. When assistant magistrate Li came out to answer these demands, the students would not listen. The hsien Communist Party committee then sent its propaganda chief to explain the matter, but they would not listen to him either. One of them shouted: "All the big chiefs are in the hsien committee!" At this, the students stampeded to the hsien committee headquarters.

There, they stormed into all its offices and, with whoops and shouts, turned things upside down. A number of the students attempted to rob the organisational department of its archives but failed because cadres intervened. They then reversed the hsien committee's signboard and wrote on its back: "We crush counter-revolution by revolutionary means!"

"*Cadres kidnapped on two occasions*"—Captain Shangkuan Ming-hsien, director of the Conscription Bureau nearby, made an effort to stop the students, saying: "You ought to be more vigilant now that reactionary slogans have appeared." Cadre Hu Tzu-chiao of the Youth League hsien committee explained to the students: "Don't be fooled by counter-revolutionary elements!" This stirred up a frenzied uproar. "What? You say we are counter-revolutionary elements!" the students charged. One of them pulled out from his pocket a rope, bound up Hu Tzu-chiao and hauled him off to the school.

At the evening meal, someone said: "Director Shangkuan says the First Middle School is a nest of counter-revolutionary elements." Yang Sung-tao was quick to seize this opportunity and instigated: "What! He calls us counter-revolutionary elements. Let's go and talk it out with him." He incited the students: "If we can't get him, let's bring his gun back here." They then headed for the Conscription Bureau but found Shangkuan not in. Someone pointed to the ammunition depot upstairs and said: "He must be there!" At this, the students swarmed toward the depot but were stopped short at the door by the cadres guarding it. Somehow, Shangkuan was seen in the hsien committee office and at the first shout, the students turned and crowded into the place. He was dragged out along the ground straight to the school. Teacher Yu Hsin-ping held him up around the waist with the students demanding that he turn over his gun. Shangkuan explained: "I never carry a gun." He added resolutely: "I'm all for your righteous demands. But your erroneous demands I'll never support even if you kill me." He was locked up in the garden.

At night, the hsien committee sent some ten cadres to the school to persuade the students to release the conscription director. They called an emergency meeting of teachers, announced the enrolment percentage and asked the teachers to calm the students . . . when the emergency meeting of the teachers was held in the school to discuss the hsien committee's proposals for the resumption of classes, Yang Sung-tao, Chang Liang-shao, Yu Hsin-p'ing and Wang Shao-ping quickly walked out and headed straight for the classrooms and student dormitory to inflame the students with: "Your action today was righteous, though we did not organise well. We are going to renew the disturbance in an organised way tomorrow. So, go to bed early today for the big day tomorrow." At the end of the meeting, Wang Chien-kuo went over to the students to make sure that they had the encouragement they needed.

June 13

On the morning of June 13, a large slogan appeared on the school's notice board: "Wuhan student strike has borne fruit; enrolment has increased to 10,000 from 30 to 50 per cent. Why then cut our enrolment from 26·3 per cent. to 5 per cent. Is this action of the Government reasonable? We are determined to act and oppose it!" Breakfast over, students of the ninth class of the third grade paraded around the campus, shouting to other students to come out, calling those that refused names such as "traitor," "shameless," and threatening a good beating for the dissenters. Thus, except for those of the first, second and fourth classrooms who remained in class, all the students, numbering about 800, went on the streets. Many of them brought new ropes, ready to use them at the first opportunity.

"*Repeated attempts to bind up magistrate*"—When the students reached the hsien People's Council office, Magistrate Han Mao-ling received their representatives. He criticised their action of the previous day as having gone beyond the limits of democracy and told them that they were wrong to post up reactionary slogans, tear down public property and kidnap cadres. The students booed. On the question of enrolment, the magistrate explained: "Its percentage is definitely 26·3. Unified national enrolment is a question beyond the power of Hanyang hsien to solve. I will convey your opinions to my superior, but it is my responsibility to make the matter clear to you." At this juncture, Yang Sung-tao instigated the students to bind up the magistrate. Several attempts by students to get near the magistrate were foiled by his cadres. Some students expressed agreement with his answers to the questions, but others yelled: "We cannot represent all the students. You go and deliver the answers." Scarcely had the magistrate moved when the students charged forward, surrounded him and pushed him to the ground. Cadres helped him to his feet. The students cried to the cadres: "You are henchmen of the magistrate." They charged: "You are trying to attack students." A rope was flung by a student behind and those in front of them bound up Teng Liang and two other cadres with it.

"*Students storm into hsien committee office to beat up cadres*"—When cook Wang Ta-tsai of the hsien committee saw in the street two students hauling cadre Chu Chia-cheng with a rope around his neck in the direction of the school, he decided to intervene. He demanded that the students should release the cadre immediately. His demand having met with no response, he forced the rope out of the students' hands and set Chu loose. One of the students attempted to grab the rope but Wang Ta-tsai subdued him and dragged him to the hsien committee headquarters. Thereupon, a number of students ran panting to the hsien People's Council office and cried to the other students there: "Schoolmates! hsien committee has bound up three of our students, and is hanging them up and beating them." At this, the students turned and ran to the hsien committee headquarters only to find that the students had already been set free. But Yang Sung-tao incited them: "Let's get in there!" Wang Chien-kuo cried at the top of his voice: "Schoolmates! hsien committee has bound up three of our students, remarks, the students crowded into the hsien committee headquarters, broke open its door and attacked every cadre they met. They beat cadre Li Pang-cheng unconscious. Cadre Chen Chi-huei was covered with bloodstains from being bound with a rope. The students pulled Li Yu-chiao by the hair, threw him to the ground and rained blows on him. Student Hsu Ssu-wu posted upstairs by Wang Chien-kuo whistled and Yang Sung-tao shouted: "Bind the secretary!" Thereupon, a number of students drove the secretary of the hsien committee into a corner of the room and prepared to tie him up and beat him. It was at this moment that several hundred workers arrived on the scene.

"*Workers and peasants rise to counter-attack*"—Even on June 12, workers and peasants had been very unhappy about the riot which the students had started. Students sent to the countryside to solicit support from the peasants met only with reproof and censures. "Now you have a full belly," the peasants told the students "and instead of studying at school, you are creating trouble." When the students bound up Director Shangkuan of the Conscription Bureau on the night of June 12 and posted reactionary slogans on the workers' glorious deeds board, workers voluntarily met together and decided to stop these unlawful actions in order to preserve public order. They agreed with the trade union chairman that they should send twenty representatives to the school to negotiate for the removal of the reactionary slogans from the workers' glorious deeds board and for the termination of the riot. When the workers heard on the afternoon of June 13 that the students had beaten up cadres of the hsien committee, they voluntarily stopped work. Before long, 600 to 700 workers gathered, determined to protect the Government organisations and the leading cadres. The hsien committee had to advise them to hold their hand. As the students beat up one cadre after another, the workers decided otherwise but promised that they would use words and not fists when mediating. They then headed for the school. There they were also assaulted by the students. This provoked the workers. They caught a number of students by the arms and dragged them out of the building. Disconcerted, the students satisfied themselves with binding up five worker representatives and seven cadres and retreated.

Finding that their own men had been kidnapped by the students, other workers rushed to the school. Neighbouring peasants, having heard that the students had beaten up cadres of the hsien committee, sped into the town, shouting: " Support the Communist Party. Support the People's Régime," and " Oppose the unlawful actions of the First Middle School students." The situation was tense, as the workers, peasants and students were all in the school grounds. The magistrate had to rush to the school. He advised all to sit down and appoint representatives for negotiations, and leave arbitration to the Government. He demanded that the kidnapped workers and cadres be released immediately. But Yang Sung-tao now went among the students and instigated them to " bind up the magistrate." When worker Tang Hsin-yu of the Electric Power Station and worker Yi Kuo-ching of the Oil Mill heard this, they roared: " He is the magistrate we have elected. We'll see who dares to bind him! " They nabbed Yang Sung-tao on the spot.

Representatives of the workers and peasants brought up three demands: (1) Cessation of the unlawful actions of the students. (2) Severe punishment to be meted out to the persons responsible. (3) Immediate resumption of classes. The magistrate accepted the demands. Student representatives, knowing that they were in the wrong, failed to appear.

"*Counter-revolutionary elements wanted to kill Party cadres in school*"—When the workers and peasants had left, rumours again started spreading in the school. These were: "146 students have been beaten up, two fatally; the hsien committee has hired the workers to suppress the students and has stood them a meal in a restaurant for this. The workers get three yuan per head for a day of beating up. Peasants get three work points for one swing of a bamboo pole." Slogans appeared demanding the "arrest of culprit Chao Lien-chi (secretary of the hsien committee)." Teacher Chang An-chien conspired with several students to murder Principal Han Chien-hsuan and other Communist members with a knife and a pointed iron bar. Supper over, the students again surrounded the office building and made several attempts to storm in and grab the principal. Student Tang Hui-min climbed up the stairs with a knife but a teacher grabbed him in time to snatch away the knife.

"*Scheme to enlarge the incident*"—Deep into the night, Wang Chien-kuo and others organised scores of students and posted them at key points in the school as patrols with knives, javelins and clubs in order to create a tense atmosphere. He sent student Hsu Ssu-wu to organise a secret meeting with more than ten students and to map out "three resolutions and nine measures." The meeting wanted to have its representatives walk to the provincial authorities to submit petitions, to continue the strike and to demand the "punishment of culprit Chao Lien-chi in the form of exile to Sinkiang for land reclamation and of Han Mao-ling by depriving him of his official post." The meeting then drafted "A letter to the people of the country," "A letter to the compatriots in Wuhan," "A petition," and "A letter to the *Hupeh Daily*." Chang Liang-shao supplied the required stencil with which to mimeograph and distribute the "petition" and "A letter to the people of the country." Wang Chien-kuo urged student Hsu Ssu-wu to get a letter of introduction with which to tender the petition to the provincial authorities and instructed him to threaten violence if the letter were not issued.

During the night, Yu Hsin-ping spread the rumour: "3,000 Kuomintang troops have occupied the Chujushan [fifty li from Tsaitien] and students of the First Middle School have gained control of the lower reach of the Han River." The students then prepared themselves to storm the hsien broadcasting station to tell the people of the hsien "the truth about the hsien committee organising workers to beat up students." They plotted to attack the electric power plant and, when the electricity was cut, to rob the ammunition depot and break into the hsien jail. Workers of the power plant found more than ten students equipped with clubs and bludgeons near it. The workers put up electrified barbed wire and government organisations and units were on guard around the clock in case of any counter-revolutionary disturbances.

June 14

On the morning of June 14 the students called on Wang Chien-kuo for a conference, sending meanwhile representatives to the rural districts to disrupt worker-peasant relations. They prepared for an all-school meeting to struggle against Han Chien-hsuan and Chou Ping-hsien.

"*Truth established and class resumed*"—Secretary-General Chao Ke-chien of the district committee and the hsien committee had got to the bottom of the incident. They called in Wang Chien-kuo and solemnly pointed out to him: "The incident has gone beyond the limits of democracy and is a question of antagonism between the enemy and the people." In the afternoon, Chao Ke-chien called the students to a mass meeting, and proved that counter-revolutionary elements had been behind the riot. The hsien committee at the same time sent a large group of cadres to the villages to explain the truth of the matter and organised people in all walks of life to inspect the scene. At the request of the masses, the hsien judicial organ put Yang Sung-tao, ringleader of the riot under arrest, and the incident was closed. The students went back to class.

[*People's Daily. August 8*

* * *

NANKING

Nanking University—Students go on the streets

Rightist Liu Ching-kun, Lecturer in the Department of History, published an essay entitled "What has harmed Nanking University," in which he compared the people's Nanking University with the puppet Central University before the liberation when Chiang Kai-shek was president, and said that Nanking University "was in adversity": his words were: "Aged and amputated, today's Nanking University is an ill match for the glorious Central University of former days."

Liu Ti-sheng [real name, Liu Chin], Assistant Professor in the Department of Chinese, called upon the Communist Party to "liberate" the Chinese people for a second time. . . .

Lei Kan [real name Szu-tu Chien], student of the Department of Geology, brought forward "twenty principles," counter-revolutionary in nature, including "Fight for democratic liberty," "Support the views of Committee Member Lo Lung-chi," "Marxism-Leninism needs amendment," "The Kuomintang Revolutionary Committee should be on an equal footing with the Communist Party" and "Abolition of special privileges of the Party and Youth League."

Wang Yun-hui, student of French in the Department of Foreign Languages, cried frantically: "In my opinion, ten million out of the twelve million Party members should be killed during the present rectification." He dreamt of mobilising students to stage street processions and of filing a petition with the Provincial Committee. But he failed to secure the support of the majority. Only some ten people responded.

The anti-Party attacks launched by the rightists of Nanking University were specially manifest in the incident in which over thirty students were mobilised to post bulletins in front of the *Hsin Hua Daily* [on June 1—*Wen Hui Pao*, June 28]. In the bulletins they sharply asked the *Hsin Hua Daily* why it did not report the news of the students' "democratic upsurge" in their university. They asked, since the *Wen Hui Pao* reported the "democratic wall" of Peking University, why did the *Hsin Hua Daily* not report the democratic wall of Nanking University? They inveighed against and satirised the reporters and the editor of this newspaper.

But the posting of bulletins aroused a chorus of opposition among passers-by. A worker by the name of Fan indignantly rebuked the students, saying: "You rectify in the school. What are you here for? You are handling contradictions among the people as if you were up against enemies."

Another worker asked the masses around him: "Do you all agree that we tear down the bulletins?" The masses answered unanimously: "Agreed." Thereupon some of the bulletins were torn down. . . .

The next day, several students went secretly to post bulletins in front of the newspaper office. They were again surrounded by the masses. They scented something wrong, removed their Nanking University badges and returned after receiving this set-back. . . .

[*People's Daily. July 12*

Beaten back into the university, these rightists still did not own up to their defeat. While continuing to make plans for organising 600 students to stage demonstrations and rumouring, "The students of

Peking University are already demonstrating and Premier Chou has pledged support to them in a message," they at the same time solicited " support " from all quarters usurping the name of the Students' Association. . . . When the students did not fall prey to their guile, they summarily pieced together a " delegation " of some ten people to " petition " the provincial committee of the Chinese Communist Party. After this they tried to negate the leadership of the Party committee in the university and the provincial committee by cabling to the central committee and calling upon it for " support." They also intended to seize the broadcasting station and to dissolve the Students' Association. . . .

For a time a small number of students, owing to their lack of political experiences, were bewitched by the " facts " fabricated by the rightists or even believed them to be true, and thus wavered in the storm of the class struggle; . . .

[*A letter to the people and students of Kiangsu from the Students' Association of Nanking University. Hsin-Hua Daily. (Nanking.) July 6*

*

What other Nanking students said

The rightists . . . launched frantic attacks on the Party. . . . They said: " Marxism-Leninism is a theory. To regard it as the guiding ideology will result necessarily in doctrinairism," " Marxism-Leninism is a theory of capitalist society, it is now out of date." They demanded the termination of the courses of Marxism-Leninism and the removal from the schools of the branches of the Communist Youth League, and the Young Pioneers.

Tan Tien-shi of East China Water Conservancy College . . . said that he was a slave in the new society. . . .

[*Wen Hui Pao. June 29*

* * *

CHENGTU

Students beat up police

On the evening of June 3, when a *Wen Hui Pao* report [June 2, p. 3] of the beating up of Ch'ang Chin-pai, a teacher at Huaiyuan hsien Primary School in Anhwei, began to circulate among students of the Second Normal School of Chengtu, the students began to lose their heads. . . . On June 10, " An Open Letter " signed by one " Fo Hsiao " also appeared. In it the writer said: " The Communist Party is skilled only in organising riots and disturbances and in repressing the people, but is incompetent at running schools." He also viciously called the Communists "empty-headed and unlettered ignoramuses," called upon the students to "sweep away from the leadership posts of educational work those mountebanks and impostors whose heads are full of irons and chains," proposed that "the Bureau of Education should recall Principal Hsu (a Party member and Vice Principal of the school). Some students spoke out against these reactionary views at the time. On June 11–12, more and more big-character bulletins appeared, most of which demanded that allowances should be raised so as to be paid over twelve months in the year and that the pay and social status of primary school teachers should be raised, expressed support for Ch'ang Chin-pai, and demanded severe punishment for the culprits. On the afternoon of June 12, a small number of students began going out on the streets to stick bills and posters. Meanwhile, the Bureau of Education called an emergency meeting at its office of committee members of the students' union and the students' monitors of the various classes of the school, at which officials of the bureau tried to reason with them, promised them that their demands would be met as soon as possible, and asked them to carry on as usual and not to worry. After supper, three of the students of the school went to Yenshihkou to stick bills and posters. The students were seen by some of the workers of the Chien Chin Iron Works, who prevented them from sticking more bills and took two of them, T'ung Wan-li and P'ei Yuan-fu, both members of "Tatung-tang" (a counter-revolutionary group in the school) to a police station. One of the students escaped and returned to school, declaring that the other two students were being detained in the police station and that they had been beaten up by the police. Thereupon, more than two hundred students rushed out of the school, proceeded to the police station and surrounded it. Rightist P'eng Lin-jung of the school hurried to the scene when he received the news, in order to add fuel to the flames. As a result, the students became intensely excited. They shouted slogans, stuck bills and posters everywhere, and beat up the chairman of the workers' union of Chien Chin Iron Works and three workers. Some of the policemen were also beaten up. The people nearby, angered by the unruly action of the students, came up in large numbers to question the students. Their numbers increased, till at one time more than two thousand people were gathered there, blocking up the traffic. A primary school teacher, speaking with indignation to the students, told them how hard life was for primary school teachers before the liberation. . . . One peasant, a manure porter who happened to pass by, said to the students: "It takes more than three peasants to support one student, yet you still want to make trouble. If you do not heed my warning, I shall club you with this stick." Some of the residents also angrily reproved the students . . . asking them how they could expect to bring up the coming generations well when all they were concerned about was their own pay even before they had completed their training. Thus, justly and rightly reproached, the students realised their own unreasonableness and dispersed at about 11 p.m. leaving about twenty of their schoolmates as representatives. Responsible comrades of the Public Security Bureau and the Bureau of Education then called a meeting of the student representatives and some thirty representatives of the workers, teachers, residents and shop assistants gathered there. Under the weight of criticism and persuasion from the other representatives, the students made a preliminary criticism of their own error in creating a disturbance in the streets, and then returned to the school after midnight. . . .

On the afternoon of June 13, the Bureau of Education again called a meeting of committee members of the student union and student representatives, explaining to them why it had been decided the previous winter to pay them their allowances for eleven months only in a year. In order to persuade the students to take a reasonable attitude as soon as possible, the Bureau of Education also invited people's congress delegates, People's Political Consultative Conference members and outstanding teachers to take part in the persuasion. Finally, the great majority of the student representatives expressed agreement with the Government's measures and willingness to abandon their unreasonable demands. . . . The findings of an inquiry committee showed that no worker had beaten up any students, but that on the contrary the students had struck the workers and some policemen. Having ascertained the truth, the students of the school began to realise that they had been deceived by rightists and counter-revolutionaries and admitted the error of having created a disturbance in the streets. That brought the incident to a close. . . .

[*Chengtu Daily. July 9*

* * *

TSINGTAO

Student unrest at Shantung University

On June 3, while students were absorbed in their studies, Yu Chan-hsueh, a rightist student of the Department of Physics, and Mou Hsin, a rightist student of the Department of Chinese, were secretly discussing the report on " Blooming and Contending " activities at Shantung University, published in the same day's *Tsingtao Daily*. At that time the other students had not yet read this paper.

Yu Chan-hsueh instantly reported the " good tidings " to the whole class, to whom he said by way of instigation: " The report of the *Tsingtao Daily* is a complete misrepresentation of the facts. Students of the Department of Chinese have begun to write bulletins in ' protest ' to the newspaper. What shall we do? "

Mou Hsin returned to the Department of Chinese and agitated to students there in a similar manner, trying actively to win over them to his side. Rightist Chiang Pao-fu and Wang Chun-cheng immediately pledged their sincere support and joined forces with him. After lunch, they stayed in the dormitory and hurriedly wrote a number of bulletins and " protests." Then, leading a group of blind followers, they marched to the " democratic tribunal " and maliciously agitated the students there who had not yet seen the newspaper. They read aloud the slogans which they had prepared in advance, like: " We oppose the control of *Tsingtao Daily* by a few men; the newspaper should echo the popular voice," " Do you listen to Chairman Mao, or to doctrinairism? Shameful tailism! " " Reporters, listen to our denunciation of the ' three evils ' written in blood and tears! " " Down with *Tsingtao Daily*! " and so on. Right on the spot, some students objected to their ignominious acts. But, at their instigation, a small number of students fell prey to the deception. Accordingly, led by " generals " Mou Hsin, Chiang Pao-fu, Hsia Wei-cheng, also a rightist, and Wang Chun-cheng, and headed by motor-cycles, this *grande armée*, over 100 strong, marched murderously toward the newspaper office, where they joined forces with several students of the Department of Physics who, led by rightist Ti Keh, had already been creating trouble.

They unreasonably rejected the suggestion of the newspaper office that they should post the bulletins inside the room and sit down for talks in the recreation club. They savagely insisted that the comrades in charge of the newspaper answer their " queries " and " protests " before the masses. Together with some others, Mou Hsin barred the entrance of the newspaper office so that the masses might not come in. They also viciously mocked at and insulted the comrades in charge of the newspaper. By then, a crowd of pedestrians had gathered outside the newspaper office; traffic was blocked. Those making trouble inside also shouted slogans aloud. In the general confusion somebody cried:

"Down with Communism!" In order to settle contradictions and to ease traffic, comrades in charge of the newspaper promised to consider their unjust demands. Thereupon most of the blind followers went back to the University, leaving behind more than ten people, including Mou Hsin, Chiang Pao-fu, Hsia Wei-cheng and Chou Shan-cheng to "talk" with the newspaper office.

While this was going on, the "democratic tribunal" in our university held heated debates against the trouble-makers; rapidly formed a force in opposition to them; wrote slogans; hastened to the newspaper office to explain that as the trouble-makers were a minority of minorities, they could by no means be taken as representative of the students of Shantung University; and resolutely censured the unjust acts of the trouble-makers.

By this time, the pedestrians had been paying attention to the slogans posted in front of the newspaper office. When they had grasped the situation, they were extremely angry with the trouble-makers, rebuked them, and told them to tear down the bulletins. When this just request was turned down, they became even more indignant, and resolutely tore down the slogans themselves because they slandered the Party newspaper. They also entered the recreation club to take part in the forum. They rebuked and queried the trouble-makers, who became dumbfounded and destitute of arguments. Some of them admitted their mistakes, but still insisted on such absurdities as "our motivation was sound" and "this is not democracy in its broad sense." But, under the merciless rebukes of the masses, they had to admit their mistakes. Thus, in appearance at least, the troubles created in the newspaper office came to an end.

Chiang Pao-fu, however, did not own up to his defeat. While the masses were departing, he and Shih Jo-ping, an employee in the university press, entered the office of the comrades in charge of the newspaper and rebuking them pointed out that the newspaper "did wrong to mobilise the masses against the students," that "the Constitution allows students to post bulletins." They threatened that they would "denounce" the comrades in charge of the newspaper to the *People's Daily*. (We do not know if this denunciation was ever made.) Thereupon, Yang Feng, a rightist among the workers in the newspaper office, concurred in their views and leant his support to the erroneous acts of the trouble-makers. Under the stern rebuke of the comrades in charge of the newspaper, they left in great disorder.

After supper that same day, over 1,000 teachers, students and workers gathered in front of the "democratic tribunal" to discuss the incident at the newspaper office during the day. . . . When the tribunal was declared open, rightists Chang Chuan-tseng, Chiang Pao-fu, Hsia Wei-cheng and Ti Keh, exploiting the tribunal under the control of rightist Li Teh-chun, who was working there (because Mou Hsin was disabled by hoarseness), mounted the platform in turn and made extremely ignominious rumours and evil speeches. They said that the newspaper report in question was a complete distortion of the " Blooming and Contending " situation in the university, that it painted living conditions in rosy colours, formulised everything and idealised everything. They alleged that the Party committee in the university was not determined to " bloom and contend " freely, that the road had been burst open by the masses. They claimed that it was the " Democratic Newspaper " of the Chiu San Society, and not the Party committee, which led the masses. In order to deceive the masses, even falsehood was not beneath them. They rumoured: " The masses who argued against us in the newspaper office today were there by invitation of the newspaper; they were not the true masses! " They said that the newspaper office had come secretly to record speeches. (In reality, it was the broadcasting station which came openly to do so.) They claimed that the newspaper office detained their representatives. They also said that plain-clothes men attended the scene of the newspaper office incident. (In reality, public security officers had already told them that they were there to maintain order.) They said that the newspaper office was " ignominious and shameless " in using the masses to " oppress " the students. They said that the newspaper office had concocted false photographs; and so on. Their speeches were vivid and eloquent, masterpieces of defamation and rumour-mongering.

Chiang Pao-fu was even more absurd than the rest. He rumoured that strikes were going on in higher institutions in Peking, that people there were posting bulletins on buses. At this instant, those rightists who were ordinarily quite civil people and looked not unlike university students with badges on, thought that their poisoned arrow had hit the mark, that the " May 4th spirit " had revived. One and all, they brandished their fists. Their looks were murderous, their eyes aglow with ferocity. They were like wolves and tigers. . . . The poisonous anti-Party, anti-socialist spirit pervaded the " democratic tribunal " which they had seized by force. They were drunk with what they supposed to be victory. . . .

The night deepened. The audience was worn out. The " heroes " could think of no more lies to win the applause of the masses. The " democratic tribunal " was declared closed. . . .

On June 4, Mou Hsin, Wang Chun-cheng, Hsia Wei-cheng and others " aired " their reasons before the Political Consultative Conference, when they also demanded: (1) That the crimes of the *Tsingtao Daily* be denounced before all the people of Tsingtao; (2) That the newspaper be denounced before the journalistic circles of the whole nation; (3) That all colleges in the country rise in protest against the " slander " made by the *Tsingtao Daily* against the students of Shantung University; (4) That accusations be placed before the Central Committee of the Party. . . . To " corroborate " their statement that the *Tsingtao Daily* " mobilised the masses against them," the rightists made separate investigations . . . a certain Yu Hung-tzu, an employee on the private side of the jointly operated Oil Store of the oil and fat industry in this municipality . . . supplied information on the " situation," claiming that the masses in question were bribed, were the workers of the *Tsingtao Daily* in disguise, were unemployed workers hired by the Federation of Democratic Youth.

But the eyes of the masses could accurately distinguish the true from the false, the right from the wrong. Chairman Mao's report and the editorials of the *People's Daily* provided us with powerful weapons. The anti-rightist struggle began. . . .

[*From a public statement by the faculty, students and workers of Shantung University. Tsingtao Daily. Tsingtao. July 18*

* * *

TSINAN

Shantung Normal College—

" In defence of righteousness and human rights "

. . . a well-organised, directed, disciplined and financed reactionary clique. . . . Information disclosed up to the present points to Chang Yu-sung, who posed as a translator in Peking, as the immediate director of this reactionary clique. This Chang Yu-sung had translated certain literary works by European and American writers. . . . The major members of this clique were Chuang Wei-shih, Li Ching-sheng and Tai Tien-ching, teachers at the Shantung Normal College. . . . Some students were actually won over by the clique to be used to disseminate its propaganda materials. . . .

This reactionary clique successively printed in Peking seven kinds of propaganda materials . . . printing 100 to 300 copies of each for dissemination within the Shantung Normal College and in various areas of the country. . . .

On a handbill printed by the clique, Chang Yu-sung wrote "Our War Song," with the sub-title "Launching a Holy Structure to Remove the Three Evils in the Shantung Normal College," to urge all to "respond to the call" and "join in the rectification movement in defence of righteousness and human rights. . . ."

At precisely this time, Chang Yu-sung published in the *Wen Yi Pao* an article entitled: "I raise My Head, Thrust Forward My Chest, and Join in the Fight. . . ."

[*NCNA. Peking. July 28*

* * *

KWEILIN

"Anti-Party storm" at Kwangsi Normal College

In June this year an anti-Party storm broke loose in Kwangsi Normal College. . . . They believed that "the Communist Party has changed qualitatively since it seized power, is going downhill and will one day topple down." They spoke slanderously of the Party, saying: "The Communist Party monopolises all the power in China today. All you can do is flatter it and pander to its every wish. You will be in its good books by simply shouting 'I support . . .' and 'Long live . . .' all the time. What you really think does not matter. . . ." They said that "the Liberation Army is at present formed largely of raw recruits inexperienced in combat and with low fighting morale" and that "they are discontented with life in the army." Thus they formed the conclusion that "eventually there will certainly be riots and uprisings in China."

It was student Pao Chu-t'ao's view that the present-day society was worse than feudal society. He said: "Peasants in the days of the T'ang dynasty were oppressed, but they nevertheless enjoyed some measure of freedom. Now our peasants have not even the freedom to say more than what is expected of them. . . ." Pao Chu-t'ao also put forward his own political views. He said he wanted to build a "new society" of "Eastern Communist economy plus Western democracy. . . ."

He said: "The system of unified purchase and sale is a mess, and supplies to the market are short or irregular." He took exception to our system of personnel records and said: "The system of personal dossiers was a ruler's tool with which the Tsars dealt with revolutionaries." His attitude toward realist literary theories: "I utterly ignore them." He thought that all literary works produced in the socialist countries were stereotyped and too generalised. He wanted acceptance of the literary thinking of Western Europe in its entirety. . . . He maintained that man should have " absolute freedom " to develop himself. He showed his perverseness by saying: " I will resolutely refuse to do anything I am ordered to do, although it may be a good thing." He often compared himself with satisfaction with Don Quixote.

Early in June, reactionary articles like " To the Oppressed " and slogans like " The Oppressed, Unite! " appeared in the college, and these were inwardly applauded by the anti-Party group. . . . Pao Chu-t'ao also said as if intoxicated: " All the people are openly opposing the Communist Party. The time has come to overthrow the Party! . . ." they decided to write " guiding articles " and publish a wall newspaper to be known as " The Battle Cry. . . ." Of these, Pao Chu-t'ao's " Discussion with the Dean on the Object of the Blooming and Contending Movement " was the core of an anti-Party declaration. . . . He argued: " The Chinese people know how to conduct their affairs. It is the 600 million people, not the Party, who have inexhaustible strength. Only the sectarians and those who think that the Party is supreme will think that the salvation of the people and the nation depend on the rectification of the Party. . . ."

On the afternoon of June 6, the anti-Party group gathered together about a dozen " activists," who had already come out in their true colours, and held a meeting with them in the great hall of the college. It was proposed at the meeting to " organise a ' blooming and contending ' committee to lead the movement and substitute it for the students' union." After the meeting, Pao Chu-t'ao and his friends decided to " demand that the leadership make public its personal dossiers, pay allowances for the students' board during the summer months, suspend classes during ' blooming and contending,' and refrain from taking reprisals." They planned to introduce these demands at a free-speech meeting in the form of four resolutions. Later the students' union, acting under pressure from the anti-Party group, issued a circular calling a general meeting of students for free " blooming and contending." Pao Chu-t'ao immediately made an appeal from the broadcasting room to the students to take part in the " free blooming and contending meeting." At that meeting Huang Hsien-fan and other rightists spoke, and Pao Chu-t'ao read aloud his reactionary declaration, " Discussion with the Dean on the Object of the Blooming and Contending Movement." This was followed by reactionary speeches, in which such views as " Party and Youth League members are ' plain-clothes men ' " and " The Soviet Union is guilty of aggression against China " were expressed. . . .

Later, under his manipulation, the "committee for blooming and contending" adopted an anti-Party telegram addressed to the Provincial People's Council, saying: "Dean Liang is incompetent to lead the blooming and contending movement. Please ask Ch'en Man-yuan to come to this college as soon as possible."

Pao Chu-t'ao's small group took an active part in, and aggravated further, the anti-Party activities of other reactionary students of the college, including their seizure of the broadcasting room . . . and the demonstration demanding the suspension of classes and publication of personal dossiers, and the subsequent surrounding of the personnel office of the college. . . .

The students of the Normal College, greatly incensed because the "committee for blooming and contending" had dispatched the anti-Party telegram to the Provincial People's Council at Pao Chu-t'ao's instance without first consulting them, held a general meeting and resolved to dissolve the "committee for blooming and contending. . . ." Pao Chu-t'ao falsely said to his confederates that "the act [the dissolution of the 'committee for blooming and contending'] was prearranged by Dean Liang," and that he "would go to Peking to see officials of the Party's central leadership." He also swore: "We may let our heads be chopped off and our blood flow, but our spirit must not yield! . . ."

Lo Shen-yun himself wrote a number of letters to the *Kuang Ming Daily*, *Wen Hui Pao*, *Kwangsi Daily*, *People's Daily*, the Communist Party Central Committee and the Communist Party Kwangsi Provincial Committee, to "let the whole nation know that 'blooming and contending' is being suppressed in Kwangsi Normal College and to win the support of the people. . . ."

Looking for "support and guidance," Pao Chu-t'ao had made friends during "blooming and contending" with rightist Huang Hsien-fan, professor of the Department of History. . . .

Then the anti-rightist struggle began. . . . It was found out that Pao Chu-t'ao, Chang Chan and Lo Shen-yun each had an ugly personal history. They have all erred in the revolutionary ranks and have been punished. . . .

[*Kwangsi Daily. Nanning. October 3*

* * *

SOOCHOW

Fomenting trouble

Rightist Hsueh Tien-han . . . is a member of the Soochow Municipal Preparatory Committee of the Kuomintang Revolutionary Committee and head of the Seminar of Languages at Soochow First Middle School. . . .

On June 16, falling easy prey to the venomous letter sent by rightists in middle schools and Tungchi University in Shanghai . . . students of Soochow First Middle School called a meeting, at which they adopted three " resolutions," asking the government " to rescind the ruling on direct admission into universities of students from worker and peasant short-course middle schools " and " to make arrangements for all senior middle school graduates who fail to qualify for higher studies." They were also getting ready to write letters to Chairman Mao and to the State Council. Thereupon, Hsueh Tien-han promptly offered his advice. He said: " A letter addressed to the Chairman or to the State Council by a school will certainly be sent back and will serve no purpose. . . ."

At the instigation of Hsueh Tien-han, three senior students invited delegates of other schools to a joint meeting. They were ready for action, and the trouble-making students sent out 143 letters to middle schools all over the country to foment trouble. At this very moment, Hsueh Tien-han did his utmost to advocate a representative meeting of graduates and a letter to the municipal education bureau in the name of all teachers and workers to show their support to the students' demand for such a meeting. . . .

[*The Chinese Youth Newspaper. August 15*

* * *

NANCHANG

Rightist group at Linchuan Normal School

A rightist group headed by students Fu Lin-hui and Yang Kuo-hsing . . . During the period of " blooming " and " contending," the group openly applauded the " Party empire " view of the Chang-Lo alliance, praised Ko P'ei-ch'i for his " outstanding ability and surpassing courage," approvingly described Lin Hsi-ling and P'u Hsi-hsiu as " first class women," and tried to collect all rightist views and speeches for future use. This rightist group vainly hoped to abolish Party leadership. They sweepingly belittled the series of great achievements of socialist transformation and socialist development, and described the anti-feudal agrarian struggle as a " retaliatory measure." They called the agricultural co-operative movement a " repressive measure " against the peasants, who " were forced to submit, or they would have no land to till." They also declared that " the system of unified purchase and sale has caused starvation among the people." For the purpose of stirring up enmity between the Party and the masses, rightist Yang Kuo-hsing went to sell his erroneous views to law-defying landlords and rich peasants in the countryside, criticising the cadres for being " political opportunists " and " lords " and trying to disrupt the unity of the cadres and the masses. . . . Criticising the cultural and artistic activities of the nation, these rightists said: " The new society restricts the creativeness of the literati," " The individuality of the people is cramped," " Party spirit is an evil curse," " Generalisations and stereotyped products of writing are attributable to Party spirit and also to the restrictions imposed by the socialist realist principles of creative writing," and so on. They took an intense dislike to the splendid results of the movement for the suppression of counter-revolutionaries, attacking the movement as an " attempt to manufacture a White bogy." They regretted that they had not got in touch with Hu Feng earlier, and were quite willing to be " Hu Fengites. . . ." They maintained that the principal conflict was the " conflict between the Soviet Union and the United States," misrepresented Sino-Soviet unity and called China " a pawn of the Soviet Union which has lost its national dignity," and described the close friendship between the Soviet Union and China as [China's] " cringing servilely at the feet of imperialism " and a " relationship between the master and the slave." Everyone knows the justice of the resist-United States and aid-Korea campaign, but the small group of rightists had the effrontery to call China an " aggressor." They also called the existing system of compulsory military service a sign of China's " bellicosity."

For the purpose of discrediting the leadership of the Party, the rightist group called the Communist Party, the Communist Youth League and the Young Pioneers the " rule of the trinity " which was " not much different from Hitler's rule," and condemned the Communist Youth League as " an organisation of plain-clothes men " of the Communist Party for the supervision of youths. They slanderously described the leaders of the people and the state as " persons who ride in sedan chairs " who formed a " feudal dynasty imposed on the people." They also declared that " the power of the Party is in the hands of only Mao Tse-tung and Chou En-lai," and did everything to discredit them.

" Attempt to re-create the Hungarian incident "

They declared that the society was in a " mess " and another " revolution " was necessary. With this end in view, they advanced the preposterous view that " social development is not governed by objective laws, but is determined by man," and likened such social development to an "invisible wheel." Obsessed with the idea that "guns are less powerful than pens, because guns can only kill a man's body, whereas pens can change man's ideas," they decided to challenge the people with pens in the hope of overthrowing the people's government. . . .

As a result of penetrating exposures, the rightist group admitted that they had tried to form a reactionary party to be known as "Cosmos Party," to procure arms, and to carry out counter-revolutionary subversive activities. . . .

In the school, they systematically dealt blows to Youth League members and class cadres, isolated the masters of the classes, and tried to undermine the school administration. The rightists advocated "revolution by violence," for which they would need men. So, it was their desire to make friends with and win the support of other students. . . . They even wildly thought to seize the municipal offices of Fuchow and create a minor Hungarian incident. Thinking that they had the support of their many friends, they planned to "win over the Liberation Army through persuasion by the wives of army officers" and declared that "a mere call would make the peasants rise. . . ." These madmen secretly planned that it would be necessary first to seize the political nerve centre of Fuchow—the headquarters of the Communist Party district committee and district administrative offices—if they were to take control of Fuchow. Then they would seize the key communication centre—the railway station and the post office. Finally, they would seize the bank, and "the situation will be under control. . . ."

The oldest member of the group is only twenty-two, and the average age of the members is nineteen or twenty. Almost all of them have come from bourgeois, feudal landlord or rich peasant families. . . .

[*Kiangsi Daily. Nanchang. September 6*

* * *

PEKING

"An emergency conference convened by Chang Po-chun"

Chang Po-chun, First Deputy Chairman of the Democratic League; Minister of Communications, invited several famous scholars to an emergency conference in the People's Political Consultative Conference's Cultural Club at Nanhoyen on June 6 at 10 a.m. for the purpose of discussing the present situation and deciding on action. Present at the conference were Tseng Chao-lun, Ch'ien Wei-ch'ang, Fei Hsiao-t'ung,

Tao Ta-jung, Wu Ching-chao, Huang Yao-mien and Yeh Tu-yi, director of the general office of the Democratic League. In addition, Shih Liang, Minister of Justice, Hu Yu-chih (who withdrew from the conference), Chin Jo-nien and myself were also invited to the conference, probably for the purpose of enlightening us on the present situation. . . .

Chang Po-chun said that the situation in the schools was quite serious and asked those present to study and consider how the China Democratic League should do its work during the movement. Fei Hsiao-t'ung, sociologist, was the first to express his opinion, saying that the university students had been set in motion and their feelings had been worked up. Judging by the problems brought to light during the campaign, it appeared that the situation was quite serious. He had heard it said that two students in Peking University alleged that they had been wronged during the campaign for rounding up counter-revolutionaries, and that some had begun to weep on hearing their story. "We intellectuals cannot tolerate such things. Things are simply too dark. A new emotion arises in my heart today. I sympathise with the students in these matters that are brought to light. Once the students are aroused to action, the situation is likely to deteriorate. The students are looking for leaders everywhere. If teachers join in, there will be a bigger trouble. Of course it is easy to put it down. Three million soldiers would put it down but public support would evaporate and the Party's prestige among the masses would be finished." He said that the trouble today was mainly the product of the system. Non-Party people had no authority and Party and League members exercised authority and usurped power. "I think it is not a question of the style of work of individuals but a question of system. I have declared I will not join the Communist Party as an expression of my attitude (interrupting him at this point, Ch'ien Wei-ch'ang said: 'I will definitely not join the Communist Party'). Some say: Without Party nomination I cannot be anything. I don't think so. Let us see whether the masses support me or not in an election campaign."

Tseng Chao'lun, Deputy Minister of Higher Education, said: "The students have many problems today and things have reached a saturation point. Once they are in the streets, the townsfolk will gather together and the situation will worsen. For the masses are also dissatisfied with the Party today. . . ." He said that in the early period following the liberation, the students had wanted to settle down to study because of the unsettled times preceding it; at that time, they had got more lessons and Party prestige had been high so that there had been calm for some years.

But the situation was different now. The Party had estranged itself from the masses to a serious extent. Because of this and the impact of the Polish and Hungarian incidents, the situation had reached a critical point. The present situation was much the same as that on the eve of the eighth plenary session of the United Workers' Party of Poland. It was possible that the Party had made a mistake in its estimate of the present rectification campaign. Possibly the Party had thought higher intellectuals would pose many problems while young students definitely could not pose any problems. In the event it had been just the opposite and the Party had been forced into a passive position. There had been trouble in the University of Communications in Sian. The situation in Shanghai might be more serious than in Peking.

Ch'ien Wei-ch'ang, Vice President, Tsinghua Un., took the view that the special feature of the students' movement was its search for leadership and that, if teachers took the lead, there might be great trouble. "Parents of some students recently wrote to me, asking me to dissuade their children from making trouble. I did, but the students were determined. It really looks like the eve of the May 4th Movement. They would not heed the advice of their parents in the same way as we would not accept the advice of our parents when we were students. . . ." "The students are looking for leaders and hoping that we will come forward to speak for them. But it is difficult to speak for them. Some in Tsinghua University suggest that President Chiang should resign and Ch'ien Wei-ch'ang should be appointed President."

Tao Ta-jung explained the serious situation in the Normal University. He said that the Party leadership in the Normal University had many troubles but so far dared not admit its mistakes. Most of the trouble concerned the campaign for rounding up counter-revolutionaries and the question of wage scales. . . . Some students of Peking University had asked the students of the Normal University to go out on strike. Some said the present situation was without precedent since the May 4th Movement. . . .

Certainly Chang Po-chun showed his appreciation of the above speeches. . . . Here are some important points from what he said that day:

"Students of the Hankow school under the Ministry of Communications will present a petition. Students strike in other places, and the situation is serious. . . . If the students appear in the streets and are followed by the masses, things will get out of control."

He went on to say: "I am in favour of large-scale development of the democratic parties. At least one or two million members should be recruited and all non-Party people should be drawn into the organisations . . . democratic parties ought to penetrate the hsien level—only thus can they fulfil their supervisory role. . . ."

"The present rectification movement requires non-Party people to express opinions. The consequences of this, I think, were estimated by the venerable Mao: the democratic parties always put forward criticisms politely. But the estimate was incomplete. It was not thought that the Party could have committed so many mistakes. The problems brought to light have far exceeded the estimate, and really the 'task has been over-fulfilled.' They are in a dilemma; to go forward is no good, to retreat is no good. Our Democratic League has the responsibility of helping the Party. . . ."

[*From an article by Min Kang-hou (Standing Committee, CDL). People's Daily. July 4*

Premier Chou refuses to comment

After the meeting, Shih Liang suggested that the advice of the leadership should be sought and that the matter should be discussed with Premier Chou. She also said that she would mention the matter when she saw Premier Chou in the afternoon.

On June 7 the State Council was in session. Shih Liang told me that she had discussed the matter with Premier Chou the evening before, that the Premier made no comment. She asked me to take up the matter with the Premier again. At the meeting, I wrote a memo to the Premier telling him that the situation was rather grave and that the attitude of the informants was quite sincere. The Premier again made no comment.

I was myself inclined to agree with their judgment of the situation. I also agreed to talk to the Communist Party about this. I felt that the democratic parties could still do something in this connection. As to the question of who lit the fire, it is difficult to say. If it is said that it was my anti-Party and the anti-socialist speeches which fanned up the sentiments of the masses, that's a different problem. In all honesty, I neither ordered nor hinted directly that fires should be lit. . . .

[*Speech by Chang Po-chun at a meeting of the CPWDP. NCNA. Peking. July 3*

* * *

Rightists in the Youth League

They described the work of the Communist Youth League during the past few years as " a mess," attempting thereby to weaken our confidence and to dissipate our morale. . . . Rightist Chou Ching-tsai even went so far as to publish in the Honan Provincial Institute of the League " Suggestions for the Abolition of the Communist Youth League," in which he openly suggested that during the period of peaceful construction the Communist Youth League had lost the justification for its existence. . . .

The rightists inside the League wildly attacked the leadership of the Party, promoted the mood of distrusting the Party, did not execute the directives and policies of the Party, and detached the League from the leadership of the Party. In this connection, rightist Hsu Hsueh-ming of the Hsining Municipal Committee of the League openly advocated that the League should discard the status of being a " satellite " and " assistant " to the Party. He frantically decried the relation between the Party and the Youth League as that between the leading and the led. He distorted this normal relation into " the relation between the governing and the governed, the oppressing and the oppressed. . . ."

In a variety of ways the rightists manifested their hostility toward and struck against the guiding ideology of the Youth League—Marxism-Leninism—and opposed political and ideological education among the youths. Waving the anti-doctrinairism banner, rightists Sheng Yu-chiu and Liu Lo-shan opposed the study of Marxism-Leninism inside the League, opposed the analysis of youths' ideological problems from the stand of the class and imputed the many erroneous ideas of youths to insufficient knowledge or even to insufficient understanding. . . . The rightists aroused the youths to suspect the new society and to entertain discontent against the Party. . . .

In this way, the setting up of " The 100 Flowers Society " by T'an T'ien-jung and other rightists in Peking University confused the direction of scores of students for a time, who, but for rescue by the Party, would have been taken prisoners by the rightists. It is in such a manner that the rightists exploited the innocence, the impetuosity, the individualism, the liberalism and other weaknesses of the youths. . . .

League branches collapse—Rightists within the League have also done their utmost to attack the relationship between the League and the masses, to create discord in the League and to dissolve the League organisations. In this connection, rightist Chou Ching-tsai groundlessly rumoured that the existence of the Youth League aroused the discontent of the youths at large, produced and nourished sectarianism, subjectivism and bureaucratism. In one of the sub-headings in an article in the *Tientsin Ching Nien Pao*, rightist Hsiao Ti compared the relation between the League and the masses to that between "cats and mice. . . ." The rightists within the League have caused the organisations to be dissolute and the morale to be lax. Certain League branches have collapsed simply because of one or two rightists in them. . . .

People may ask: How is it that rightists appear even in the progressive organisations of the Youth League and among the cadres of the League? We answer: . . . In times of peace and prosperity, individual elements belonging to classes different from ours found their way into the League. Part of them came of landlord and bourgeois families, and had, to a varying extent, been poisoned by their original classes. . . .

It should be added here that the rightists form a very small number within the system of the Youth League. . . .

[*The Chinese Youth Newspaper. August 2*

Leading Youth League rightist

Tung Hsueh-lung, alternate member of the Central Committee of the Communist Youth League and Deputy Secretary of the Yunnan Committee of the Communist Youth League, has been found to have consistently engaged in anti-Communist Party and anti-socialist activities. . . .

Tung Hsueh-lung is a rightist who wormed his way into the Communist Party. . . .

At a staff meeting of the Yunnan Committee of the Communist Youth League, he openly said that "the main contradiction of the League at present is the contradiction between the League and the Party" and that "the Party's grip on the League is too tight." Tung incited low-level cadres to "throw back" the directives of the Party committee, with a view to resisting and defaming the leadership of the Party and demanding from the Party "the League's right of independent activity. . . ."

After the League paper was criticised by the Party committee for erroneously carrying cartoons which distorted the life of the workers,

Tung Hsueh-lung told personnel of the League paper: "That is not a mistake. Do not 'bend with the wind.' . . ."

He further criticised the League's work, stating that the main shortcoming was "excessive restrictions" upon youth, thereby turning them into "robots." He also stated that the students today had been educated into "yes-men" who did not dare "express their aspirations," and that the situation "was worse than in feudal times." When he saw a reactionary poster, he hailed it as a sign of "active thinking by the students."

Tung Hsueh-lung further took advantage of his position in the *Border Region Youth*, a League paper operated under his direct leadership, to materialise his scheme of changing the paper's nature. . . . He praised the *Wen Hui Pao* for its deftness in "grabbing news" and instructed the reporters to specialise in reporting the so-called "dark side. . . ."

Ling [Yung?] -ping, deputy chief editor of the *Border Region Youth*, pointed out that in the course of blooming and contending the paper once almost changed its special characteristics and political line. Its role in directing rural youth was greatly weakened. . . .

Tung Hsueh-lung . . . after his return to Kunming from Peking . . . greatly acclaimed Peking University's democratic wall, which posted big signs attacking the Communist Party. . . .

After a reactionary poster bearing the words "Down with the Communist Party" appeared in the League school of the Yunnan Provincial Committee of the League, he still reported to the students: "There are no rightists in the League school." At a staff meeting of organisations of the provincial committee of the League, during which the rightists attacked the Party on the questions of suppression and eliminating of counter-revolutionaries and investigation of cadres, Tung Hsueh-lung openly hailed and supported them, although he was a member of the leadership team. . . .

Tung Hsueh-lung openly attacked Secretary Wang Yu-hui of the provincial committee and asserted that the latter "deviated from reality and should be sent to the lower levels for training." He also criticised Deputy Secretary Tsui Yun, saying that the latter was incompetent and "cannot achieve anything great. . . ."

Tung Hsueh-lung was in the habit of deceiving the League organisation. . . . He told people that he was a "guerrilla hero" before the liberation of Kunming, but actually he never participated in the underground guerrilla warfare in Yunnan. He simply wrote a story about himself after hearing some stories about guerrilla warfare at a meeting. . . .

[*NCNA. Kunming. August 26*

9

WRITERS AND ARTISTS

DURING the twenties and thirties, Marxism and left-wing ideas generally probably had a greater vogue among writers than among academics; and while the universities sought refuge in Nationalist-controlled areas when the Japanese war broke out, a significant proportion of the writers trekked northward to Communist Yenan. There, in 1942, Mao Tse-tung himself laid down the conventional Communist line that art must serve politics. His speeches indicate that already even the Party writers resented such a policy and were worried at the subordination of general humanist values to the dictates of Party strategy; but the cause was sufficiently heroic for doubts to be submerged and some good works to be produced.

After 1949, the quality of literary work fell considerably. The Communist Party, having achieved its victory, no longer had any tactical need to give writers any leeway, to permit deviations from the stolid norms of socialist realism. Like the other intellectuals, the writers were subjected to ideological remoulding and forced to endure the same endless sessions of criticism and self-criticism. Those who had lived in Nationalist-controlled areas, the majority, had their bourgeois past subjected to merciless scrutiny. Writers and creative artists generally were sent to farm and factory to absorb the true subject-matter of socialist realism and had to submit the resulting work to the critical cynosure of their colleagues. Under such conditions the writers' enthusiasm seems to have wilted.

Finally, in 1955, a lesser Communist writer named Hu Feng revolted against the demand for a political and Marxist orientation for art and its creators. In its counter-attack against Hu Feng-ism, the Party attempted to root out any lingering desires for artistic freedom still preserved in cultural circles. Hu Feng himself was arrested, allegedly because he was conspiring with the Nationalists.

But with the general " thaw " in 1956, Mao Tse-tung charted a more liberal policy with his slogan " Let a hundred flowers bloom, let a hundred schools contend." This permitted writers greater variety in subject-matter and technique; while abandoning none of its long-term aims of ideological conformity the régime was prepared to free art from its political leading strings for the sake of encouraging creation. As the student Lin Hsi-ling pointed out, the new line conceded most of Hu Feng's demands. Cultural circles responded with cautious enthusiasm. Literary magazines sprang up all over the country, old plays were revived. A few controversial stories were written, the most important being *Young Newcomer to the Organisation Department*, by a young Party writer named Wang Meng, which depicted the demoralisation of a Peking Party cell.

The new trends soon alarmed the Party orthodoxy. In January and February, Ch'en Yin, Ch'en Ch'i-t'ung and other members of the armed forces propaganda department sounded a warning against such " poisonous weeds," but their *démarche* was officially rejected as pouring too much cold water on the hundred flowers policy. (Later, in June, Ch'en Yin and Ch'en Ch'i-t'ung were personally attacked in the *Wen Yi Pao* (the *Journal of Literature and Arts*); see below " Can we lead dramatic groups as we would lead an army? " and " Do not forget the particular characteristics of literature.")

When the rectification campaign started, the official Writers' Union called a number of forums. The reported remarks were not very startling though they revealed an undercurrent of dislike for Chou Yang, the Deputy Director of the Party's Propaganda Department encharged with supervising the cultural field. (Chou Yang's views were also attacked in an article in the *Wen Yi Pao* at this time.) More pungent comments on Party cultural policies appeared in the pages of the *Wen Yi Pao*, for which one of the Deputy Chief Editors, Hsiao Ch'ien, was later held responsible. A subtler attack on socialist realism was made by the young Communist writer, Liu Shao-t'ang (who, it was revealed at the forums, had also had his differences with Chou Yang), in a long article in *Literary Studies*; in effect, it was an attempt to justify the virtual abandonment of Party control over the arts.

All this was on the surface. There was no indication of any deeper activity until suddenly, two months after criticism had been halted, the régime suddenly accused Miss Ting Ling, a leading novelist and Stalin Prize winner, of combining with other prominent writers in a plot against Party leadership of culture. Virtually all the information to be released was contained in the initial announcement and it offered little indication of the truth of the affair. The case of the anti-Party clique among the painters (which was alleged to have links with Ting Ling's group) is as mysterious. But one can conclude from these reports that, despite years of indoctrination, a large number of writers and artists have not abandoned their own standards or ceased to desire release from the compulsions of Party cultural policy.

"Applauding 'Let a hundred flowers bloom'"

I cannot help but laugh out loud when I recall the way we used to approach literary works in the past. In evaluating the merits and demerits of a literary work we used to apply the following formulae:

Works produced after the Liberation:	Good
Works produced before the Liberation:	Bad
Works originating in the Soviet Union and fraternal countries:	Good
Works originating in capitalist countries:	Bad
Works taking positive characters as leading figures:	Good
Works taking reprehensible characters as leading figures:	Bad. . . .

I now dare to read books which I dared not read before. When I have read the *Dream of the Red Chamber*, *Western Travels* [classical novels] and *Romance of Tears and Laughter* [modern novel], and when I have read works by Hugo, George Sand, Dickens and Zola, I feel like walking into a new hemisphere. My vision suddenly broadens and there is a feeling that some of the works which I have read in the past are so superficial and monotonous. . . .

Even if one read poisonous works, one would not necessarily become bad suddenly, especially if one has a certain amount of analytical ability. Therefore I am prepared to take an extensive walk in the literary garden of the world, and when I come across poisonous weeds, I would even pick them up and play with them. It is also for that reason that I advocate that there should be full freedom in reading literary works. . . .

[*Wang K'uei-lung. Chinese Youth. No. 10. May 16*

*

Writers' forums

Tsang K'o-chia: " . . . In the past, when we were in Chungking, there was nothing Party and non-Party writers could not say to each other and in Shanghai we were quite intimate, but in Peking it is different. Intimate conversation between friends has decreased. . . . The Party writers are somewhat arrogant. In the past, people have said that the writers from the old areas [the old 'liberated areas' refers to the northern provinces occupied by the Communists after 1935, where a number of writers took refuge after the Japanese invasion] are the main force and those from Chiang-controlled areas [*i.e.*, the writers who took refuge in Chiang Kai-shek's wartime capital, Chungking] are not worth much. There are a few Party members who consider themselves upper class. . . ."

Hsieh Chun-chien: " . . . The Writers' Union has not done enough in the direction of encouraging creative work and officialism is quite serious. It does a lot of work for young writers, but little for the old writers and has not inquired about writers who are not members of the union. . . ."

Chin Jen: " . . . In the past few years our country's literary and artistic policy has been wavering, in general following the Soviet Union. I think we ought to have an independent literary and artistic policy. . . ."

Pi Yeh: " . . . The work of the literary and artistic world is spring-time work, but my life has been a wintry one. A wall of ice separates the Party members and non-Party people, often causing one to beware and not dare to approach. . . ."

Huang Ch'iu-yun: "The fact that rectification cannot be developed in the literary and artistic world and that the lower levels have worries and little courage is related to the judgment of the upper levels. I feel that in general the judgment of the upper levels is not great. Not long ago, Comrade Chou Yang, Deputy Director, CCP's Propaganda Department, criticised Liu Shao-t'ang as 'not knowing the immensity of the universe' [*i.e.*, not having a sense of proportion]. This was not very nice and could affect people's positive nature. There were a few leading comrades whose view of Wang Meng's novel was quite different at the beginning and at the end. Comrade Chou Yang at first did not welcome this work, but his views as expressed to the Press showed a change—but one cannot see how the change came about. . . ."

Li Ho: "Whether or not a play is performed is often decided by one sentence from a responsible comrade of the propaganda department. When we were putting on *The American Way of Life*, Comrade Chou Yang said the most important thing for us was to struggle against the enemy and we had not mirrored American life correctly. Comrade Chang Kuang-nien [Chief Editor, *Wen Yi Pao*] said we had wasted our efforts. So we just didn't do the play. . . ."

Shu Wu: ". . . Theoretical criticism is very difficult to do. It seems as if with Chairman Mao's 'speeches' [*i.e.*, at the Yenan literary forums in 1942] all problems are solved, as if in them all truths have been finally expounded. But Chairman Mao's 'speeches' are a programme, they don't solve all problems. They open the way of truth; we still have to travel the road. . . ."

[Held by the Party group in the Writers' Union in late May and early June. Wen Yi Pao. No. 11. June 16

*

A writer's appeal for creative freedom

I think that Chairman Mao's speech delivered at the Yenan forum on Literature and Art consisted of two component parts; one was composed of theories of a tactical nature with which to guide the literary and artistic campaigns at the time, the other was composed of theories involving general principles with which to guide literary and artistic enterprises over the long run. . . .

Now what kind of historical conditions were prevailing at that time? These were the most trying times during the anti-Japanese war when the Kuomintang Reactionary Clique was wavering in its resistance to Japan, indulging on the sly in activities which savoured of capitulation and betrayal, and also adopting towards the people a highly oppressive policy. Hence there existed the phenomenon of being divorced from the masses and their works being divorced from politics. . . .

Therefore, we had to carry out thought reform for the writers and artists, insisting that they should penetrate into the ranks of the workers, peasants and soldiers, and penetrate into practical struggles, and that they should produce timely works in direct service of the anti-Japanese war. Even if these works were bricks and stones, so long as they could be used to strike the enemy, they were good enough. . . .

Owing to the fact that the life that these works reflected belonged to a definite period and that the creative processes of the writers were hurried and brief, the artistic content of these works was generally very poor, and the intellectual content extremely limited. . . .

If we were to use today the same method of leadership and the same theories as were used in the past to supervise and guide writers' creative works, they would inevitably only perform the function of achieving " retrogression " rather than progress.

We cannot but admit that since the liberation of the country, our guiding theoretical ideas have been conservative and at the same time profoundly influenced by doctrinairism from abroad, which to a considerable degree has hindered and stunted the development and prosperity of literary and artistic enterprises. . . .

The root-causes of formalisation and conceptualisation lie in the dogmatists mechanically, conservatively, one-sidedly and in an exaggerated way carrying out and elaborating upon the tactical theories which Chairman Mao used to guide the literary and artistic movement at that time. . . .

Literature and art do not serve politics by mechanically serving a certain policy, nor with creative works which conform to the constitution, Party regulations and the letter of the law; they mainly do so through the class-nature of works, through encouraging people, and through the function of aesthetic education of the people's moral qualities. . . .

The subject-matter of creative works also should be divided into primary and secondary; the authors should do their utmost to acquaint themselves with the life of the mass of the workers and peasants, so as to deal with the subject-matter of the mass of workers and peasants. Of course we cannot apply rigid rules and administrative methods to compel authors to do so. . . . I am not, like Ch'en Ch'i-t'ung, putting such subject-matter as " domestic affairs and boy-and-girl romances " into a category irreconcilably opposed to such subject-matter as the lives of the workers, peasants and soldiers. Such an argument is in fact extremely ridiculous. Do we mean to say that the workers, peasants and soldiers have no " domestic affairs and boy-and-girl romances "? Do we mean to say that we must only use the following type of subject-matter when we are writing about workers: " the furnace fire is flaming red, the wheels of the engine are turning, the iron press is clanging . . ."? Do we mean to say that in writing about the peasants we can only use the following type of subject-matter: "Ahem! Ahem! Ahem! Let's exert ourselves and work with renewed vigour, so that the produce will be an inch taller"? Do we mean to say that in writing about the soldiers we can only use the following type of subject-matter: "Pick up your rifle! Charge! Kill!"? Do we mean to say that we can irrevocably sever "domestic affairs and boy-and-girl romances" from labouring, production and warfare? . . .

The fact is the value of a work is not in the long run determined by whether or not its subject-matter and theme are portentous or not; it is determined by its intellectual significance expressed through artistic forms as well as by its artistic powers of persuasion. . . .

To deny that political standards rank as the most important is in effect to deny the class nature of art, and to deny that art is a weapon, a tool, and to regard it merely as a flower vase.

But just as I have said before, this is not committing myself to the dogmatic and sectarian argument which holds that the evaluation of political standards—namely, the evaluation of a work's intellectual content and educational significance—is determined solely by whether the subject-matter and the theme of that work is portentous or not. . . .

In order to follow the tradition of realism, we must make a clean sweep of all dogmatic and sectarian theories and their influences. We must also admit that so long as authors possess and constantly strengthen a Communist world outlook, the methods with which they approach their creative works can vary. To lay down a set of universal creative methods based on fixed definitions is to fetter and smother author's creativeness. . . . To carry on the tradition of realism we must be truly faithful to the realities of life . . . we should not in the name of "realistic development of the Revolution" whitewash life and alter the true face of life. These realities of life must have the characteristics of the age and mark of time; we cannot equate the realities of 1957 with those of 1967. . . .

[*Liu Shao-t'ang. Literary Studies. No. 5. 1957*

Articles from Wen Yi Pao

(Journal of Literature and Arts)

"Throw open the window and speak plainly"

During the past two or three years a theory that writers should deal with essentials has suddenly become the vogue. The Arts should, of course, reflect the essentials of things, but once it is turned into a doctrine, this theory is likely to do a good deal of harm. . . . If you write about the comparative backwardness of a peasant, or an old worker's jealousy of other people's success, the dogmatists will tell you: "What you have written are not the essentials of the peasant and working classes. No good." If you proceed to revise according to their suggestions, you would have to cut off all the branches and leaves of art, leaving only the dead and dried trunk. In the eyes of the dogmatists, this is the way that literature should take to serve politics. . . .

When writing about the struggles between peasants and landlords, or between workers and capitalists, of a period before the liberation or even earlier, you are also obliged to put in a Communist Party member as an underground leader in order to reflect correctly the essentials of history. There is a joke that goes like this: After reading a manuscript on a farmers' uprising towards the end of the Ming Dynasty, a young editor with no knowledge of Chinese history said unhappily: "This praises the spontaneous struggle. Why not point out the Party's leadership? . . ."

[*Yao Hsueh-yin. Wen Yi Pao. No. 7. May 19*

"From comrades to Red specialists"

. . . the assumption that "Communist Party members are made of unusual stuff" evidently carries a connotation that the broad non-Party masses are made of common stuff. This may well have been a justifiable assumption in the early days, which, when applied today, becomes obviously unscientific and unrealistic. Whether or not a man is made of unusual stuff is mainly determined by his conduct in the Revolution; his possessing or not possessing a Party card has nothing to do with it. . . . Even if we were to overlook the unscientific and unrealistic nature of this assumption, and presume it to be true, I still fail to see what there is to be proud of when an entry is made in the history book to the effect that amongst 600 million Chinese people, only ten million odd are made of unusual material, and the rest made of common stuff. . . .

[*Ch'eng Ch'ien-fan. Wen Yi Pao. No. 7. May 19*

"A type of person who seems to be always in the right"

There is a type of person amongst us, who seems to be always in the right. When doctrinairism was in high favour, his articles were not only shot through with doctrines, but also lent support to other people's doctrinairism—doctrinairism of all types. At a time when crude criticism was seen as "strict adherence to principles," apart from writing many articles of the crudest kind, he actually encouraged the growth of a militant atmosphere in which friends and foes were indiscriminately dealt with. He was then, no doubt, in the forefront of the times, very much in the right. Soon a change came; doctrinairism was at last exposed as a great enemy of Marxism-Leninism, and the kind of crude criticism which recognises no friend or foe was attacked as a serious mistake. One should have thought that this was the time for these people to take stock and come out with some frank admissions; but no, on the contrary, they have been busy ever since producing articles castigating doctrinairism and crude criticism. As if he could by one proverbial magic wave set at naught all he had written, said and done in the past. Now as always he is marching ahead of the times full of vigour and pomp, still very much in the right as he is the personification of "rightness," whilst others are idiots born to make mistakes and accept his instructions. . . .

[*Hsu Chun-yu. Wen Yi Pao. No. 8. May 26*

The hardships of literary critics

At present everyone is discussing what the important contradictions in the literary and artistic world are. As I see it, the major contradiction lies in the fact that our literary and artistic creations and the demands of the broad masses of the readers are not in tune. The middle school students on the whole still accept the works we print. But the university students do not find them interesting enough and are not satisfied. Their interest is in reading foreign novels. Our most pressing task at this time is how to get down to solving this problem. . . .

In the minds of the leadership, there is a simplified theory as to the relationship between world outlook [*i.e.*, political stand] and creative work. The low quality of our creative work is not unrelated to this simplified theory. That world outlook directs creation cannot be doubted; but the direct control of creative work exercised by world outlook is limited to the writer's point of view in examining things and to his basic attitudes; it cannot directly control the writer's actual experience of people's mental attitudes, emotions and so on. . . .

In the last few years, writers have on the whole read a good few books, but why have a number of people not written any books yet? If we say that when their thought has progressed [*i.e.*, when they have absorbed more Marxism] they will be able to write books, then why is it that in the last seven or eight years the thoughts of the writers have progressed but they have still not written any books? I consider that the influence of world outlook on creation is indirectly and partially involved, but in the past we have opportunely neglected this point. . . . The leadership look at the relationship between theory and creation in too simplified a manner and so their methods are inevitably inflexible and influence the development of creative work. . . .

The writers often grumble at the laying down of many rules and regulations by the critics, but are the rules and regulations imposed on literary and art criticism so few? During the last few years, I have written very few articles, but even from this small experience it is not difficult to comprehend the difficulty of writing critical articles. One cannot be rude, one cannot ridicule, one cannot use smart phrases; one must pay attention to authorities [*i.e.*, the classics of Marxist criticism], to the famous writers, the new forces [*i.e.*, young writers], the leading personnel [*i.e.*, Party propaganda bureau officials], the old gentlemen, unity. One must consider the editor's plans, the opinions circulating in current Soviet magazines, and your own retreat in the event of future policy changes. With that many "pay attentions" and "considerations" in one's head, one's personal intentions get smaller and smaller. . . . Previously when I wrote an article, leaving whether it was bad or good aside, at least when I'd written it I felt cheerful. Now when I write articles it is often just to fulfil my duties; also, time is very short so that I am not even satisfied with some articles.

[*Huang Yao-mien. Wen Yi Pao. No. 9. June 2*

"Can we lead dramatic groups as we would lead an army?"

The Political Department of the Military Committee [presumably the Military Committee of the Communist Party] is still leading the Dramatic Groups in the same way as they used to lead the Propaganda Corps in the past. . . . Comrade Lan Ma [artistic superintendent] revealed to this correspondent: "The stumbling-block which hinders the progress of dramatic groups today is the fact that certain leading comrades are ignorant of the arts, and they do not lead a Dramatic Group in a manner appropriate to the special characteristics of artistic organisations. . . ."

When the names of two non-Party members appeared in the play bill as being the leading players at the time when *The Underground Great*

Wall was being rehearsed, two Party members kicked up a terrific row over it. The result was that the leadership had to recast the play replacing the two non-Party members by the pair of cantankerous Party members. . . .

In the Dramatic Group, the relationship between the director and the actors is not one of artistic co-operation. Because the rank of a director is higher than that of an actor, the relationship is one between a superior and a subordinate—the rehearsal stage is like a battlefield. Comrade Ch'en Ch'i-t'ung is a special case in point. He, being a deputy head of the propaganda department under the Forces Political Department, becomes even more powerful and can get away with anything when he comes to the Group. . . . Woe betide the actors when he becomes their director. Comrade Li Wei-hsin said: "His theory is: To make you toe the line, he must first break down your pride." How does he break down others' pride? By rebukes, rude and savage rebukes. Whenever he is at a rehearsal, the whole rehearsal room is filled with a threatening warlike atmosphere, with every actor trembling in his shoes. When *Hundreds of Rivers and Mountains* was being rehearsed, he punished an actor by marching him at the double just because he thought the fellow did not look like a Red Army warrior. . . . At rehearsals, one always catches him swearing . . . "bitch," "stupid swine," "rice bucket. . . ." He can sack an actor who happens to be a bit late in making an entry. Chu Chi was once late in turning up due to nervous tension; Ch'en Ch'i-t'ung said: "I want to check up on your past history. . . ." Young actress Po Hui-wen said to me: "As soon as I enter the rehearsal room, my heart is in my mouth, all my creative inclinations are gone. It is out of the question for an actor to talk of artistic creation in such circumstances. . . ."

[*Chang Pao-hsin. Wen Yi Pao. No. 9. June 2*

"To Comrade Liu Chih-ming"

I am an ordinary employee of the Chinese Youth Arts Theatre. . . . Deputy Minister Liu! Do you or don't you know the excitement that overtook us all when the comrades heard that you were coming at nine o'clock on the morning of the 18th? The comrades in the theatre lost many a night's sleep in preparing for this unusual meeting. . . . When the hands of the clock indicated nine and there was no sign of your arrival how worried we became; when your car pulled in at the theatre and into the Conference Hall you walked, there was such terrific clapping from the audience to greet you. During each comrade's speech, every one of us was all agog watching intently your reaction to it. We had the greatest expectations of you because you represented the Ministry of Culture in the central government and we believed that you would definitely take up cudgels on behalf of the masses and encourage them to speak their minds freely so that proper solutions could be found for the long-accumulated problems under the leadership of the Ministry.

You may still recall the remark of someone: "I have only just now found courage to break through my apprehensions because the Minister himself is taking part today . . ."; and another voiced the remark: "For eight years my innermost thoughts have been bottled up, they can be released at last. . . ." Many comrades dwelt upon their personal experiences of their talents being long buried, of repressions and blows sustained; other comrades called attention to the lack of respect in the theatre for learning and the curtailing of the freedom to create due to doctrinairism, that in extreme cases even violence was used to suppress criticisms; and many others with deep sorrow spoke of the vulgarity, of the boastfulness and the sycophancy prevailing in the theatre—this is because these traits are at a premium, being to the taste of the bureaucrats. . . . Eventually you spoke. These were your "invaluable instructions" to our forum. Without beating about the bush you admitted the seriousness of the problems of the theatre. However, you attributed the responsibility for them to the Ministry of Culture. In this way you transferred lightly to your own shoulders the serious problems of the theatre. . . . You thought too many made up the forum, you thought that the crowds should not have given way to outbursts of their feelings, you thought that we should have studied the relevant documents before coming to the forum. . . .

On hearing those great words shudders ran down our spines . . . we had reason to wonder if this meeting was not a waste of time.

Comrade Minister! If you will forgive my frankness, you are far from understanding the masses here, you have grossly underestimated the level of our awakening, therefore your talk will not prove of much value. That probably was your second meeting with the comrades in the theatre during the past few years! In spite of the fact that it is only a few li from Tung Sze to Tung Tan, and it takes only a few minutes to get here by car from the Ministry of Culture, the Ministers are too busy to have talks with us. That was why on that occasion all of us, not wishing to miss the rare opportunity of meeting you and in view of the seriousness of the theatre's failings, took courage in both hands, brushed aside all misgivings, and poured out our pent-up views in your presence without reservation. In such circumstances, outbursts of excited feelings were unavoidable, as we were not able to contain ourselves. . . .

An intelligent leader has a way of mobilising the crowds in an intrepid confident manner, allowing the people to bloom and contend boldly! The unintelligent leader is inclined to be uneasy about the crowds, creating undue restrictions and encumbrances in their way. . . .

[*Wang Cheng. Wen Yi Pao. No. 9. June 2*

"Whom does the People's Literature Publishing House serve?"

Whom does the People's Literature Publishing House serve? The reply is very simple. It mainly serves the interests of the people who are running it and those related to them. . . .

Those who happen to be inside the circle of the leadership of the House, irrespective of whether or not they are in the employ of the House, all enjoy privileges denied to the outsiders. These people have in a matter of a few years had their pockets well lined, become well fed and rich. . . . When it comes to the ordinary translators without connections they indulge in hair-splitting and fault-finding; as regards the scale of fees, the number of volumes to be printed, and the time of publication, these are none of the translators' business. . . . To people wielding authority and well connected with the House, the door of finance is wide open. For instance, "an old hand" in the translation circles in Shanghai recently handed over one of his old translations to the House for publication. It was considered by the editors to be of very poor quality and unacceptable; this, however, did not prevent the man in charge of the House from demonstrating his generosity by paying him a lump sum of 2,000 yuan in fees. . . .

[*Wang Tsung-wen. Wen Yi Pao. No. 10. June 9*

"The voice suppressed beneath the lid"

The Deputy Secretary of the Provincial Council, Comrade Lin Hu-chia, for one, is a person hard to deal with. . . . His leadership in the field of literature and the arts is uncouth and tyrannical, ignorant but pretentious. . . . He, in his painstaking report, urged *Chekiang Literature and Arts* to publish more works coming from the workers and peasants, saying: "If only you could abstract all the good points out of a hundred plays written by dramatic groups in the villages and blend them into one play, there you would find the makings of a good show." This created a situation in which the editors found themselves busy "working overtime" over [rewriting] the works from worker and peasant sources, whereas works by the intellectuals found it hard to get an outlet in their own province [this refers to the past], with the result that all were frustrated to distraction, and at the same time did not dare speak out (the problems are simply innumerable). Once at a meeting held "in pursuance of democracy," a certain author, not being able to contain himself any longer, gave Comrade Lin Hu-chia a piece of his mind: "... the dogmatic style of works shown by Comrade Lin Hu-chia is bound to do harm to the Party's tasks; he should cultivate an elementary appreciation for the literature and the arts before passing judgment upon literary works." From then onwards this comrade was repeatedly summoned for individual talks by the local Party Division and became an object of struggle at different meetings large or small; he eventually got the sack, and his rank was reduced into the bargain. During the purge of counter-revolutionaries he was under a cloud for ten months mainly on account of this (being accused of being "anti-Party" and "an inferior type"). . . .

In order to strengthen "ideological work" in the literary circles, the Provincial Council has appointed a number of people unversed in literature and the arts to lead . . . cultural organisations: the appointment of Comrade Lin Hu-chia's wife, Comrade Wang Ku-ming, to the post of Deputy Director of the Provincial Bureau of Culture is a case in point. This also accounts for the strange incident associated with the Provincial Literary League: a few years ago a certain Deputy Secretary General actually asked a painter to paint a crowd scene, with instructions that a portrait of Chairman Mao be incorporated in the centre of the picture, with every peasant wearing a smiling face, because everybody was happy and joyful . . . and many other similar *faux pas*. . . .

[*Anonymous letter to the editors of Wen Yi Pao. No. 10. June 9*

"Do not forget the particular characteristics of literature"

To say that literature is subordinate to politics is not tantamount to saying that literature is politics and that literary work comes under the heading of political work. To confuse the two is to disregard the characteristics of literature.

In his book of essays, *To Raise the Standards of Literary Work in the People's Liberation Army*, Comrade Ch'en Yin repeatedly asserted

" literary work is an effective instrument of political work and a powerful instrument for resolving ideological problems." This way of reasoning is one-sided. . . .

Comrade Ch'en Yin is a leader in the field of Forces literary work, whose views must be listened to by writers in the Forces. If they were really to go about their creative work in accordance with his demand which pays no regard to historical conditions, nor with practical reality, the result could only be to lead writers to be divorced from life and to write willy-nilly about things they are not familiar with. . . .

[*Chou Chi-fu. Wen Yi Pao. No. 11. June 16*

* * *

The anti-Party clique among the writers

An anti-Communist Party clique, headed by the writers Ting Ling and Ch'en Ch'i-hsia, opposing Party leadership in literary work and striving for personal power has been revealed at the current meeting here called by the Communist Party Committee in the Union of Chinese Writers, the *People's Daily* reports today.

Both writers, who are members of the Communist Party, launched an attack against basic Party policies in collaboration with the Shanghai *Wen Hui Pao,* then controlled by the Chang Po-chun-Lo Lung-chi rightist alliance. The Ting Ling-Ch'en Ch'i-hsia clique took advantage of the Party's campaign to improve style of work by sending their followers to incite cinema workers and writers.

The basic positions of this clique include: rejecting leadership and supervision by the Party and its policies, principles and directives on literary work; building an anti-Party alliance in violation of Party principles; destroying Party unity through provocations; propagating bourgeois individualism and advocating hero worship.

It was also disclosed that this anti-Party clique had planned to launch an all-out attack against the Party and divide the writers at the coming national writers' and artists' conference scheduled for this October. They also schemed to use their followers to turn the organ of the Chinese Writers' Union—*Wen Yi Pao*—into their mouthpiece. . . .

Ch'en Ch'i-hsia has admitted his crimes against the Party at the meeting, but Ting Ling has still refused to.

The poet Ai Ching and another Vice Chairman of the Writers' Union, Feng Hsueh-feng, made self-criticisms for their help to Ting Ling and Ch'en Ch'i-hsia in their anti-Party activities. . . .

[*NCNA. Peking. August 7*

*

"Widespread murmuring" among the people

Tseng Yen-hsiu, a Communist Party member and Vice President and Deputy Editor-in-Chief of the People's Publishing House . . . attacked the Party with these slanderous remarks: "Profound indeed are its contradictions with the masses!" "The dissatisfaction of the people with the Party in power and their indignation are expressed by widespread murmuring. . . ." "Dirty and decadent things have contaminated a considerable portion of the Communist Party during the last eight years. . . ." He said: "When the Kuomintang returned to Nanking and Shanghai to indulge in corrupt practices at the end of the anti-Japanese war, its prestige dropped greatly in the course of a couple of months. Our Party is not as bad as the Kuomintang, but since it took over the cities seven or eight years ago, some signs of resemblance have now emerged. . . ."

[*Report of a People's Publishing House Forum. NCNA. Peking. July 12*

*

Classical literature neglected

Hou Tai-ling [Editor, Antiquarian Publishing House]:

"Many specialists in classical literature have had to change their profession because classical literature has not received due attention. Few books devoted to classical literature have been published, and it looks as though the scholars of classical literature will find themselves without successors."

Ku Hsueh-chi [Editor, People's Literature Publishing House] pointed out that certain leaders of the Classical Publishing House and the People's Literature Publishing Service knew nothing about classical literature, but pretended to know; they distrusted and disregarded the views of the specialists. All this had been deleterious to the work of managing the business and organising manuscripts. . . .

[*Reported in Kuang Ming Daily. May 23*

*

National treasures

Ch'en Ts'ung-wen . . . said that during his recent tour of inspection, he had seen many invaluable cultural treasures that had been excavated in recent years in different districts . . . these cultural treasures had long been dumped in stores without being sorted, and very little use had been made of them, while many university history professors who were in desperate need of them in their research work were denied access to them. . . .

Cheng Chen-to: " The disregard for cultural treasures today is really a serious matter. . . ." For instance, the method of preservation applied by the Palace Museum was unscientific and there was not a single store-room with controlled lighting, temperature and humidity. He had repeatedly suggested installing thick curtains in the old Palace picture gallery where the well-known pictures were exposed to sunshine, but nothing had come of his suggestion. . . .

[*CPPCC cultural forum reported in Kuang Ming Daily. May 25*

Libraries

Chang Shen-fu [Director, Peking Library Research Department]:

" Hundreds and thousands of books have been dumped in stores to rot without being sorted; this is really heart-rending. . . ."

[*At a librarians' forum reported in Kuang Ming Daily. May 25*

Chinese traditional painting held in contempt

Kao Hsi-shun [traditional-style painter]:

" Although the Central Institute of Fine Arts is the highest institute of learning for fine arts, the Chinese traditional school of painting is held in contempt. The teachers of traditional Chinese painting are not respected and there is a grave paucity of students in their classes. Why, if the Government has a programme to train young artists in this field, should this state of affairs exist? . . ."

Hsu-Yen-sun [traditional-style painter]:

" The disdain for Chinese traditional painting has now become so widespread that if we wish to reverse this trend we must re-indoctrinate ideologically the minds of the present generation."

Wang Shen-chih [traditional-style painter]:

" In the Central Institute of Fine Arts even water-colour work has become a victim of the sectarianism which has consigned Chinese traditional paintings to the lavatory, leaving us without hope and in spiritual agony. Conditions are unfavourable for traditional-style painters and there is a grave shortage of good quality paper and water colours which are sorely needed. . . ."

[*CPWDP forum reported in Kuang Ming Daily. June 5*

*

The fate of a painter

The case of Li Ku-chan, which was recently told in the *Peking Daily*, the capital's local newspaper, shows the sort of revelation that is now being made. It is a direct commentary on why Chinese creative art has seemed so sterile in these last years of "socialist realism."

Li was a fairly well-known artist, though not of the first rank, and was a good professor at the Central Institute of Fine Arts. But soon after the Communists came to power, officials said that he and another professor called Wang Ching-fang were reactionary and so both were dismissed from the teaching staff. . . .

He and Wang tried to learn to paint in the new style but their efforts were not considered successful by young cadres who said they were "unqualified" to join the Association of Fine Arts. Wang's efforts at painting were torn up in front of him and it was this sort of treatment, Li said, that led to his friend's death.

After being dismissed from the College he was given a pension of eight yuan [just over £1 sterling] a month while he was out of a job and this could be collected once every ten months! Li was then sent to work in a department making designs for pottery and from there was assigned to a job selling tickets in a cinema box-office. When patrons were few or unenthusiastic about the film being shown he had to go out into the streets to hawk the tickets. . . .

Li admitted that he began to drink heavily because he was so unhappy. . . .

During this time of poverty he was forced to sell most of his possessions, his wife procured an abortion for herself and he often stayed in his house for days as he had no money to go out and could not get a job. "In such conditions how could I be expected to create an expression of the 'New Age'?" Li asked. . . .

Li said that he gave up painting and whenever he tried to dispose of some of his old work he was told that they were no good at all. But once when some Soviet visitors came to the College and asked to see his paintings these were displayed, but were taken down immediately the guests had gone. . . .

After that students wanted him to teach them but the College apparently did not want this so they found him a job as a " common employee " at a research institute. But beyond hearing that he has the job Li knows nothing more—what it entails or even what a " common employee " is.

The reporter of the *Peking Daily* . . . concluded his story:

" In fact, under the policy of the Central College of Fine Arts to stamp out the Chinese [traditional] art of painting Li was only one among a number of old painters sacrificed. What makes the old painters most worried is that, apart from the reverses they have met themselves, if things go on like this there will be no next generation of Chinese painters."

[*David Chipp. Reuter. Peking. May 23*

*

The anti-Party clique among the painters

Chiang Feng, director of the Central Institute of Fine Arts and concurrently deputy director of the China Association of Artists and secretary of its Party organisation . . . has long refused to implement the Party policy of continuing and further developing the national art traditions and of unifying traditional Chinese art, on the pretext that traditional Chinese art is " unscientific," " backward " and " cannot serve politics. . . ."

In the middle of May the rightist clique headed by Pang Hsun-chin, of the Central Institute of Handicraft and Art, under the pretext of opposing the leadership of the handicraft industry administration bureau, advanced a so-called ten-point proposal, simplified regulations governing " the democratic operation of schools," and other anti-Party programmes. These programmes were advanced with Chiang Feng's support and direction. . . .

Chiang Feng also said: " I do not agree with the practice of the Party committee system in schools. I also reject it. . . ."

At the May 25 meeting, certain participants carried oil paintings and sculpture works, and this was meant to look like a demonstration against the Party. During the course of the meeting, certain participants shouted: " A number of Comrades of the Party organisations of the Ministry of Culture and of the China Association of Artists formed a sectarian group to injure Chiang Feng, throw out oil paintings, discredit modern Chinese drawings, sabotage unity, and foment disintegration.'

When the meeting was over, Chiang Feng and others urged that the minutes of the forum be published in the *Wen Hui Pao* and distributed in various parts of the nation. . . .

Chiang Feng said: "What was achieved in the suppression of counter-revolutionaries? Many people have said that the achievements in the suppression of counter-revolutionaries are the important thing, and that errors are unavoidable in a mass movement. Such a viewpoint is terrible!"

Chiang Feng also uttered such slanders as this: "Life is undemocratic in the Party. . . ."

[*NCNA. Peking. July 28*

Chiang Feng's henchmen were found in all the fine arts organs in places like Peking, Hangchow, Shanghai, Shenyang and Chungking. . . . Elements of Chiang Feng's anti-Party group also have intimate connections with members of the Ting Ling-Ch'en Ch'i-hsia anti-Party group. . . .

The major strategy adopted by this anti-Party group was, in the name of "opposing the sectarianism in the Central Propaganda Department and the Ministry of Culture," to win over the masses; to use as anti-Party instruments the schools, publications, exhibition work committees, studios, oil-painting training classes and sculpture training classes under their control; all this in an attempt to usurp from the Party its supervision over works of art, turning them towards the bourgeoisie. Party leadership was practically abolished in the Central Institute of Fine Arts, which was under the sole control of Chiang Feng. In the same institute the Communist Party organisation had substantially changed into an instrument for the anti-Party activities of Chiang Feng's group. At an early stage in the rectification campaign, the Party organisation in the Central Institute of Fine Arts, manipulated by Wang Man-shih and Hung Po, "drove" the masses to attack the Ministry of Culture. . . .

Once, when Ch'en Ch'i-hsia attended a banquet, a member of Chiang Feng's anti-Party group admitted right out that their group of people "were like the Peteofi Club." After the Hungarian incident, estimating the situation, Ch'en Ch'i-hsia told Chiang Feng: "Now that living standards are so unequal in town and country, it needs only one call to make several tens of thousands of people rise. . . ."

[*NCNA. Peking. August 14*

* * *

The revolt in the film industry

From the slanders levelled by rightists of the various units under the films organisation, it is clear that the rightists inside and outside the Party have a programme to follow, which is anti-Party as well as anti-socialist. That is:

(1) To oppose Party leadership: When the rightists declare that the Party does not understand the motion picture business, is a "layman," is "interfering with the industry's administration," and that the "studio must be run by art workers" and led by "experts," their intention is to negate the Party leadership and to wrest leadership from the Party. Rightist Wu Yung-kang of the Shanghai Motion Picture Studio demanded the opening of movie studios of the Democratic League for which Wu Ying and Pai Cheng wanted a reshuffle of the leadership as otherwise it would not be a thorough purge; . . . the rightists in the orchestra under the Changchun Movie Studio snatched "dictatorship for eighteen days"; . . . Lu Pan held that only the director should have a say. . . .

(2) To oppose the policy of making motion pictures serve politics: They state that serving workers, peasants and soldiers is the cause of the formalism and generalisation of our films; they care only for art and not for politics; they oppose ideological remoulding; they seek to oppose Marxism-Leninism and promote revisionism under the name of anti-doctrinairism; they oppose centralism and unity under the name of anti-bureaucracy.

(3) To prevent the people's motion picture industry from pursuing the socialist line: In this attempt, they seek to deny the superiority of such a system and refuse to learn the Soviet experience, stating that that would throttle creativeness; . . .

(4) To negate the success we have achieved in the field of motion picture industry during the past eight years: They exaggerate certain defects and errors, stating that "all pictures made before liberation were booking office record breakers," but the pictures produced today "nobody wants to see"; they judge from the booking office record the value of a picture: . . .

[*Wang Lan-hsi, Director of the Film Administrative Bureau in Chung-kuo Tien-ying (Chinese Motion Pictures). No. 1. January 8, 1958*

10

BUSINESS MEN

THE Communist Party needed the managerial skills of the Chinese business class just as it needed the knowledge of the scholars. It came to power declaring that for the moment it would be conducting a " bourgeois-democratic " and not a " socialist " revolution and that private enterprise would be tolerated and indeed encouraged. Chinese capitalists, completely embittered with the Nationalists as a result of the economic chaos and official corruption of their last years of power, welcomed the change of régime and for a time their firms flourished. The end of this honeymoon period came in 1951 when the Party launched a " five-anti " campaign (anti-bribery, tax evasion, theft of state property, cheating on Government contracts and theft of state economic secrets) against the business community. This campaign enabled the state to take over considerable private assets and consolidated Party control over the capitalists. Many of them were driven to suicide and production in the private sector of industry dropped sharply for a time. The decisive change occurred in January 1956 when, to keep pace with rural collectivisation, private firms were abruptly changed into jointly managed state-private concerns. The theory was that the business men would be retained as managers and paid compensation for the expropriation of their property.

The criticisms in this section make it clear that in practice the experience of the shrewd Chinese business class is going to waste due to the intolerant supremacy of the state representatives in the joint enterprises—and there was some suggestion during this period that they should be withdrawn. The question around which most discussion in business men's forums revolved was whether the Government should pay 35 per cent. or 100 per cent. compensation. The proposal for complete compensation does not seem to have aroused much comment when first mooted in January, probably because people were too wary to take it up; later a number of capitalists disagreed with it largely because they thought it was not in their political interests. Both the proposal for total compensation and Jung Tzu-cheng's revelation of the devaluation of private business assets when the Government was settling the price at which it would buy out show that the Party leaders, if they were not confiscating, were pursuing a policy of enlightened self-interest. It is interesting to note that the prospect of paying out any more in compensation was distasteful enough for them to mobilise the workers on this question; these cases of workers " speaking up " are a major exception to the general absence of counter-criticism during May and early June.

Another point brought out by the criticisms is that while China's sixty-eight showpiece " millionaires " have been accorded the kind of treatment that might impress foreigners and overseas Chinese business men with the régime's pragmatism and tolerance, many of their smaller colleagues have been in dire economic straits.

" We need not have any fear "

PEKING **May 11**

Yen Shao-ching [Member, Peking ACFIC], describing the attitude of Peking industrialists and merchants, said: " They want to contend but are trembling with fear. Many still have misgivings. . . . Some are afraid that they will be ' encircled and attacked ' if they express wrong opinions."

Chang Nai-ch'i [Minister of Food] said:

" In contending, one must not be afraid of one-sidedness; there are bound to be errors and shortcomings but there is no cause for fear. . . ."

In conclusion, Chen Shu-t'ung [Chairman, ACFIC] said:

" Only unity can ensure victory. But while there is unity, views are different on some things, that is to say, there are contradictions. In dealing with this problem, the Communist Party will first ' Let a hundred flowers bloom, let a hundred schools contend ' to expose the problems and contradictions and then start a rectification of style of work. But this rectification campaign concerns the Communist Party and not us. Therefore, we need not have any fear. . . ."

[*Forum held by ACFIC. NCNA. May 12*

*

The "Buying out over twenty years" proposal

PEKING

Li K'ang-nien:

"I am Li K'ang-nien, a Shanghai business man, Director General of the jointly managed Hung Hsing Textile Factory, General Manager of China Watchmakers, Manager of Ts'ui Chung Textile Factory, and the proposer of the so-called 'Li K'ang-nien's Suggestion of twenty years of Fixed Interest' or 'Buying out over twenty years' as headlined recently by the newspapers. In actual fact, there is nothing in my suggestion to indicate a demand for the fixed interest to be for twenty years; nor do I wish to extend the duration of compensation to twenty years. . . .

"I submitted a written proposal at the 1st Session of the 2nd Shanghai People's Congress on January 8 this year in which I . . . made three suggestions:

"1. I would advise the Government to issue 2,200 million yuan (People's Currency) worth of Chinese People's Republic's Industrial and Commercial enterprises' Reform Compensation Certificates, in accordance with the figure of 2,200 million yuan arrived at as a result of assessment of property and capital. At the same time, the Government should withdraw the shares or partnership contract held by the capitalists so as to enable the capitalists to sever all relations with the enterprises. Four payments a year are to be made in connection with these certificates; in other words, the total sum to be paid out each quarter will be 27,500,000 yuan, and the total sum for each year will be 110 million yuan; taking into consideration the fact that 220 million yuan have been paid out during 1956 and 1957, there only remains 1,980 million yuan to be paid out to the capitalists. The remaining 220 million yuan can be used as lump sum rewards or consolidation money for the capitalists' agents, the directors and comptrollers and those capitalists in need of help, in order to cut their links from the enterprises concerned. Whatever is left over, if any, can be handed over to the All-China Federation of Industry and Commerce as funds for mutual assistance among private-side personnel.

"The Chiaotung Bank, I submit, can be entrusted with the above-mentioned work. Those unwilling to receive such compensation certificates should be at liberty to decline the offer and the Chiaotung Bank can, in such instances, either retain them on their behalf, make donations with them, transfer them to other people, or hand them over to the national treasury at the request of the people entitled to the certificates.

"In cases where people entitled to compensation certificates relinquish their compensation certificates—an act indicating their willingness to relinquish exploitation—they should, after having obtained the receipts for their donations or contributions to the national treasury, be allowed to regard such receipts as evidence of relinquishing exploitation and should be allowed the opportunity to join the trade unions and strive for labour insurance treatment. In this way, a person can doff his capitalist class 'hat.' . . ."

[The two alternative suggestions are less important—*Ed.*]

[*Kuang Ming Daily. June 6*

The question of expropriating capitalists

PEKING **May 13**

Some held that "buying out" was state help to the bourgeoisie; others held that it should be viewed as the legitimate interests and reasonable profits to which the bourgeoisie was entitled; still others held that it should be regarded as state outlay in socialist development, money well spent to have the bourgeois enterprises turned over to the state in perfect shape.

All those present at the forum approved the boldness with which Li K'ang-nien proposed "buying out over twenty years. . . ."

Some took the view that, inasmuch as the Government enforced a "buying-out" policy it should buy out to the end and that, on the basis of 5 per cent. per annum, it would take twenty years to complete the "buy out. . . ."

Many persons considered it quite unnecessary to pay fixed interest for twenty years. They said: With the period of interest payment fixed for seven years and with further help given by the state at the end of the seven years in case of hardship, industrialists and merchants in the main will be able to maintain a reasonable livelihood. . . . Further, they saw several disadvantages in the proposal for extending the period of fixed interest payment to twenty years: (1) Increase of contradictions between the bourgeoisie and the working class. When the state fixed the period of interest payment at seven years, much had to be done to persuade and educate the worker masses; a proposal to extend the period to twenty years would certainly cause objections on the part of the working class. Besides, all people of the country would have a bad impression of the bourgeoisie and accuse them of insatiable greed. . . . (2) The proposal for extending the period to twenty years would certainly be unacceptable to those small industrialists and merchants who owned only a few thousand yuan share capital and got very little in interest payment and who urgently hoped to remove the bourgeois label and become part of the working class. (3) An unfavourable effect on the transformation of the bourgeoisie. It was said that the Chinese national capitalists were characterised by their willingness to accept the leadership of the working class and willingness to follow the socialist path. The national capitalists must therefore seriously reform themselves and give up exploitation at an early date so as to become workers living by their own labour. . . .

Opinion was also divided on the year from which the " buying out " should be counted. . . .

[*Forum held by CDNCA. NCNA. May 13*

Capitalists oppose " buying out over twenty years "

SHANGHAI **May 15**

During the discussion, the majority disagreed with the view of Li K'ang-nien. They took the view that Li did not clearly understand the buying out policy, regarding buying out as a " deal " and " repayment of principal. . . ."

If the buying out is extended to twenty years, it would mean that after the building of a socialist society, the private personnel would still live on the sweat and labour of the working people. That would be disadvantageous to the unity of the people of all strata. . . .

It was recognised during the discussion that Li K'ang-nien represented in certain ways the views of some industrialists and merchants and that, consequently, his proposal deserved further discussion.

[*Forums held by CDNCA and ACFIC. NCNA. May 15*

" Middle " capitalists and " buying out over twenty years " proposal

TIENTSIN **May 18**

Chen Yu-tsao [Assistant Superintendent, Second Plant of the Tientsin Dyestuff Chemical Company] expressed the opinion that, in proposing

" buying out over twenty years " Li K'ang-nien of Shanghai spoke mainly for the middle capitalists. " Large capitalists have no living difficulties because they get more in interest payments and higher wages. Small capitalists do not receive much interest payment each year; therefore, they want to get the bourgeois label removed as soon as possible and are not in favour of extending the ' buying-out ' period. Only the middle capitalists who have certain living difficulties and whose investments amount to a significant sum welcome the extension of the ' buying-out ' period. However, if the ' buying-out ' period is extended, workers will accuse the capitalists of insatiable greed, and a new change is likely to be brought about in the class relations."

Many persons shared the view expressed by Chen Yu-tsao. . . . Some industrialists and merchants in Tientsin backed up Li K'ang-nien in his proposal. Jung Tzu-cheng [Chairman, Hopei ch'u ACFIC] . . . held that most of the national bourgeois elements had raised their fortunes by dint of industry, frugality and work. He, for instance, began his career as an apprentice and had worked all the time. He was in favour of Li K'ang-nien's proposal for " buying out in twenty years."

[*NCNA. May 18*

Workers start to defend the Party

SHANGHAI **May 20**

The Shanghai Federation of Industry and Commerce called a forum of some thirty old workers today to discuss contradictions in the factories.

The discussion was centred on the question of withdrawing the state representatives from state-private enterprises and extending the period of interest payment to twenty years. All these workers, with a record of over ten years' service, were opposed to withdrawal of state representatives from state-private enterprises and extension of the period of interest payment to twenty years. . . .

None of the old workers subscribed to the view of some industrialists and merchants who proposed " twenty years of interest payment." " All the workmen in our mill and myself," said Yin Yung-kang of the Minfu Dyeing and Weaving Mill, " consider the proposal as one of dragging the feet of socialism." A number of old workers commented: " A socialist society will be built during three five-year plans: twenty years of interest payment means preservation of exploitation in a socialist society. . . ."

The fact that the Press was crammed with reports on defects caused great discontent among the old workers present at the forum. Chen Chan-an of the Shanghai Electricity Administration Bureau expressed this opinion: "The Press is crammed with reports on defects; as a matter of fact, the achievements of the Communist Party are the main side of the picture. It is not fair to ignore these achievements." He and many old workers declared: "Capitalists want to 'contend' but we workers also want to 'contend.' We hope the Press will publish our opinions and let the public judge for themselves which is fresh flower and which is poisonous grass."

[*NCNA. May 20*

CANTON **May 21**

The Canton Federation of Industry and Commerce called a meeting of workers from some state-private enterprises on May 21 to discuss whether state representatives should be withdrawn from the state-private enterprises. . . .

Representative Kuo Yu of the trade union of food trades in the central district did not share the view that state representatives had no technical knowledge. He said: "The state representatives are not as good as the capitalists in matters of production technique but have one very important technique—the technique of doing mass work. Good work depends on the mobilisation of the masses. Can capitalists, long accustomed to exploiting others and unlikely to understand the hardship of workers, mobilise the worker masses? The state representatives are different. The vast majority of state representatives are cadres enjoying prestige among the workers who are willing to place confidence in them and accept their leadership. . . ."

Objecting to the proposal for an extension of the period of interest payment to twenty years, Wu Chih-chin said: "I consider seven years is very long and state assistance to be great enough. . . ." In excitement she declared: "Existence of exploitation means non-existence of socialism and extension of the period of interest payment to twenty years is dragging the feet of socialism. It means unwillingness to accept transformation and unwillingness to give up the life of capitalists."

Workman Liang Tsu-jen quoted a proverb: "Greed is so insatiable that a snake wants to devour an elephant" to describe the proposal for extension of the period of interest payment to twenty years. . . .

[*NCNA. May 23*

Marxism-Leninism often inappropriate to China

TIENTSIN **May 30**

Jung Tzu-cheng [Standing Committee member, Tientsin ACFIC; Assistant Manager of the Tientsin Municipal Rubber Company] said:

"The Communist Party has treated the Chinese national bourgeoisie according to the theories of Marxism-Leninism. It should be noted that most of the works of Marxist-Leninist theory were written a long time ago. In many cases, application of these theories in China is quite inappropriate.

"For instance, it has been asserted in political economy classes that when an independent worker turns into an exploiter, he will quickly spend all his original capital and depend on the labour of others for his income. This theory does not apply to the Chinese national bourgeoisie. We are diligent workers who spend less than we earn. . . .

"The central authority has told us that it will buy out our enterprises and will pay half the price, confiscating the rest. In reality, however, the actual prices paid by it in carrying out the buying-out policy are as good as confiscating more than half of the capital amassed by the private sector through exploitation.

"Prior to the conversion of our enterprises to state-private joint operation," Jung Tzu-cheng said, "the tax bureau attached great value to almost everything owned by us in order to impose more taxes. At the time of the conversion of our enterprises, however, the value of our property became so low in the eyes of the industrial and commercial authorities that we, the private sector, suffered a reduced share in the enterprises . . . the total value of the property of private enterprises in China was reduced from the original 4·5 billion yuan, before conversion to state-private joint operation to 2·2 billion yuan afterwards," Jung Tzu-cheng charged. . . .

[*NCNA. June 16*

Business men's other complaints

Ostentation in state industries

PEKING **May 15**

Ma Ch'un-lin [Deputy Secretary General, Shenyang ACFIC]:

"In the past, Shenyang industrialists and business men . . . were able to evolve a set of skilfully calculated, parsimonious, flexible and ingeniously thrifty small-factory or small-shop management methods. . . .

"What's the position now? On the one hand, the factories have become enlarged, and we have the slogan: 'Watch the nationalised factories'; while on the other hand, those administrators, instead of living up to the real spirit of the socialist managerial system, put the cart before the horse, indulge in ostentation and pomposity, with the result that there are a multiplicity of departments and sections all trying to pass the buck, and that the documents have to go on long journeys for stamping. The procedure for ordering goods, too, becomes very complicated; their attitude towards the customers is arrogant and overbearing, and they play fast and loose with the workers. Factory production follows the general pattern—nothing doing at the beginning of the month, attending meetings in the middle of the month, overtime towards the end of the month. . . . The set-up is enormous and there is much overlapping, and there are more men than jobs. Some people have submitted views opposing such red-tapism and bureaucracy . . . they have been received with derision and with attacks from those bureaucrats, such as 'meanness,' 'small-workshop style of work,' 'undermining the system,' and so on. . . ."

[UFWD forum. Kuang Ming Daily. May 16

Irresponsible statements, sectarian attacks

PEKING **May 17**

Kao Chen-sheng [Secretary-General, ACFIC in Hopei Province]:

"We must carry out the rule of law in earnest. All are equal before the law. There should not be one law for the working class and another for the capitalist class. . . ."

Pi Ming-ch'i [Chairman, ACFIC in Tientsin]:

"Whenever unlawful elements among small tradesmen or handicraft workers are found committing breaches of the law, the newspapers without discrimination lash out against the national capitalist class as a whole. I regard all these as indications that sectarian attacks are being levelled against the national capitalist class. . . .

Great is the national capitalist class! It has accepted the peaceful reforms offered by the Communist Party and Chairman Mao. Great are the achievements of its reformation! Greater still are the working class, the Communist Party and Chairman Mao! To reform industry and commerce peacefully is the creative development of Marxism-Leninism in China. . . ."

[Forum of business circles throughout the country held by CP. UFWD. Kuang Ming Daily. May 18

The fate of small capitalists

PEKING **May 18**

Sung Lien-fu [Deputy Secretary General, ACFIC in Hupeh Province]:

Life is hard for those with large families to support. . . . The problem of livelihood is the biggest problem confronting the middle and small men in industry and commerce today. . . . Also after the start of joint management, there have been cases in which the working hours have been from morn till night, as long as sixteen or seventeen hours per day, which adversely affects the health of those concerned. A shift system must be introduced in those instances to ensure adequate rest. Care should be given to those pregnant women employees who are not getting adequate rest before childbirth. . . ."

[Forum held by CP. UFWD. Kuang Ming Daily. May 19

Business men not trusted

PEKING **May 20**

Hu Tzu-ang [Vice Chairman, CDNCA] said:

"The personnel representing the private sector [*i.e.*, in joint state-private firms—*Ed.*] though having positions possess no power. . . . Many reasonable suggestions emanating from private sector personnel receive no support and the private sector personnel do not receive proper care and attention as regards living conditions. . . ."

Yang Hsi-shan [CDNCA]:

"Many a problem of human relations still exists between the public and private sectors, the main one being the lack of confidence in and support for the private sector personnel. For instance, there is a certain shop where, when the shutters are put up for the evening, keys are given to the public sector personnel, whereas the private sector personnel are left without keys."

[Forum held by CDNCA. Kuang Ming Daily. May 21

Problems of personnel work

PEKING May 20

Shou Mo-ch'ing [Deputy Head, Executive Office, ACFIC]:

Now that classes had been fundamentally eliminated and the movement against counter-revolutionaries had been pretty well wound up, it was worth considering if it were necessary for the personnel departments to maintain their security system. . . . "Non-Party people are excluded from personnel work—the All-China Federation of Industry and Commerce is no exception" (at this point the director of the Communist Party's United Front Work Department, Li Wei-han, butted in asking the Deputy Secretary General of the All-China Federation of Industry and Commerce, Huang Chieh-jan, whether this was true. Huang replied: "Yes"). Shou then suggested: "The Party ought to make this problem the focal point of an inquiry in its rectification campaign." He thought that it was not good enough that during each campaign the personnel cadres were deemed beyond reproach. . . .

[*At a business men's forum. Kuang Ming Daily. May 21*

Why business men are apathetic

PEKING May 21

Kuo Hung-wei [Canton Committee, CDNCA] said that:

The private sector personnel had their own views about sick-leave and wages; they often left their work in their enterprises promptly every day, saying: "Who is there to care for you when you fall sick through your being positive and there is no money for medicine and your wages are reduced?" Often the material on problems of their legitimate interests that got sent up to the top met with procrastination or was shelved or ignored.

[*Forum held by CDNCA. Kuang Ming Daily. May 22*

"The Sword of Authority"

PEKING May 22

Ning Szu-hung [Deputy Manager, Pen and Writing Brushes Industrial Company, Shanghai]:

"Personnel work, labour-wages work and public security in the industrial and business departments and the mining enterprises and so on are all led by Party comrades. . . . They listen only to one side—namely the staff and workers, thus leading to great bias . . . especially towards the Personnel Department. People hold it in respectful awe and keep it at a distance, regarding it as holding 'the Sword of Authority.'"

"There is a saying in the Shanghai China Shipbuilding Factory, 'For every Lo-han [A Buddhist monk who has passed the stage of novice —*Ed.*] there is a Kuan-yin' [Buddhist Goddess of Mercy—*Ed.*], meaning that all the wives of the Party cadres in the factory have got jobs in the factory. The relation between staff and workers used to be one to six, but now it is one to one-point-eight. This is a result of the development of nepotism."

Chu Sung-ling [CDNCA]:

"The technical abilities of many of the private-sector technicians have not only not been put to good use, but many of the technicians are kept in idleness. . . ."

[*Kuang Ming Daily. May 23*

The difficulties of business men

PEKING **May 25**

Huang Yen-pei [Chairman, CDNCA]:

"We have just returned from an inspection tour of Shanghai, Wusih and Nanking. . . . During the past inspection tour I have found in many jointly operated enterprises discriminatory practices against personnel representing private interests. In some factories such practices reached the degree of absurdity. One factory in Nanking, for instance, asked the personnel representing the private interests to go away when the Party members were to give reports on the revolutionary martyrs whose tombs they had visited during the ancestor-worshipping festival. . . . The personnel representing the private interests dare not put forward their views for fear of retaliation. The reason for this is that personnel management is under the exclusive control of the Party committee. If you were to commit any offence against the Party, some time later the person in charge of personnel management would transfer you to a post you did not like, to render you harmless. . . .

[*NCNA. May 25*

On Party leadership of industry

PEKING **May 30**

Tung Shao-ch'en [Standing Committee, Tientsin ACFIC]:

"I had the shock of my life when I saw my own proposal headlined in a newspaper 'Withdraw Public Representatives' in huge black characters. The consequence was that I was immediately pulled up by some people 'Do you want to usurp the leadership of the Party?' 'Do you want to start a revolt?' This is not only 'putting the cap' on me, but a steel helmet, at that." He then went on to elucidate once more his proposal. He said that at a forum called by the *Ta Kung Pao*, which he attended, all those present spoke of the bad relations between the public and the private sector in the jointly managed enterprises, and the frustration the private sector personnel felt as a result of having positions but no power; and whilst they could draw fixed interest and high salaries, they felt they could find nothing to do. Therefore, it was suggested that the jointly managed enterprises should, under the leadership of the Party branches, hand over the responsibility of overseeing national plans and conducting practical affairs to responsible people with ability on the private side. A few test cases could be chosen for a one-year experiment to see if this idea would work, and if we should wish to put this measure into practice. . . .

[*Kuang Ming Daily. May 31*

Fears and complaints of provincial business men

PEKING **June 1**

Mai-mai-ti-ni-ya-tzu-ha-jih [Chairman, ACFIC in Sinkiang] said that the relationships between different nationalities in enterprises were anything but normal and that a chasm still existed between them. For instance, in some enterprises, the managers and directors of factories of minority nationality did not possess the same powers as their Han counterparts. . . .

Lu Ting-hua [Chairman, ACFIC in Honan Province] said that . . . although he was a manager of a factory, he had to subject himself to a search every time he took a parcel out, whilst on the other hand, the workers and even nannies did not have to put up with that. . . .

[*Kuang Ming Daily. June 2*

Obstructions for Shanghai technicians

PEKING **June 6**

Hu Tzu-ang [Vice Chairman, ACFIC; CC. CDNCA]:

According to surveys made in Shanghai there are seven to eight thousand senior technicians in Shanghai, therefore the total number for the whole country will, of course, be much larger. Most of them are not being used in the best manner possible and are indeed " sitting on cold benches." The reason for this is:

1. Positions without power—the public sector often feels that having given them positions it has been magnanimous enough.
2. Misuse of trained personnel through personnel mismanagement.
3. Lack of trust in technical personnel—the engineers are not even allowed to study the blueprints of the complete process.
4. Inadequate support. Not giving materials when they are experimentally manufacturing new products.
5. Lack of encouragement—for instance, in Canton an employee of the private sector who invented an omnipotent sewing machine was only awarded one sweater.
6. Suppression of democracy. Whenever the private sector has any views to offer the public sector is quick to pin the label of " Anti-Leadership " upon them. . . .

[*Kuang Ming Daily. June 7*

Party's attitude towards capitalists' criticisms

PEKING **June 8**

The forum of business men sponsored by the United Front Work Department of the Central Committee of the Communist Party concluded today.

A speech was made by Li Wei-han, head of the United Front Work Department . . . before the meeting closed.

Li Wei-han said: " Friends! Comrades! . . .

" Altogether twenty-five sessions have been held since the forum opened on May 15, and 108 persons have spoken. It may be said that there has been much enthusiasm for the forum and that views have been fully expressed. . . .

" Nearly all the speeches made at the forums have touched upon the question of relations between state and private-side personnel in joint enterprises. . . .

" The system of state representatives in joint enterprises is a basic system, the object of which is to guarantee the socialist direction of the enterprises and state leadership in these enterprises. To accomplish this object, state-side personnel must take the responsibility for ameliorating the relations between themselves and private-side personnel. Complete confidence should be placed in all those patriotic private-side personnel who are willing to serve the cause of socialism, so that they may have the powers and assume the responsibilities proper to their positions. . . . As for private-side personnel . . . they have before them the dual task of participation in socialist construction and self-reform. . . .

" There are some people who oppose ideological reform. They assert that there is no longer any exploitation by capitalist elements and the fixed interest paid them is not exploitation, that there is no longer . . . any class difference, between capitalist elements and the workers. . . . Such views and attacks are revisionist attacks on Marxism-Leninism carried on under the banner of anti-doctrinairism, and are a struggle between bourgeois ideology and working-class ideology, or in practice a struggle between socialism and capitalism. . . ."

[*NCNA. June 8*

11

CIVIL SERVANTS

THE non-Communists who help man the present Chinese governmental machine were brought up in a *milieu* similar to that of the university intellectuals, were educated like them in Western ideas and techniques. Their criticisms indicate that waste and inefficiency, the traditional disease of the centralised Chinese state with its vast bureaucracy, is greater under Communism, partly because the views of non-Communist experts are ignored for political reasons, partly because there is a compulsive urge to achieve big results quickly in order to please superiors and achieve targets.

Cause for discretion

Yuan Chin-chang [Vice Director, Law Bureau, Kansu Provincial Congress; Vice Chairman, Kansu Province, KMTRC]:

"Some say: 'When the official is at fault, the Yamen servant gets beaten, and when the Yamen servant is at fault he gets beaten by the official,' from which we can imagine the frustration of the non-Party cadres. Fitting big caps is a frequent occurrence; caps such as 'impure motives,' 'capitalist class working style,' 'jeopardising revolutionary enterprises,' 'undermining the prestige of the Party,' etc., have been fitted to quite a number of non-Party cadres; therefore people take a knowing-it-to-be-wrong-but-preferring-to-say-little-about-it attitude towards the style of work, speech and behaviour of the Party-member cadres and treat the work of their organisation as 'none of my business; leave it hanging on one side.' . . ."

[*Kuang Ming Daily forum. Kuang Ming Daily. May 26*

*

Is the Party luring the enemy forward?

PEKING: *State Council* May 27

Kuai Shih-tsai, member of the People's Political Consultative Conference National Committee who works in the Law Codification

Bureau, pointed out that a state of confusion existed in the promulgation of laws and decrees and the issuance of directives by the State Council, its various offices, and the different Ministries. He stated that sometimes a lower organ received directives from several quarters on the same subject, and this increased its difficulties in handling the matter. . . .

Kuai had just returned from an inspection tour in Shantung. . . . He said that in some areas no distinction was made between the Party, the Government and the co-operative, and some co-operatives were undertaking the registration of marriages and census registrations. Some Communist Party district committees could veto a directive of the provincial people's council. . . .

Wan Hei-tzu, councillor of the State Council . . . stated that . . . from the central Government level down to the local organs, there were too many assistant posts. . . . He referred to a certain hsien where there were more than ten deputy magistrates; some organisations at the hsien level had one cadre, while all the other workers were directors and vice directors of departments. . . .

Hsu Hsing-chih, councillor of the State Council, criticised certain high-ranking cadres for treating themselves as privileged people. He stated that Peking Hospital specially looked after high-ranking cadres of Class Seven and above. This care for the cadres was understandable. But some senior cadres even included their dependants among those enjoying free medical services. Some of them went to the extent of sending into the hospital children suffering from slight colds. Others, as soon as the weather got cold, sent their parents to live in the hospital. . . .

[*State Council forum for its non-Communist officials. NCNA. May 27*

The State Council is the root of bureaucracy

May 29

Fan Po-tsai, councillor of the State Council, considered the State Council to be the root of bureaucratism, for if bureacratism did not exist at the top level, it would not exist at the lower levels.

Yang Yu-ching, councillor of the State Council, pointed out that . . . there were . . . loopholes in those laws and regulations already made, so that they were tantamount to being non-existent. . . . The State Council had now a large following which it could not control. Any organ with the needed funds could erect buildings and employ personnel. This indicated that their capacity for administrative control did not meet the needs of the situation. . . .

Li Yi-ping, councillor of the State Council, criticised some people for abusing the prestige of the Chairman [*i.e.*, Mao Tse-tung—*Ed.*], indiscriminately quoting the words of the Chairman in order to stop people from freely expressing their views. He instanced the case of the reform of the written language, which was clearly something monopolised by a few people. In the discussions on this matter, somebody quoted Chairman Mao's views, saying that the Chairman supported Romanisation, and this stopped many people from giving expression to their own thoughts. . . .

[*State Council forum for its non-Communist officials. NCNA. May 29*

The eighteen-storey pagoda

June 4

Yu Sui-hsin, councillor of the State Council . . . considered that the structure of state organs embodied too many levels, and that a directive from the State Council only reached the primary level after going through channels even longer than descending an eighteen-storey pagoda. This was a very powerful cause of bureaucratism. Departmentalism still existed in various departments, each attempting to pass on responsibility to the other. With the large number of organs and their colossal sizes and with the very rigid control exercised over the lower levels, with the upper levels busy all day long in making arrangements, transmitting orders, holding conferences and issuing printed documents, matters needing urgent attention at the lower levels could not be disposed of quickly. In factories and other enterprises, the proportion of non-productive personnel was also too great. There was, for instance, a factory with 600 employees, and of them nearly 170 belonged to the administrative staff. . . . Yu recommended that the central Government should delegate a portion of its authority to the local authorities. . . .

Lo Tzu-wei, who works in the Central Handicraft Industry Administration, tabled ten viewpoints before the State Council, *viz.*:

With reference to personnel arrangements in the State Council, in all eight offices of the Council, there was at present only one Vice Director who was not a Communist Party member. Should not this situation be given consideration? The question which existed in these offices today was that the views of the different offices were often at variance, so that there had emerged a process, in the handling of problems, of "study and further study, consultation and further consultation, and procrastination and further procrastination. . . ."

[*State Council forum for its non-Communist officials. NCNA. June 4*

*

Inefficient land reclamation

PEKING: *Ministries of Agriculture and Land Reclamation*

Hsiung Yi and Hsi Cheng-fan, two soil experts, told this correspondent that during recent years government departments concerned with reclamation had proceeded with their work blindly without sufficient data about soil to guide them, with a resulting enormous waste of manpower and material resources. . . .

When it was decided to reclaim a piece of pasture land in Inner Mongolia, a large force of technicians and agricultural workers was organised and tractors were brought over to start the work of digging irrigation channels and obtaining water supply. The enthusiasm for collective labour was indeed impressive. But when the earth was turned over, it was found to contain large amounts of salt and alkalis. How could it be cultivated with salt rising to the top after the earth had been turned over? The leaders did not see the seriousness of the problem, and continued to dig more than 50,000 acres of land. The result was that only 1,000 acres was fit for cultivation. The reclamation force had to be withdrawn . . . although they had not a small number of young cadres studying soil conditions, they did not use their services properly. When these young cadres were given an assignment, they were ordered to finish it with "shock tactics" within a short period. These young cadres without sufficient scientific training, though hard-working, could not obtain data about soil to serve as a basis for reclamation and agricultural planning because they had not mastered the basic methods of study in soil. . . .

[*Kuang Ming Daily. May 10*

Excessive optimism leads to grain shortages

May 17

Non-Party Democrat Mo Ting-shen, wet paddy and wheat specialist, . . . criticised the failure of personnel of the Ministry to make appropriate arrangements for the planting area for grains and economic crops, and the neglect of grain production. The leaders of the Ministry said in 1951 that it had more grain than it needed and that it had decided to switch over to cotton production. "The Grain Production Bureau chief Wang Shou and I felt that this was a passing phenomenon on the completion of land reform and that it could not be a sign of real sufficiency. We did not agree with the switch. Our opinions were submitted to the inter-party conference where we objected, in particular, to any large-scale development of cotton production in the south-western area. Responsible personnel of the board and bureau concerned dissented. Thus, in 1952, cotton was grown over a large area and, in 1953, a situation of tight supply of grains presented itself. . . . Wuhu, Anhwei Province, which had gained for itself the name of an abundant rice-producing area, yielded last year only 480 catties *per capita*. . . .

[*People's Daily. May 18*

"Not even the Kuomintang could have been any worse"

Leading member of the Peasants and Workers' Democratic Party branch at the Ministry of Agriculture and a rightist in that ministry, Tseng Hsien-pu stated: "I do not understand, after all, what the Ministry of Agriculture is doing." In his opinion, the summing-up report of the agricultural production conference of each year always followed the established pattern of stating "accomplishments as essential, and defects inevitable. . . ." He implied that the Ministry of Agriculture was actually doing nothing other than fooling people with certain fabricated reports. He also abused leading cadres of the bureau and department directors and above in the Ministry of Agriculture for playing "cats and mice" and slandered the leading cadres of the Ministry whose working styles, he asserted, were so bad that "not even the Kuomintang could have been any worse. . . ."

At the suggestion of Shen Tseng-kan, Liu Kuo-fang spread a rumour through the large-character bulletins to the effect that, because of the popularisation of Sinkiang experience in cotton cultivation, "several tens of million mow of cotton fields reduced production" last year and consequently "coupons for two metres of cloth are good for only one" this year. . . .

At the Ministry of Water Conservancy, rightist Li Yu outrageously libelled the democratic life of our country and charged that "the

Communist Party promotes pseudo-democracy, which is much worse than the imperialist democracy. . . ."

[*NCNA. August 1*

Rightists in the Ministry of Agriculture

In the Ministry of Agriculture, a small reactionary clique . . . attacked and maligned the Communist Party on many sides. Shen Tseng-kan . . . asserted that "sectarianism constitutes the main current" and that "sectarianism will inevitably lead to subjectivism and bureaucratism." He maliciously implied that it was sectarian to claim that the Communist Party should assume the responsibility of providing leadership. . . .

Liu Kuo-fang, too, insanely condemned the Communist Party for "one-Party dictatorship," and bellowed that "democratic parties should participate in all aspects. . . ."

The three members composing the clique also unanimously denounced the movement to suppress counter-revolutionaries and demanded establishment of a "committee for the exoneration of counter-revolutionaries" to redress their grievances. Kuo Shu-fan . . . proclaimed "injustice" everywhere and insanely declared that "if something (meaning a Hungarian incident) should ever occur, I will also take part in it. . . ."

[*NCNA. August 14*

*

"I don't even dare tell my own brother"

PEKING: *Central Meteorological Bureau*

Chu Ho-chou [engineer]:

"When I was Deputy Director of the Tientsin Meteorological Bureau, whilst enjoying the confidence of the Party organisation, I was regarded as suspect by the Party cadres under my leadership. Every day, when I left off work to go home, they would make all sorts of clumsy attempts to search my briefcase to see what it contained. I thought this quite unpleasant. . . ."

Wang P'eng-fei [engineer]:

"As a result of repeated political campaigns in the past many people have become reticent. . . . I don't even dare tell my own brother about my work. . . ."

[*Kuang Ming Daily. May 18. (Date of forum not given.)*

Defects of secondary technical education

PEKING: *Ministry of the Machine Industry*

Chou I-p'ing, Director of the Education Department of the First Ministry of the Machine Industry, told this correspondent . . . that in the past the educational period of our secondary technical schools had been from two and a half years to three years. The curriculum had been the same as that of the four- or five-year system in the Soviet Union. It had been compressed to increase its "density" without any reduction of its contents. Therefore, the students had been subjected to too heavy a burden and had suffered from "indigestion. . . ." He said we had dogmatised and embalmed some good educational experiences of the Soviet Union. . . .

[*Chang Chung-hsiao. Kuang Ming Daily. May 10*

*

Welfare groups controlled by the Party

PEKING: *Ministry of the Chemical Industry*

Ch'en Chin-Po: "The Welfare Committee and Mutual Aid Committee are both in the hands of Party men. Some subsidies are granted in secret; no discussions are held in cases where some section chiefs and directors are concerned. . . ."

Shou Lo and Kao Shu-ch'ao and other engineers were furious at the sectarianism shown by the way letters of introduction were all printed with the words "Party Member" and "Youth League Member." In cases where the person concerned was neither a Party nor a Youth League member, the two headings would be deleted and the word "masses" inserted in their place. The engineers said: "What we are sent out to discuss are not political but technical problems. We will not probe into anything that is not within our terms of reference. What is the meaning of adopting these markings? If we are not to be trusted why not stop sending us?" (The two Ministers present, P'eng and Liang [P'eng T'ao, Minister of the Chemical Industry; Liang Ying-yung, First Deputy Minister] both said: "Well put. This way of doing things is inappropriate.") (Reporter's footnote: The Ministry of the Chemical Industry abolished the aforesaid letter-headings on the evening of May 16 and gave instructions that new letter-headings be printed.) . . .

[*Forums of non-Communists on May 14, 16, 17.*
Kuang Ming Daily. May 18

*

An excess of inferior Russian translators

PEKING: *Ministry of Buildings*

Shen Ta-miao [translator]:

"There are seven or eight Russian-language colleges in our country mass-producing translators. . . . And yet the leadership has given little thought to the future of these graduates. At the moment our country possesses several tens of thousands of Russian language workers—how many more will we need from now on? . . . The leadership always says: 'The cultural exchanges between Russia and China will daily grow increasingly broader; the things we want to translate from the Russians are as limitless as a sea of mist.' This kind of talk is 100 per cent. meaningless, and springs from abstract ideas."

Someone said on this point: "Even if the translatable material is vast, it is not something the vast majority of our translators today can tackle. Quantitatively there is a surplus of translators, but qualitatively their standards are inadequate. . . ."

Liu Cho said: "The Ministry of Higher Education ought to be held responsible for blindly training Russian language translators and also for the serious shortage of translators for other languages. . . ."

[*Kuang Ming Daily. June 3*

*

The mistress and the slave-girl

PEKING: *Ministry of Foreign Trade*

Yen Wen-chieh, director of the European and American Research Unit of the Quotation Research Office and right-winger within the Party . . . advocated that the Party should limit its leadership to the problems of "the direction of the road to socialism as well as important questions involving lines and policies. . . ."

Yen Wen-chieh thought that numerous Party member cadres of the middle and lower echelons (including cadres with rank equivalent to bureau chief of the central Government) were unfit for the offices they held. He looked upon them as "ignorant and useless persons" who owed their livelihood to the Party. . . .

Yen Wen-chieh outrageously slandered the "three-anti" and "five-anti" movements and the movement for the suppression of counter-revolutionaries by saying: "People who have gone through these movements themselves will remember the terror and feel their flesh creep whenever they think of them," and "At that time, everyone felt that he might be the next victim and there was general terror in society. . . ." He said: "The scenes of struggle were more unbearable than prison. . . ." "I feel that these struggles might force some people who originally had no intention of becoming counter-revolutionaries to join the counter-revolutionary camp," he added.

He even clamoured: "No matter what their achievements are, these movements cannot be launched again." He said: "We must demand that the Government lay down a stipulation to the effect that the ordinary organs and organisations may not inaugurate any struggle meetings unless they have obtained the approval of the Procuratorate-General and that such meetings must be conducted under the auspices of a court of law."

He said: "Death to those whose false charges led to the death of other people" and "Imprisonment for those whose false charges led to the wrongful imprisonment of other people. . . ."

No freedom of speech or thought

Yen Wen-chieh also thought that there was no freedom of thought and speech in the country and within the Party. He said: "People are not free to think and talk as they please. . . ."

Concerning the interpretation of articles written by the leader, he slanderously and maliciously said: "It looks as if one article [*i.e.*, Mao Tse-tung's speech on "contradictions"—*Ed.*] is enough to solve all the theories and work problems in the world. . . ." "If the things written by a man have to be explained in numerous ways before they can be understood by other people, we can very well go without them."

For the sake of allowing thought and speech to "open up," he "suggested" that there should be published more newspapers of the "current style" (referring to those published at the time when the right-wingers launched their rampant attack and the Party temporarily took no action to strike back). "With this kind of public opinion available, even without the rectification campaign, people would be forced to manage their affairs with greater care and to have regard for the opposition view and popular opinion. . . ."

He wrote that at present some people "speak and write as instructed or simply to flatter. . . . When their writings or speeches are read or heard, one has the feeling of chewing the muck-worms and wanting to vomit."

He said that the leaders and those led by them, the leaders and the people, and the upper and lower echelons were related to each other like the " master " was related to the " slave." He said: " A ' slave-girl ' is the dowry or appendage of her ' mistress.' She has to win the favour and avoid the hate of her mistress. In her spiritual world, there are only submission and flattery. She looks upon the swallowing of the saliva of her mistress as an honour. This is the philosophy of the ' slave-girl.' . . ."

Yen Wen-chieh openly opposed the counter-attack made by the *People's Daily*. Apart from speaking at Party conferences and sending two articles to the *People's Daily*, he also addressed an " urgent appeal " to the Party central committee. . . . He attacked the *People's Daily* for using the headline " The People Have Not Asked Ko P'ei-ch'i to Make These Utterances " [June 6] and said: " Does this mean that it has been verified by plebiscite? I think that Ko P'ei-ch'i also represents some of the people in the society. . . ."

Yen Wen-chieh joined the revolution at Yenan in 1938. He was admitted into the Communist Party in 1942. He came from a landlord family. He has now become a spokesman of the bourgeois right wing within the Party and has openly rebelled against the Party.

[*NCNA. July 23*

*

A Communist attacks the leaders

PEKING: *Ministry of Geology*

On June 8, after the rectification campaign had begun, Hsueh I [Director of the Policy Research Office of the Communist Party Administrative Staff Office in the Ministry of Geology] published a 14,000-word article on " The System of Reforming and Using Cadres." In his article, Hsueh I maliciously attacked the organisational systems of the Party . . . accused the leading cadres of lacking knowledge and of being ordinary and lazy. He said that the leading cadres solely relied on their membership and seniority in the Party and the legal status given to them by the state to assume leadership. . . . He even voiced support for the statements made by other rightists calling for a system of rotation in exercising state power and for freedom of forming a new Cabinet by the one which won at the election. . . . He wrote articles refuting the *People's Daily* for the unfair treatment given to Ch'u An-p'ing. . . .

Hsueh I . . . a member of the Communist Party for eighteen years . . . during the War of Resistance against Japan as well as the strenuous struggles for land reform and suppression of counter-revolutionaries, was criticised and punished by the Party a number of times for sympathising with the landlords and opposing the suppression of counter-revolutionaries. . . .

[*NCNA. July 23*

*

Blind imitation of Russia

ENGINEERS

T'an Chen-hsiung [Deputy Chief Engineer, Ferrous Metals Planning Department, Ministry of the Metallurgical Industry] says that learning from the Soviet Union has hitherto been a doctrinaire process, and just strict copying. . . .

Yen Shao-hsi [an engineer, Planning Bureau, Ministry of the Metallurgical Industry]:

During the peak period of last year in particular, the leaders only wanted everybody to overcome conservatism. They said too few factories had been built in the past and wanted everybody to map out more plans quickly. Money was no object. In these circumstances, the attempt to attain the " world level " was made. Minister Wang Ho-shou of the Ministry of the Metallurgical Industry and Vice Premiers Li Fu-ch'un and Po I-po have all admitted that it is right to blame the leadership for all these mistakes and faults. . . .

The standards and scales we have adopted are mainly Russian without being modified to suit Chinese conditions. For example, the sites of some factories have not enough ventilation facilities. We do not understand the actual conditions in which these standards are applied in Russia and have thus blindly applied them in our own country. Due to pressure of work, the planners have no time to study and find out these things. Besides, the leaders do not understand technical problems anyway. At all events, they simply refuse to approve your plans whenever they are found to be not in conformity with Soviet standards. . . .

[*Kuang Ming Daily forum. June 8*

" Let us stand up, shout and make trouble "

ENGINEERS

Wang Kuang-ying, a rightist in the Non-ferrous Metals Bureau, said: " The Communist Party has changed for the worse; the minority exploits the majority."

Rightist Yuan Chun-jung of the mining bureau, insinuated that Party membership could be obtained under certain conditions, including supply of information, flattery, violation of the law and discipline, and idealism instead of materialism.

Rightists even urged abolition of the Communist Party and execution of its members. In addition, they distorted all facts and completely denied the achievements of the Communist Party. . . .

A rightist element in the Non-ferrous Metal Research Institute openly proposed "to demonstrate from one street to another in the May 4 spirit."

Another rightist element wrote in a wall slogan: "Let us stand up, shout and make trouble." These rightists even prepared a name list of all leading comrades and openly urged them to resign. . . .

A rightist element in the Non-ferrous Metal Research Institute shouted: "Suppression of counter-revolutionaries is not proper."

[*NCNA. Peking. July 27*

*

Disdainful treatment of non-Communists

PEKING: *Institute of Socialism* [1] **May 20**

Chang Chen [former Nationalist general, Deputy Governor, Honan Province] gave an account of how for several years between the time of his revolting in sympathy [*i.e.*, with the Communists—*Ed.*] and the time when he got the post of member of the Physical Culture Commission he had had nothing to do and he felt miserable. At the time when he was Chairman of the National-Style Physical Training Commission, in accordance with the policy of "To study and organise so as to move forward step by step" he was able to get some work done. In September 1954 he invited Chairman Ho Lung [Marshal; member, CP's Politburo; Chairman, Physical Culture and Sports Commission—*Ed.*] to review a combined display of traditional physical culture at Tientsin. Chang Chen described it thus: "Chairman Ho Lung being dissatisfied with it, burst into a fit of temper then and there, saying 'No good.' He also said he knew all along that I was no good, and went on to say that 'I do not want you even as a Commission member!' This caused me to go red all over. . . . I have my failings and am of low standard and mistakes are unavoidable in my work. What you should do is to

[1] The Institute of Socialism was founded especially to provide courses in Marxism Leninism for non-Communist officials and intellectuals.

educate me and bring me up to the required standard, but you should not humiliate me, despise me and ignore me. . . ."

[*Kuang Ming Daily*. *May 21*

Aristocratic schools

May 22

Yang Chao-chun [staff member, National Education Department; Ministry of Education] submitted views on the schools for children of cadres. He said: "The masses have strong feelings about the fact that only the children of the senior cadres can attend those 'artistocratic schools. . . .' Whilst the cadres today want to identify themselves completely with the masses, and to break down 'the walls,' fill up 'the moats,' nevertheless they still allow their children to continue to receive 'privileged education'; therefore these youngsters grow up in privileged and pampered conditions, and their life and scope of knowledge become narrow; quarrels often occur between fellow students. One would say: 'My father is a director of a bureau'; another would say: 'My father is a Minister who supervises your father.' Or else they quarrel over whose family has more cars. The teaching personnel also feel that these 'heaven-pampered children' are quite a handful. . . ."

[*Kuang Ming Daily*. *May 23*

A comprehensive programme

May 23

Yu Yung [Committee of Experts, Ministry of Communications] . . . made more than ten suggestions on state work.

1. The Party and the administration should be kept separate, and the latter should not be replaced by the former. The Party can only enunciate policies and measures, but cannot issue commands and orders.

2. Encourage freedom of speech. It should be permissible for private individuals to run newspapers and periodicals so that diverse views can find expression. . . .

3. Investigations be carried out to find out the deviations and errors that occurred during past campaigns.

4. Criminal law and civil law be enacted with all speed. . . .

11. People's Deputies and members of the People's Political Consultative Conference should not be produced by consultations among various departments; they should be produced by elections.

[*Kuang Ming Daily*. *May 24*

Freedom of the person unrespected

May 27–31

Ku Chih-chung's speech was on the problem of thoroughly implementing the Constitution. He said that the freedom of the person as provided by the Constitution had not been respected by certain people. Although citizens had the right to appeal to the law against state personnel for unlawful acts or dereliction of duties, yet no one had ever exercised this right. The fundamental reason for this was that struggles against contraventions of the Constitution had not been effectively carried out. . . .

Ch'en Hsin-kuei [alternate member, Central Committee, CDL] said that the succession of storms in the past was one of the factors contributing to the creation of contradictions among the people. . . . The past few campaigns had produced a number of repercussions, the most serious being the growth of idealism. For instance, arbitrarily laying down the number of objects for attack beforehand without having ascertained the facts. . . .

Some people said that during a campaign "one must attack others if one wishes to avoid being attacked oneself."

In conclusion, he proposed:

1. The Party in its rectification movement should make a point of examining the credit and debit sides of past campaigns.

2. There should be a summing-up of the past few campaigns, which should be published in the newspapers in order to encourage public discussion.

3. The Representatives of the National People's Congress and members of the People's Political Consultative Conference should hold an inquiry into the problem of the suppression of counter-revolutionaries, in accordance with Chairman Mao's directive. A special committee ought to be set up to deal with the matter and its rulings should be made public.

4. People struggled against in public during past campaigns should be rehabilitated in public too.

5. Thorough inquiries should be made into the cases of innocent people who committed suicide for fear of struggles and persecution. Their reputations should be restored and families looked after. . . .

Shou Ch'ung-yi's speech exposed the concern for privilege, lack of discipline and lawlessness of the Personnel Department of the All-China Federation of Industry and Commerce. . . . The Personnel Department was known to have written anonymous letters falsely accusing a certain comrade of being a counter-revolutionary in retaliation for his criticism of the Department. The comrade of the Personnel Department responsible for this misdeed, instead of receiving due punishment for it, had been upgraded twice running. . . .

Wang Yu-tse said that arrogance and complacency were rampant among Communist Party members who had been spoilt by the victories of the revolution. . . . If someone had had the audacity to point out the failings of Communist Party members before the start of the rectification campaign, he would have evoked the concerted attack of Party members and their so-called positive elements. These comrades were apt to identify Party membership with the Party itself, so that, whoever criticised Party members as individuals received the label " anti-Party." That is why the masses took good care to respect Party members but give them a wide berth. . . .

[*Kuang Ming Daily. June 3*

*

" The Three Abominations of Li Shih-chun "

NANKING

Li Shih-chun is a member of the Central Committee of the Kuomintang Revolutionary Committee and is concurrently Director of the Bureau of Civil Administration in Nanking. On May 23, at a forum called by the Communist Party Kiangsu Provincial Committee, Li Shih-chun made his venomous attacks. . . . [*People's Daily*, July 14.]

Li Shih-chun hates first of all our public security system. He has said that our public security personnel are (countless like) " the hairs of a tiger " and that " public security personnel are dreadful and hateful." Another rightist, Wu Ssu-kuang, deputy director of the Bureau of Handicrafts Industries for Kiangsu . . . threatened to " kill all public security personnel one day. . . ."

Li Shih-chun also hates our personnel management departments. He calls our personnel departments the " Court of the King of Hell," where " there is, in addition to big and small spirits, the King of Hell himself." He also calls the personnel dossiers " The Record of Life and Death. . . ." There are other rightists who decry our personnel departments, calling them " secret police organisations. . . ."

There is a third abomination for Li Shih-chun: he hates the party spirit of the Communists. He has said: " The Communists weigh every word and action of non-Communists carefully," that the Communists were "icily cold," that they "judge other people solely from the standpoint of class struggle. . . ."

[*NCNA. Peking. July 14*

*

An intra-Party rightist attacks collectivism

SHENYANG

Chang Hai-tao, Communist Party member and Director of General Office in the Marine Products Supply and Marketing Company . . . not only defamed collectivisation, but also distorted the policy of unified purchase and unified sale. He undermined the worker-peasant alliance by saying that as the peasants could not even subsist on the foodstuffs which they produced, the workers and the peasants "were too unequal." He . . . even carried his madness to the extent of saying that in Taiwan the average income of the people exceeded that on the mainland. He called cadres in the personnel section little special agents; claimed that the Party newspapers reported glad tidings but covered up sad news, singing praises to merits and virtues only. He deliriously clamoured for what he called "Letting the masses see the colours of the bowels of the Communist Party. . . ." Rightist Chen Kuang of the People's Bank . . . frantically claimed that the "three evils" could never be eradicated unless the Party ceased to exist. . . .

[*From a report on the anti-rightist struggle in Liaoning Province. Shenyang. NCNA. August 5*

12

DEMOCRATIC PARTIES

DEMOCRATIC parties also held forums for their members at which those not important enough to be invited to the Communist Party forums for leading non-Communists were able to have their say. It was at a meeting of the Democratic League that Ch'en Hsin-kuei took Ch'u An-p'ing's views on " the world belonging to the Party " to their logical conclusion. These forums were all in Peking.

Nominal nature of the Defence Council

PEKING: *Kuomintang Revolutionary Committee* **June 3**

Wang Wen-hao . . . referred to the fact that Huang Yen-pei, while Minister of Light Industry, had wanted a list of the directors of the departments of industry of different provinces, but was refused the list for security reasons. Wang said if a man like Huang, who was then Vice Premier of the Government Administration Council and Minister of Light Industry was denied confidence, it would be a great joke for other people to expect to have authority to go with their posts. . . .

T'sai T'ing-k'ai also spoke at the meeting. He considered that sectarianism existed to a serious extent in the Physical Culture Commission. He said that the National Defence Council was only a nominal organ without any practical significance and could be dispensed with. He himself as a member of the National Defence Council [1] had nothing to do. . . .

[*NCNA. June 3*

The " double-track " system

PEKING: *Kuomintang Revolutionary Committee* **June 5**

T'an T'i-wu referred to the method by which the Communist Party led the state. There was now one set of structures in the Government,

1 The precise nature and functions of the National Defence Council (whose *ex-officio* Chairman was Mao Tse-tung) had always been obscure since it had no official control over the Ministry of Defence. This statement of T'sai T'ing-k'ai indicates that it is simply part of the " united front " façade, an organisation on which former Nationalist generals like himself can serve without having to be entrusted with military plans and secrets.

and another set of structures in the Party. She referred to this as the double-track system. She wondered if this were not the cause of all problems arising in work today—such as those relating to the " wall " and the " moat," and the three great " isms." She said the set of structures inside the Party was " completely of one colour," not associated with the masses. It was originally claimed that the Party would undertake the control of ideology and policy only, but in practice this scope had already been exceeded, and the Party was directly issuing orders to the people, while the government departments did not have authority. . . .

" The different departments within the Communist Party should be made into different committees under the Standing Committee of the National People's Congress.

" Party groups may be organised in the Standing Committee of the National People's Congress, and non-Party people should be asked to participate in its work."

T'an T'i-wu also suggested that the policies of the Communist Party should be realised through the laws and decrees enacted by the state. She did not agree with the practice of the Party issuing directives within the Party separate from the laws and decrees of the state.

[*NCNA. June 5*

*

Chairman Mao must " develop his thesis "

PEKING: *China Democratic League*

Ch'en Hsin-kuei [alternate member, Central Committee, CDL]:

" The system adopted by the Soviet Union and the New Democracies is the dictatorship of the proletariat, through the vanguard of the working class—the dictatorship of the Communist Party. Is it any wonder that sectarianism thrives on a system which regards all outside the Party as pagan elements? This is a theoretical problem: What do we mean by the dictatorship of one party? How can the democratic parties supervise a one-party dictatorship? Chairman Mao will have to develop his thesis further. Subjectivism was once an object for rectification in Yenan, but it only grew worse as a result. The dictatorship of the proletariat is the " root " of it all. Unless we go to the source of the troubles we will only aggravate bureaucracy and sectarianism by trying to combat them. . . ."

Ch'iu K'o-hui: " Privilege mindedness is not simply an infection that has spread as a result of city life following the liberation, it is also a by-product of the absurd hierarchical system which besets the whole country. For instance, the discrepancy in material rewards between a Minister, a director of a bureau, a director of a department, a head of an office, a chief of a section and the ordinary rank and file cadres is far too excessive, and the distinction between them far too marked. . . . Talk of sharing hardships with the masses in a hierarchical system such as ours! . . ."

[*Reported in Kuang Ming Daily. June 8*

Proletarian dictatorship is the source of sectarianism

PEKING: *China Democratic League*

Ch'en Hsin-kuei [alternate member, Central Committee, CDL], who had on more than one occasion expressed such an erroneous view, at this meeting continued to defend his own viewpoint. He said that he fully agreed with Ch'u An-p'ing's view that the idea of "the world belongs to the Party" was the root of all sectarianism. He guessed that Ch'u An-p'ing was possibly afraid of being accused of being a "revisionist," and so did not go on to point out the source of this idea of the "world belongs to the Party." He himself thought that the source of this idea was the proletarian dictatorship.

Ch'en Hsin-kuei proceeded to elucidate his views further. He stated that the Stalinist mistakes in the proletarian dictatorship of the Soviet Union, and the Hungarian incident arising out of the proletarian dictatorship in that country had proved that the political system of the proletarian dictatorship was open to question. He added that the proletarian dictatorship was in effect the dictatorship of the Communist Party. In this way, the Communist Party, in implementing its policies, in exercising its leadership of the country, must first rely on the members of the Communist Party, next rely on the members of the Communist Youth League, and then rely on those who had sided with the Party. Under such circumstances, it would be unbelievable if sectarianism, subjectivism and bureaucratism did not emerge; it would be difficult to imagine that the idea of the "empire of the Party" would not be evolved.

Before the meeting was closed, Ch'en Hsin-Kuei again took the *People's Daily* to task. . . . He described the counter-criticisms of anti-Communist Party and anti-socialist views in the Press the last few days as "accusations" flying around. . . . He added indignantly: "Frankly speaking, if one is a counter-revolutionary, one would certainly not issue those statements which the papers consider mistaken; rather one would assuredly talk about the greatness of the Communist Party and so forth."

[*Kuang Ming Daily. June 10*

✱

Handling of Complaints

PEKING: *Chiu San Society* **June 5**

Chu Tsung-jang [Ministry of Health] thinks that to pass back people's letters of complaint to the organisations complained about is not the correct way to deal with such matters, because the persons who wrote the letters are bound to be retaliated against by the organisations concerned which are bedevilled by bureaucracy and sectarianism.

[*Kuang Ming Daily. June 10*

" Ch'u An-p'ing's heart is in the right place "

PEKING: *Chiu San Society* **June 8**

Wei Chien-kung said: ". . . Ch'u An-p'ing's heart is in the right place, only he happens to have made some misleading overstatements which have led to undesirable repercussions. I reserve my judgment of his speeches. We should not finish him off with one blow with the cudgel. . . ."

Yun Chen said: ". . . The mistakes in Ch'u An-p'ing's speech are only too obvious. But is there something good in what he said? . . . Is it not a fact worth investigation that every establishment, every department has a Party member as its chief? The Party leadership ought to delegate responsibility to Party members and non-Party members alike, with Party members acting as a medium through whom policies can be thoroughly implemented. . . ."

[*Kuang Ming Daily. June 9*

✱

The position of women

PEKING **May 31**

Shih Liang [Minister of Justice; Vice Chairman, CDL]:

" Right up to the present day, people in all walks of life neither think much of nor respect woman. Even in the minds of some Communist Party members the remnants of such feudal thoughts still linger. There are departments which loathe to take on female comrades; others which pick on the female comrades as the first victims of redundancy. . . ."

Liu Ch'ing-yang [Chairman, CC Women's Work Committee, CDL]:

"The Ministry of Health stipulates that no one below the 7th grade can be admitted into the wards of Peking Hospital. But the fact is many mothers-in-law, wives and children of Ministers and Deputy Ministers are allowed in. It is a dubious style of work, which puts officials first and the masses last. . . ."

Lei Chi-ch'ung [Standing Committee, ACFDW]:

1. The Women's Work Committee and the All-China Federation of Democratic Women should take a more active part in legislation and resolutions concerning women. "For instance, the Ministry of Health has recently made public its decision to relax the restrictions imposed on the practice of abortion. My impression is that medical specialists are widely opposed to this. However, the Women's Work Committee and the All-China Federation of Democratic Women have so far taken no stand on this vital matter concerning the health of woman—a fact which shows their indifference towards the welfare of women."

2. The All-China Federation of Democratic Women had never shown any concern over the persecution and oppression of women. She criticised the apathy of the All-China Federation of Democratic Women towards women and its lack of fighting spirit. Incidents of rape and cruelty to women were seldom harshly condemned in the Press. Even the courts were inclined towards leniency in these cases. The League had in the past rarely come out with definite views on those issues. She hoped to see a change in its attitude.

3. The practice of dumping old cadres' wives also constituted a problem in some departments. "I consider this merits the attention of the Communist Party Central Committee's Women's Work Committee. . . ."

[*Women's forum summoned by CPPCC Women's Work Committee and ACFDW Party fraction. Kuang Ming Daily. June 1*

13

PEASANTS AND WORKERS

The Peasants

The peasants formed 85 per cent. of the 635-odd million Chinese living on the mainland in 1957. There could therefore have been nothing like general unrest without their participation; indeed, historically no Chinese dynasty has been overthrown without peasant support. The Chinese Communists themselves came to power at the head of a peasant army. Could disgruntled students and intellectuals have aroused them against the régime?

It is, of course, impossible to tell. We have little evidence as to peasant feelings. We have no reports of forums, conducted in the spirit of the early days of rectification, for the peasants as we do for the intellectuals. The forum system had not been tried at the peasant level when the anti-rightist campaign started.

But on balance, it is extremely unlikely that a major peasant uprising against the régime would have occurred. The peace and stability that the Communist régime had brought, coupled with vigorous water conservancy measures, had permitted a slight but significant bettering of material conditions according to visitors who have been able to make comparisons with pre-Communist days. It is doubtful if the long-suffering Chinese peasant who has known little enough of freedom had yet been driven hard enough by the Party officials actively to want to change a régime that had brought him that benefit—especially as he well knows the ruthlessness of the Party in dealing with dissidents. Besides, the grievances of the intellectuals must have meant little to the peasants; and the students were more concerned with individual liberty and justice than the problems of the peasants' livelihood.

What could conceivably have occurred if the mood of May 1957 had reached the villages was large-scale withdrawals from the collectives. Party officials, thrown on the defensive by the upsurge of anti-Party feeling as reported in the Press, would have been ill equipped to resist.

The evidence for this suggestion is sparse, but significant. The Kwangtung Province Party organisation admitted in May that there had been withdrawals (involving probably about half a million people) though many peasants had later changed their minds. Later, from July onwards, there were reports from a number of provinces about withdrawals during the rectification period, usually attributed to the plotting of landlords.

These reports are not surprising. The vast majority of peasants had been herded into collectives for the first time in the great drive during the winter of 1955–56. Unfortunately for the Party, 1956 was a disastrous year from the point of view of natural calamities which collectivisation could do little to alleviate. (It was revealed in June 1957 that 14,700 Kwangsi peasants had migrated and 550 had died due to the serious famine of 1956, for which senior officials responsible were dismissed. It should be pointed out, however, that this figure, if correct, is minute compared with the numbers who perished in pre-Communist times.) The novelty of the collectives and the inefficiency of their officials compounded the situation. Altogether, the first year of collective farming, far from permitting a leap forward towards the millennium, was the worst on record since the Communists came to power. The peasants, led to expect better, would have been understandably dissatisfied.

It is extremely unlikely that the resultant withdrawals from collectives were incited by landlords as officially claimed. The one report we have of withdrawals which was issued before the polemics of the anti-rightist campaign—the Kwangtung report—makes no mention of them. He would be an extremely brave landlord who, after the persecutions and executions meted out to his class, would have criticised so fundamental a Communist policy. (If landlords *were* brave enough, then the situation must have been very serious indeed.) It is anyway clear from the later reports that poorer peasants were dissatisfied with collectives and even with some of their officials and their "undemocratic ways"; and the extent of the dissatisfaction can be gauged by the Party's decision to launch an educative campaign to get peasants to see problems in perspective.

N.B.—Unified purchases and sales of grain: The hardships imposed by this policy are mentioned a number of times in this section. It was introduced in November 1953, after the bad harvest of that year. Peasants were compelled to sell their entire surplus to the state at prices fixed by the Government. Further, the size of the surplus was determined by quotas fixed in advance by the Government rather than by the amount of grain actually produced. It was probably this latter provision that gave rise to most grievances.

Peasant dissatisfaction with the Party and collectivisation

KWANGTUNG PROVINCE

The Communist Party Kwangtung Committee has courageously and thoroughly exposed the contradictions found in current work in Kwangtung.[1] . . .

The contradictions between the state and the peasants. The most salient of these are the contradiction between the planned guidance of the state and the independent operation of agricultural producer co-operatives (like the state demand for guaranteed grain yield versus the peasants' demand for more economic crops to boost their income; the state demand for the breeding of more hogs and the cultivation of more oil-bearing crops versus the peasants' unwillingness to accept state plans) and the contradiction relating to regional price differences in commercial buying and the difference in buying and selling rates. . . .

The peasants feel that the Government is paying too much attention to the cities. As a result, the workers and cadres are leading a good life while the life led by the peasants is a hard one. The cities are well supplied (with cloth and edible oil) while the countryside is short of supplies. The price of manufactured goods is high.

The contradictions between the leadership and the masses. These find main expression in undemocratic behaviour on the part of the cadres which leads to the practice of having work carried out by coercion and command and the violation of law and discipline; the refusal to make

[1] The problem of location of industry and the failure to cultivate oil-bearing crops may be peculiar to Kwangtung. The Party Committee may well have been protesting against neglect of the province by the Government in the north; Kwangtung has always been distrusted by Peking officials. But there is no reason to suppose that peasants' and workers' complaints about living conditions and the methods of officials would not be echoed in other provinces.

public the accounts which has permitted quite a number of co-operative cadres to indulge in corrupt practices; the non-participation of co-operative cadres in manual work and the payment of compensation wages to them at too high a rate. All this dissatisfies the masses. . . . From last winter, a total of 117,916 households have pulled out at different times from co-operatives in the province. At present, 102,149 households have rejoined. . . .

In places where greater changes are effected in economic reorganisation and in calamity-stricken areas, the masses have many complaints about the small progress made in the bettering of their living standards. . . .

Workers' strikes

Since last year, workers in the province have involved themselves in thirteen strikes and trouble-making incidents. The contradictions find main expression in the following points:

Irrational wage system. . . .

Want of democracy in factory management. According to the report of the Canton Committee, if all the factory superintendents in the municipality were elected by the workers, less than 50 per cent. of the existing factory superintendents would get themselves elected. . . .

The question of workers' welfare. Some of the problems involving public mess halls, lavatories, medical clinics and dormitories which could and should be solved are left unsolved. In the case of those which cannot be solved, the reason is not made known to the workers. This is also a cause of dissatisfaction among the workers. . . .

Kwangtung: a depressed area

At present there are in Kwangtung about 180,000 people who are unemployed. Although Kwangtung has started up some industries to solve the employment problem for some of these people during the years since the liberation (the number of workers in Canton has now increased to 200,000 compared with no more than 70,000 in pre-liberation days), yet because Kwangtung is not a key district for industrial construction, it can give employment to only a limited number of people. The people are universally of the opinion that too few industrial construction projects are carried out in Kwangtung and have voiced their dissatisfaction on this point. At the same time, the Government has exercised too firm a control over some of the measures which can solve the problem of employment. When some unemployed workers and poor people devise ways and means to start various handicraft industries themselves, for example, they frequently fail to obtain the necessary approval. This aggravates the dissatisfaction of the unemployed. . . .

The contradictions caused by short supply and rising prices. This is a tense problem of the utmost concern to the people of the cities and countryside in Kwangtung, which gives rise to numerous complaints. At present, the main commodities in short supply are edible oil, pork and cotton cloth. Since the liberation, Kwangtung has never completely abandoned its reliance on other places for its supply of oil. It has made no energetic efforts to develop the cultivation of oil-bearing crops. As a result, it is estimated that this shortage cannot be eliminated quickly. In the case of hogs, because of the low buying price prevalent for a time coupled with the short supply of grain, there was a drop in the number of hogs bred. At the moment, although the supply position has taken a turn for the better, the general situation remains strained. In the case of cotton cloth, where the ration has been cut, the biggest complaint of the masses is that they were urged to make new clothes last year but are called upon to wear old garments this year. They criticise us for going back on our words. As to the problem of rising prices for edible oil and pork, if we made known the cause to the people, we can still make them understand. At present, the people are most bitter at the rise in the prices of vegetables and eggs which has been caused not by underproduction but by mismanagement. They denounce the Government for allowing prices to fluctuate in the free market and for doing away with controls thus making the living standards of the people suffer.

[*NCNA. Canton. May 14*

*

Reports of rural unrest

Independent farming is better

SHENSI PROVINCE

The anti-socialist and anti-Party utterances of bourgeois rightist elements boosted the position of a small bunch of landlords, rich peasants and elements under surveillance in Hanyang, Changan and other hsien in Shensi Province. . . .

The vicious attacks were directed against the Party policies of agricultural co-operation and unified purchase and unified marketing of grains by these landlords, rich peasants and elements under surveillance. Some claimed that the superior advantages of the farm co-operative had already reached their limit. Others spread the word that co-operatives were not as good as independent operation. Still others cried that unified purchase and unified marketing had gone haywire. Some landlords and rich peasants in Changan publicly claimed that the living standards of peasants since the liberation had not been raised at all. Chang Ching-shun, a former rich peasant in a village in Hanyang, took advantage of the contradictions between the state and co-operative members on the grains issue. He said: "The blame for the excessively small shares in the grain distribution this summer can be traced to the bigger co-operative." He even publicly denounced co-operative cadres: "These cadres are going to move grain to other places. . . ."

[*NCNA. Lanchow. July 25*

"We are starved"

KANSU PROVINCE

Some members in Minch'in hsien had wanted to quit their co-operatives to go into business. Fourteen members of the Yucheng agricultural co-operative had called on cadres, demanding money and grains, yelling "we are starved." In view of this, co-operatives at Yucheng and Yushun called meetings to discuss whether or not there had been improvements in livelihood since the institution of co-operativisation. . . . The meeting came to the conclusion "if we still call ourselves poor, we are merely blind to the prosperity which we already have. . . ."

Some members of the Hsianglang co-operative, disagreeing with the principle of state first and then the individual, had refused to sell grains to the state. . . .

[*NCNA. Lanchow. July 25*

Cadres' vigour sapped

FUKIEN PROVINCE

Those cadres who became negative and incompetent under the influence of the rightist attack now stand up and work hard. Militiamen who stopped standing guard have now become increasingly vigilant and have resumed patrols for the protection of the summer crop. Some of the muddle-headed men confused by the rightist arguments against socialism have begun to see the truth. Counter-revolutionary remnants and landlords and rich peasants who had grasped the opportunity to revive capitalism have been isolated and some have been dealt heavy blows. For instance, bad element Yu Lo-ling in Minho (?) hsien seized the opportunity of the rightist attack on the Party and the people to create sabotaging rumours and to instigate peasants to withdraw from the co-operatives. . . .

[*NCNA. Foochow. July 23*

"Which is better: the landlord or the Communist Party?"

KIANGSU PROVINCE

Some time ago, unlawful landlords and rich peasants in the rural areas of Chiangpu hsien openly sowed seeds of discord in collaboration with the rightists, saying: "Unified purchase and marketing of grain is good but 480 catties is not enough to keep a stomach full." A landlord in the "May 4th" agricultural producer co-operative in Tachiao hsiang even plotted to seize the leadership of the agricultural producer co-operative, starting activities among members to elect him director of it. Landlord Chang Chi-yao of the Tuanchieh agricultural producer co-operative in Lungshan hsiang reckoned accounts with members: "Before liberation you paid me only 50 tan of grain as land rent. Now you have to pay tax and sell surplus grain totalling more than 100 tan. Which is better: a landlord or the Communist Party?" An anonymous threatening letter was posted on the door of co-operative director Li's house. . . .

[*People's Daily. July 29*

"Down with the co-operatives"

HUPEH PROVINCE

After the anti-Communist and anti-socialist wind was wafted from the cities to the countryside of Hupeh, certain unlawful landlords, rich peasants and counter-revolutionaries spread rumours and dealt blows to cadres and the masses in their attempt to cause the collapse of co-operatives. . . .

Misled by the reactionary utterances and actions of landlords, rich peasants and counter-revolutionaries, a small number of well-to-do middle peasants, who had no liking for their co-operatives, took the opportunity to attack their co-operatives. An old-type middle peasant of Sungtze hsien told a lie in order to instigate members to withdraw from their co-operatives: "The co-operatives have set up withdraw-from-co-operative offices." Old-type middle peasant Li Chi-yuan (an independently operating peasant), who had not paid agricultural tax and had not sold surplus grain for two years, gathered eighteen peasant households and, together with them, approached the Party branch secretary, shouting: "Down with the co-operatives!" When the Party branch secretary criticised him with his improper behaviour, he beat him up and pushed him into a pond. (The hsien government had decided to punish Li Chi-yuan.) In some localities, certain old-type upper middle peasants caused trouble to the co-operatives and withdrew from their co-operatives. . . .

[*People's Daily. July 29*

"The Communist Party is at the end of its tether"

HONAN PROVINCE

For a while in the past, some unlawful landlords, rich peasants and elements under surveillance utilised rightist assertions against the Communist Party and socialism to create sabotaging rumours. They declared: "The Communist Party is at the end of its tether. The time for our liberation has come." Some went about putting up reactionary posters, openly beating up village cadres, poisoning livestock, destroying autumn seeds and settling scores with the peasants. The Municipal Committee of the Communist Party estimated that a total of ninety-eight had committed such sabotaging acts and words. . . .

[*NCNA. Chengchow. August 4*

Cadres sympathise with peasants

KIANGSI PROVINCE

The Secretariat of the Kiangsi Provincial Committee of the Communist Party decided at a conference on August 2 to set in motion a propaganda movement on the policy of Government purchase and collection of grains with a view to giving peasants a correct understanding of the grain problem. . . .

It pointed out that some cadres had blindly aired grievances on behalf of the peasants. For this reason, it suggested that the ideological conceptions of the cadres be unified before the movement was launched and that acts of singing in chorus with rightist elements against collection and purchase (of grain) be criticised. . . .

[*NCNA. Nanchang. August 5*

A rightist miasma

KWANGTUNG PROVINCE

In the counter-attack against the class enemy, public security and judicial departments have arrested a number of active counter-revolutionary remnants and iniquitous landlords and rich peasants. The rightist miasma evaporates before the penetrating movement. Talk of disbanding co-operatives and withdrawing from co-operatives has quieted down. Those peasants who wanted to quit co-operatives and took home agricultural implements are now coming back with the implements.

[*NCNA. Canton. August 5*

More than 100 cases of sabotage

SZECHWAN PROVINCE

On the basis of the materials exposed by peasants in the hsien, the public security department there reported more than 100 cases that occurred in the period, January to July this year, involving unlawful landlords, rich peasants and counter-revolutionary elements, reckoning old scores with the peasants, wresting or attempting to wrest from the peasants, lands, houses and other items of property, revenging themselves on and beating up peasants and cadres, poisoning livestock, destroying water conservancy works and crops, alienating relations between cadres and the masses and spreading rumours.

[*From a report on ideological education in Shantai hsien, Szechwan Province. NCNA. Chengtu. August 6*

Attacks on collectivisation

SHANSI PROVINCE

During the " free contention and free blooming," bourgeois rightists in various hsien in Shansi viciously defamed the basic Party organisations and Party members at large. They called Party members in agricultural villages " lazy-bones " and " detectives." Kuo Hai-chen, rightist in An-yi hsien, said: " The agricultural co-operatives do not function properly, because the Party and League members and basic cadres are imperfect." Certain rightists even attacked food-grains policies and agricultural collectivisation. They tried to disrupt relations between the Party and the peasants. They said that peasants were "forced" to join agricultural co-operatives, that the Government took away food-grains from the peasants, that the living standard of peasants had not been raised. . . .

[*From a report on the anti-rightist struggle in Shansi Province. NCNA. Taiyuan. August 12*

Trouble in Kwangsi Province

KWANGSI PROVINCE

A number of former landlords, rich peasants and remnant counter-revolutionaries have launched a counter-revolutionary attack upon the peasants, the Party and the People's Government in an attempt to upset the socialist system. . . .

They seized plots of land, houses, cattle and furniture, all of which had been confiscated and distributed among the peasants during the period of land reform. . . . Some even forced the peasants to repay old "debts" incurred prior to land reform, threatening them with the following remarks: "The Kuomintang will return in August. . . ." . . . in direct response to the bourgeois rightists' call, posted such reactionary slogans as "Follow Chang Po-chun," "Democracy and freedom, and down with the Communist Party," etc. They openly incited the peasants to refuse to deliver public grain agricultural tax in kind to the state and threatened the masses by saying: "We shall beat anyone who delivers public grain to a state warehouse and break his legs." They also instigated a small number of members of agricultural producer co-operatives to withdraw their memberships, and to reap and divide the rice crops among themselves so as to upset these co-operatives. They openly rebuked cadres, drove wedges between the cadres and the masses, incited the masses to start troubles and even beat cadres and murdered rural activists. . . .

More than ten cases of violent assault upon cadres occurred in Yunghsien in July, and as many as forty-six such cases took place in Peiliu hsien in June and July. . . . Certain Party-member cadres and non-Party people made no analysis of the rightists' opinions and were even influenced by rightists' ideas, wrongly believing that co-operatives really do not have any superior quality and that the villages have really turned "very bad." All these also helped, to a definite degree, to encourage the frenzied attitude of landlords, rich peasants and counter-revolutionaries and constituted the reason why they were audacious enough to launch a counter-revolutionary attack at this time and why at the very beginning of this attack they were able to create a state of confusion in certain rural areas for a short period of time. . . .

A small number of rightists in factories attacked the Party in regard to questions such as wages, welfare and the leaders' style of work, and carried on agitation among building workers. . . .

[*Report to Kwangsi People's Congress by Deputy Governor Wei Kuo-ching, August 23. Kwangsi Daily. Nanning. August 24*

The need for rural indoctrination

To sum up, among the 1,393 households in the six co-operatives were sixty well-to-do middle peasant households imbued with serious capitalist thinking and marked by anti-socialist words and actions, sixty-four households of middle-of-the-road middle peasants, lower middle peasants and poor peasants who were dissatisfied with socialism, and fifty-two households of landlords and rich peasants who were not law-abiding or were partially law-abiding, totalling 176 households or 13·35 per cent. of the total. It can therefore be said that the majority of the peasants in the countryside supported socialism. . . .

Some Party members and cadres took a muddled view of the state of the class struggle and failed to uphold socialist principles. . . . For this reason, in conducting socialist education we must overcome rightist thinking on the part of Party members and cadres. . . .

[*From a report on the rural situation by Pan Fu-sheng, 1st Sec. Honan CP organisation. Honan Daily. Chengchow. September 20*

The Workers

One of the areas where " non-antagonistic contradictions " were particularly pressing in the spring of 1957 was industrial relations. The *People's Daily* of May 13 admitted that there had been strikes and petitions in the recent past, though it asserted that they were few in number. It ascribed the troubles to welfare difficulties and adjured officials to pay greater attention to answering complaints and explaining difficulties. A week earlier, Chou Yang, Deputy Director of the Party's Propaganda Department, had announced that workers had the right to strike if officials acted dictatorially, an unprecedented right to be accorded in a Communist state.

The complaints of the trade unionists printed here show why strikes would often be the workers' only means of protest. Chinese trade unions, they make clear, are designed to " sell " state policies to the workers rather than obtain redress for workers' grievances from the Government.

After the anti-rightist campaign started, reports came in of workers dropping their welfare demands in the general interest. But a report included here indicates that some workers, possibly influenced by critics they read or heard about, had voiced more general criticisms. This would account for the Party's September decision to launch an ideological education campaign among them to discuss such questions as living standards before and after 1949 and the correct relationship between discipline and freedom. But forums among workers on a par with those among the intellectuals had probably not become general by the time " blooming " was halted.

During the anti-rightist campaign, some trade unionists were attacked for attempting to " usurp the leadership " of the unions. They were said to have slandered Communist unionists, claiming that they themselves were sticking up for the workers. Some are reported as saying: " The people must kill the Communists," and wanting to set up " Peteofi Club " and " Hyde Park " organisations to attack the Party (NCNA, August 5). Presumably those who came under fire were of the type whose criticisms are included in this section.

As in the case of the peasants, it is difficult to assess the likelihood of workers joining students in riots. Where factory conditions were bad and officials harsh, they probably would have responded to student agitation. But it is very doubtful if, in general, the Party leadership in Peking would have been regarded as hateful as foreign imperialists were in 1919—and that would have been an essential pre-condition of serious, widespread urban riots.

" Crisis " in the trade unions

Not long ago, Li Hsiu-jen, deputy head of the All-China Federation of Trade Unions' General Office, accompanied a responsible comrade of the Central Government on an inspection tour of some areas. . . .

Li Hsiu-jen said that cases of labour trouble that came to his knowledge had one thing in common: trade unions were cast aside. These trade unions showed no concern and gave no support to the proper demands of the masses and even came forward to defend the bureaucracy of the administration and defend irrational resolutions and regulations. That is why some workers in Canton, Changsha, Wuhan, Hsinhsiang and Shihkiachwang dubbed their trade unions "workers' control departments" led by the administration, "tongues of the bureaucracy" and "tails of the administration," etc. . . . Is it not a "crisis" in the trade union work that trade unions are divorced from the masses in such a degree? . . .

When the views of workers clashed with the views of the Party and Government, trade union cadres would be at a loss to know how to handle such contradictions. They said: "We are Party members and, according to Party discipline, must subordinate ourselves to the resolutions of the Party organisations, otherwise we might be labelled 'syndicalists,' 'agitators for independence against the Party' or 'tailists,' etc., and might even be expelled from the Party. On the other hand, we are elected by the workers to speak for the interests of the workers and should subordinate ourselves to the will of the majority of workers, otherwise we would be accused by workers of 'tail of administration' and discarded by the workers." In the face of such contradictions, cadres of this type became double-faced: within the Party they would say that bureaucratic regulations were "incorrect" and should be corrected and that the proper demands of workers should be met. If their views were not adopted, they would tell the masses outside the Party—in order to maintain the identity of Party action—that the bureaucratic regulations were "correct" and should be carried out and that the proper demands of workers could not be met; or else, they would keep silent in the presence of the masses. The upshot was that right and wrong were confused and displeasure was incurred on both sides.

According to Li Hsiu-jen, the so-called "mobile change of shift," that is, a kind of extra shift system based on concentrated work and concentrated rest, was introduced in Canton Harbour last year. Each workman was required to work eight hours, rest eight hours and work again eight hours a day, that is, to work for sixteen hours a day; after working two days he was allowed to take one-day rest. Transport workers, who carried things over 100 catties in weight, were very tired after eight hours' work. The eight-hour rest was very short after allowing time for walking to and from work and taking meals. Shortly after a worker closed his eyes he had to wake up and go to work again. Many workmen got ill from overwork. And those who did not get ill from overwork were so weak that they could not carry many things; thus the wages they got (piece wage) was less than sick leave pay (75 per cent. of basic wage). Because of this, many workmen pretended to be ill, went slow and asked sick leave. 60 per cent. of the workmen did not go to work. Trade union cadres raised no objection to such an erroneous decision of the administration; on the contrary, they helped the administration devise ways and means to compel the workers to go to work (one of the means was to ask the doctors not to issue certificates of illness). Two vice chairmen of the trade union, who had formerly been transport workers, had turned into cadres within the hierarchy and forgotten the hardship of the workers. . . .

[*" On an 8,000-li tour of hurried observation " by Li Feng. People's Daily. May 9*

What is the fundamental cause behind the " crisis " in trade union work?

With great interest we read on May 9 " On an 8,000-li tour of Hurried Observation " by the New China News Agency correspondent Li Feng on his interview with Comrade Li Hsiu-jen, deputy head of the All-China Federation of Trade Unions' General Office. . . .

Is it true that all trade union cadres are, as he said in the article, " following the state line," asking money from the state and adopting a viewpoint of asking favours? From what we know of some trade union cadres of Shanghai, we maintain that only a few and not " all " adopt such a viewpoint.

But the important thing is that the primary level trade union cadres have encountered and are still encountering considerable resistance in the course of following the mass line. This resistance comes from various sides. Under such pretexts and questions as " the higher body has not made arrangements," " no system has been instituted for this," " can you guarantee? " and " who is to decide, you or I? " other bodies do not give the trade unions the minimum support and do not co-operate with the trade unions. Some often blame the trade unions for " making trouble " and " routinism." Some even accuse trade union cadres of " unprincipled compromise " with the masses. They bind the hands and feet of trade union cadres with regulations, systems and habitual administrative means, hindering them from following the mass line to solve the problems of the worker masses. . . .

Once a managing director or Party committee has made a decision, nothing can be done but to leave it as it is even though it is clearly unreasonable. And trade union cadres, even if they do not agree with it, can do nothing but try to persuade the masses to act accordingly. Even if they are called names and scolded, they can only keep silent and show a smiling face; otherwise, they will be accused of " fomenting discord " and " not being determined to carry out the will of the leadership." As to mass supervision, it is out of the question for the trade unions. Even today, when Chairman Mao's report on correct handling of internal contradictions has been widely relayed, if trade unions publish criticisms put forward by the workers against the leadership and present the widespread views of the masses to the management and the Party committees, they are questioned like this: " You are mobilising the masses to open a ' struggle ' meeting and criticise the leadership, aren't you? . . ." Trade union cadres in general . . . dare not make decisions lest they should be accused of " syndicalism," " economism " and " tailism." And no one backs them up against such accusations. . . .

Comrade Li Hsiu-jen had a great disappointment on this 8,000-li inspection tour. He said: " Originally I wanted to collect some instances where trade union cadres ' knocked their heads against the wall ' in their fight for the legitimate interests of the workers. . . ." We thank him for his good intentions and regret that he could not find anything. . . . The following thing happened in the Shanghai Knitting Factory which Comrade Li Hsiu-jen visited during 1956. Mao Hai-ken, former trade union chairman in this factory, always backed up the masses and, shortly after he had revealed some serious problems to Comrade Li Hsiu-jen, he was transferred to the labour wage department. The masses wanted to elect him as trade union chairman, but who were to back them up? . . .

We should solve the problem of how to play a supervisory role, how to support the proper demands of the masses and how to combat bureaucracy, and ensure that trade unions, in carrying out their tasks, are not afraid of any pressure applied by bureaucracy. . . .

[By ten members of the Shanghai Trade Union Council. Daily Worker. Peking. May 21

More trade unionists complain

Last year, owing to a shortage of electric power from Soochow, our factory often added a shift, arousing many objections on the part of the masses who complained: " After working six days we have to work on

Sundays." And the management added the shift without consultations with trade unions. When the trade union did not agree to the extra shift, the Party branch retorted: "Suppose the production task is not fulfilled and the state plans are hindered?" and asked the trade union to persuade the masses to work the extra shift. Once an engine broke down and operations were stopped in order to make repairs; the management wanted the workers to divide their meal hours and work an extra shift. The trade union did not agree and requested instructions from the higher body which also disagreed with the extra shift proposal; but the management itself enforced the extra shift. . . .

Not to agree with the views of Party branches means insubordination to Party leadership; not to agree with the views of the management means interference in management. Thus there is no alternative but to be hand in glove with the Party and management. . . .

[*Chien Pao-chi. Daily Worker. Peking. May 22*

"Distressing contradictions"

I am a new trade union member and was elected an official of the primary level trade union only this year. I earnestly hope to be able to do something for the workers and employees. . . . If trade unions stick to different opinions on certain matters, the majority of Party members (all of them unwilling to join the trade unions) shout: "Trade unions fight for rights and wealth against the administration," "Trade unions agitate for special position" and "Trade unions try to be independent of the management. . . ."

Being a Party member, I must undoubtedly obey Party discipline and resolutions. On the other hand, being elected by the masses as a trade union cadre, I should listen to the voice of the masses, particularly the voice of the majority of the masses. I am required to familiarise myself with their conditions and study their problems. Further, I am required to make known to them certain problems which they do not understand, and to ask their views and opinions. However, the result is that the Party branch, even the general branch of the Party, criticises me for "enlisting the masses to hit at the leadership" and "sowing discord between the masses and leaders." I am told that I should study the problems with the leadership and not with the masses and that to discuss problems with the masses means "becoming a tail of the masses." In a word, they hold that the decisions of the management must be carried out whether they are right or wrong and that trade unions should unconditionally support the management and explain to the masses the "correctness of some unfair measures."

I am regarded as a trouble-making Party member. My views run counter to reality—such is the distressing contradiction in which I find myself. . . .

[*Lo Yu-wen. Daily Worker. Peking. May 22*

*

The reason for reindoctrination of workers

In the struggle against rightist elements, workers and employees not only have drawn a clear line of demarcation between themselves and the enemy, but have also increased in vigilance, enabling them to dispel many muddle-headed conceptions. They have re-examined the erroneous thoughts which they previously had relative to democracy as against centralisation, freedom as against discipline and the individual as against collectivism. Soldiers demobilised for industrial work express solemn regrets for the demands which they previously put forward for high pay, good welfare and housing space. . . .

[*NCNA. Changchun. July 31*

14

RELIGIOUS GROUPS AND NATIONAL MINORITIES

Religious groups

Religion has been a comparatively minor problem for the Communists taking over a country whose cultural tone has been set for 2,000 years by secular Confucianism. Christianity has been a significant opponent of Communism in a European setting; but there are only about three million Chinese Christians, Protestant and Catholic. The Communists first cut their main organisational link with the West by killing or driving out foreign missionaries, against whom they were able to mobilise Chinese xenophobia. Since then, Chinese policy has aimed at making Christians completely loyal to the régime. By 1954, the various Protestant Churches had been organised into a " patriotic " national group.

The Catholics, with their close allegiance to the Vatican, were a more difficult problem. In the autumn of 1955, the Bishop of Shanghai, Kung Pin-mei, and other Shanghai Catholics were arrested as counter-revolutionaries in an attempt to stamp out the last resisters. But when they came to organise a national Catholic Church in July 1957, the Communists clearly found many Catholics still adhering to the Vatican and attacking the régime (and demanding the release of Bishop Kung).

Chinese Moslems (as distinct from minority races like the Uighurs who also profess Mohammedanism) have been treated as a national rather than a religious minority. (Since the rectification campaign they have been awarded their own Ninghsia-Hui Autonomous Region.) This is not specifically a Communist policy, for the Hui, as Chinese Moslems are known, have always been regarded as alien by their fellow Chinese, however unjustly; but it has set the Hui apart so that the spread of the Moslem religion among " true "

Chinese is far less likely. Thus the three and a half million Huis were also a minor problem, though the report included here indicates the tenaciousness with which many have maintained their beliefs.

A majority of Chinese, probably, are to some degree Buddhist. But Buddhism has never been organised as a Church and has never been characterised by fervent evangelising. Popular Buddhist beliefs, the Communists realised, could only be eradicated by decades of education and propaganda, but Buddhism as such presented no real threat to the régime. (The same applies to Taoism.) In fact, the Communists imposed a centralised organisation on the Buddhist priests, the better to control them.

These factors enabled the Communists (after the early persecutions) to adopt a "liberal" attitude of constitutionally guaranteeing religious freedom while preventing evangelising. But as the forum of May 29 indicates, here too theory and practice diverge considerably.

N.B.—The reports on Catholic and Protestant attacks on the régime presented here indicate that these attacks occurred after the anti-rightist campaign had started; but since reports of this kind are unusual, one can regard the criticisms as part of the general reaction to Mao Tse-tung's speech on contradictions.

Religious persecution

PEKING: *Religious leaders*

They thought that there were still cadres and those among the masses who did not treat religious leaders and believers with enough respect, and even discriminated against them. Some of the Christian priests remarked that in the minds of believers there was a sort of oppressiveness; and although they went to church services, on their return home they dared not admit that they were believers. Some of the people and the police interfered with the families of these believers in devious ways; for instance, the children of believers would be called for individual interviews; some school teachers would not allow children to attend Sunday school, telling them: "If you go again, we will expel you." A priest said: "My child goes to a certain middle school; he is good from every point of view but because I am a priest his application to join the Youth League has been repeatedly turned down."

Islamic imams had much to say about inter-marriage between Mohammedans and the Han—one of them said: "In particular a Han Party or Youth League member, before marrying, is obliged to join the Mohammedan religion—but this is clearly anomalous. Consequently, some Mohammedans regard marriage between Han Party or Youth League members and Mohammedans as a mockery. . . ."

A Catholic Sister said: "When we walk in the streets wearing our habit, some people abuse us, shouting 'Running dogs of Imperialism,' want to tear off our hoods, and give us stony stares." Some Catholic Fathers remarked that a believer at the Thirteenth Middle School (by the name of Tai) was the object of discrimination—a certain Youth League member wrote on the blackboard abusing him in all sorts of ways, so that everyone looked down on him.

During the discussion, the religious leaders held that the Religious Affairs Bureau of the Municipal People's Committee and other departments concerned showed insufficient concern for every religion, and did not help enough in solving problems. Some of the Islamic imams said: "The United Front Department of the Communist Party Municipal Committee does not maintain sufficient links with us, and its members rarely bother to meet us. The Bureau of Civic Affairs shows a lack of concern about our living conditions; and very little help has been given in connection with repairs to mosques this year."

Members of the Buddhist religion had similar feelings towards the Bureau of Religious Affairs. . . .

Some of the Catholic Fathers said: "The Government advocated the self-sufficiency of religions; but the question of the Seventh Hospital and the Thirty-ninth Middle School, the estates of which belong to the Church, has remained unsolved since 1950. Are they being rented, or requisitioned, or are they on loan—we can't make out why, up to the present, not a penny has been received in respect of these few hundred houses. . . ."

Some Christian priests had much to say about newspapers publishing a great deal of anti-religious articles, but not publicising religious policies in a favourable light. Some believers voiced views against their own religious leaders, alleging that they had, all along, failed to merge deeply with the masses, and had failed to help the monasteries, temples and churches in a concrete manner to solve their problems. . . .

[*Forums reported in Kuang Ming Daily. May 29*

*

Rebel Moslems in Honan Province

During the period of "big contending and big blooming" last year, upon the occasion of the frantic attacks on the Party by the rightists in various parts of Honan, the rightists hidden in the upper strata of the Hui [Hui: Chinese Moslems] nationality and the Islamic religious circles also became active. They disseminated reactionary views which undermined unity among the nationalities and cast a slur on the nationalities policy of the Party. Some of them even plotted riots and intended to sabotage the unity of the country by creating an independent kingdom. . . . They gave the utmost publicity to such reactionary fallacies as "All the Hui people of the world form one family" and "Religion comes before country. . . ."

These rightists, as they have always done, opposed the socialist system, hated the new society, described today's society as pitch dark, alleged that, while there were "more rich people than poor people" in the days before liberation, there were "more poor people than rich people" in the days after it, stigmatised the socialist system as the "system of starvation," and said that "the more numerous and greater the co-operatives are, the narrower becomes the road before the Hui people." They sabotaged the state's policies and decrees, privately slaughtered draught animals *en masse*, and speculated in edible oils and grains. . . .

They regarded with hostility the cadres and Party and Communist Youth League members of the Hui nationality. They stigmatised the Hui cadres as "tu-shih-man" [*i.e.*, enemies] and "traitors of the Hui people," and described the progressive imams as "men without a religion. . . ."

Pai Ch'ing-chang, during the period of "big contending and big blooming," slandered the Party's nationalities policy everywhere, in an attempt to instigate the Hui people to more riots. Rightists Yuan Ch'ang-hsiu, imam of Ningling hsien, instigated the Hui people to fight the Communist Party, and frantically inflamed them to attack their own hsiang and co-operatives, then to attack hsien and cities, and finally to set up an Islamic state. . . .

[*People's Daily. May 16, 1958*

*

Protestant group makes trouble

The anti-Communist and anti-socialist statements and actions of Kou Hsi-tien and Liu Ya-han, rightist Protestants operating under cover of the cloak of religion, were fully uncovered and criticised at the Kansu Province Protestant Representatives Conference. . . .

At the meeting this time, Kou Hsi-tien still frantically launched attacks on the Party, slandering the Party policy on freedom of religious belief. He also condemned Government cadres for their failure to understand the religious policy, as well as spread the rumour that the religious policy pursued in the province had ended " in a mess." He also rallied members of his small group to a meeting illegally called, and posted big-character newspapers on so-called " appeals from churches in twelve places " to attack cadres and intimidate the People's Government. During the meeting, he had himself illegally elected head of the " executive committee for propagation of faith in the West China section," in a futile attempt to carry out anti-Communist activities through the medium of this organisation, as well as infiltrate the National Self-Administration Association to usurp the powers of the leadership and disintegrate the Self-Administration movement at its roots. . . .

Liu Ya-han, another rightist element uncovered at the meeting, was a Kuomintang member and served as a mechanic in the enemy air force during 1939–49. . . .

At the meeting this time, he viciously attacked the Party, spread anti-Communist and anti-people poison, abused the national flag and picture of the leader, attacked the campaign against counter-revolutionaries, denounced the work of the Procuratorate, defended Fang Cheng-kuang, the counter-revolutionary, spread rumours accusing the Party policy on freedom of religious belief as " unread," undermined the self-administration movement, and denounced patriotic members of the faith.

[*Kansu Daily. Lanchow. February 22, 1958*

*

Defence of the Vatican by Catholic rightists

Catholic representatives' conferences, study meetings, and forums have been called recently in twenty-six provinces, municipalities and autonomous regions throughout the country to undertake the study of socialism and to propagate the resolutions of the Chinese Catholic Representatives Conference called in July last year. . . .

At these meetings, a few rightist elements hiding in the Church launched vicious attacks on the Party and socialism. Fan Hsueh-an, bishop of the Paoting diocese in Hopei Province, frantically claimed that it was " sinful " to expel imperialist elements. He also accused the People's Government of " saying one thing and meaning another," and condemned the worker-peasant alliance as " banding together like wolves." Chang Chen-kuo, acting bishop of the Szeping diocese in Kirin Province, openly advocated non-co-operation with the People's Government, and used the reactionary slogan of " kneeling down to pray, and standing up to fight " to incite Catholics to " fight " the People's Government. Liu Chien, acting bishop of the Sichang diocese in Szechwan Province, openly admitted in a big-character newspaper that he favoured the old society and spurned the new society. Wan Ku-ju, vicar-general of the Loshan diocese in Szechwan Province, openly advocated disturbances, and demanded the dissolution of Communist Party leadership and a going over to capitalism. Wang Keh-chien, priest, in the Hangchow diocese in Chekiang Province, and Sung Kung-chia, Catholic layman in Shanghai, also launched frantic attacks on the socialist system, religious policy and the campaign against counter-revolutionaries. These rightist elements also slavishly defended the Vatican's reactionary political nature.

[*NCNA. Peking. March 14, 1958*

National minorities

According to the census of 1953, there were 35·3 million members of national minorities. While they constituted only 6 per cent. of the population, they occupied (in company with Chinese settlers) some 60 per cent. of the country's area. They included 6·6 million Chuangs in the Kwangsi-Chuang Autonomous Region in the south, 3·7 million Uighurs in the Sinkiang-Uighur Autonomous Region in the north-west, and 1·5 million Mongolians in the Inner Mongolian Autonomous Region in the north.

Many of these minorities have always resented Chinese rule, which has often been brutal and harsh. The Moslem herdsmen of the north-west in particular despise the pork-eating infidel Chinese peasants. The greater efficiency of the Communists in extending Chinese control over these people would obviously tend to exacerbate such tensions. While it is quite likely that the " upper strata " of the minorities are particularly resentful at being deprived of their power as the Communists maintain, the report included here leaves little doubt that nationalist anti-Chinese feelings extend far beyond that limited group.

On the whole, the Communist leaders seemed to have wanted to handle the minorities with kid gloves, while never abandoning their determination to control and communise them. (They did not long adhere to the clause in the 1931 Constitution of the Kiangsi Soviet Republic that said that national minorities had the right to seek their own salvation independent of the Chinese if they so desired.) Communes apart, " socialist reforms " have been introduced among minorities somewhat later than among the Chinese. The Communists have provided a number of minority languages with scripts, encouraged minority cultural activities and granted formal autonomy. But their decision to launch in 1957 a campaign to eliminate " Great Han (Chinese) Chauvinism " (the tendency for Chinese officials contemptuously to dictate to the minorities), indicated that minorities had been enjoying no real autonomy.

Bearing in mind Chinese aims, and the fact that few trustworthy officials from the minority races had been trained, it is not surprising that " Great Han Chauvinism " was widespread. That would certainly seem to be the implication of the kind of demands voiced by the minorities during the rectification period. But pleas for real autonomy went far beyond what the Chinese were prepared to contemplate, and in 1958 " Local Nationalism " replaced " Great Han Chauvinism " as the major sin in the minority areas.

Tibet is a special case. By modern standards of self-determination she should be an independent country. Tibet was left out of the rectification campaign due to its status as an unassimilated minority area. However, Mao made a concession to Tibetan stubbornness in his speech on contradictions by postponing " democratic " reforms at least until 1962. This concession proved insufficient to appease Tibetan nationalism and it did not apply to East Tibet, the home of the warlike Khambas. How the revolt of the latter spread throughout Tibet is too well known to need description here.

Anti-Chinese feelings among the minorities

In the past year or two, and especially since our Party decided to launch a rectification campaign and carry out the policy of "blooming and contending," a considerable amount of reactionary or extremely erroneous views and activity has been brought to light among small sections of the upper strata of the national minorities. Of these views and activities the main ones are:

(1) *Separatist ideas and activities*—The most noticeable examples are those who, claiming that a nationality has the right of self-determination, want to establish a union of republics or autonomous republics. A few of these openly want independence, declaring that "we want independence even if that means we have to forgo socialism" and that "if Han settlers continue to come, we will close the borders!" Meanwhile, separatist or secessionist activities have been brisk among the Mongols, principally among a small number of intellectuals and students who belong to families of feudal princes, aristocrats or high officials of the former puppet Mongolian Government, or who are corrupted by bourgeois ideas. They have tried to organise their own party and government. A small number of students even organised themselves in preparation for a flight to some foreign country where they might continue to engage in activities aimed at dividing the motherland. Some students and intellectuals of the Korean nationality, too, would not recognise China as their motherland. . . .

(2) *Repudiation of Central Government and Party leadership and effort to exclude Han cadres under the excuse of autonomous rights and "nationalisation"*—Some cadres of the local nationalities in Sinkiang have vociferously expressed their disapproval of Han cadres and openly told them to "go home." They said: "This will be genuinely an autonomous region only if the Han cadres are gone. So long as they remain here there will be no real autonomy." Huang Hsien-fan, a rightist of the Chuang nationality, says: "So long as Han cadres remain (in autonomous areas), the national minorities will not be able to exercise their powers. All Han cadres should be evacuated from national minority areas." These rightists especially object to the occupying of leadership posts by Han cadres inside and outside the Party in the autonomous areas.

(3) *Opposition to the coming of Han peasants and workers to national minority areas*—In order to attain the object of exclusion of Han people some people in Sinkiang urge mechanisation of agriculture at full speed. Some Mongols advocate a partitioning into a " purely Mongolian area " and a " purely Han area," so as to separate the Mongolian nationality from other nationalities, even if the Mongols have to do without the Paotow steel complex, the modern industries and the railroad. There are also those who advocate the setting up of industrial and mining enterprises by single nationalities. There are also those who oppose the learning of the Han language, both spoken and written, and the language of other nationalities. They also oppose cultural exchanges between different nationalities.

(4) *Opposition to socialist transformation*—Rightists among the national minorities allege that the co-operative movement has been bungled and that the co-ops. are not superior in any way, that the system of unified purchase and sale is ruinous and has brought misery to the peasants, and that the movement for the suppression of counter-revolutionaries was also bungled, and that it victimised all the good men. These views are identical with those held by the rightists of the Han nationality. All the anti-socialist arguments of the rightists of the Han nationality are echoed by the rightists of the national minorities.

(5) *Hatred for and opposition to the Party*—The rightists say that " Party members are a privileged class," and that " Party leadership is rule by Great Han nationalism," and that " the national minorities are not yet liberated and are waiting for another liberation," and that " the national minorities could have liberated themselves and built socialism even without Party leadership." Rightists Wang T'ien-shi, Ou Pai-ch'uan, P'eng Po, Pu Lin, Ma Sung-t'ing and others all have organised their own groups for the purpose of opposing Party leadership. They hate especially the Party and Youth League members of their own nationalities, calling these Party and Youth League members traitors, black sheep, sycophants, and degenerates and scapegraces, and praising on the other hand the anti-Party elements as national heroes. Party leaders of the national minorities are attacked with particular vigour. Ma Sung-t'ing, a Hui rightist, declares that none of the Hui Communists know anything about their own nationality, that they have all eaten pork, and that they make the Hui girls marry the Han people. . . .

As most of these views are expressed under the banner of the nationalities and appear to support the interests of these nationalities, they have succeeded in capturing the imagination of some people and hoodwinking them. . . . Therefore, even though these views are held by a handful of men of the national minorities, we must not minimise their dangerous possibilities. These views must be seriously and resolutely criticised.

First, the rightists of the national minorities have been declaring loudly that present conditions are worse than the past and that the Communist Party is not so good as the Kuomintang. . . .

Secondly, concerning separatism or secessionism, that is, the agitation for republics and a federation of republics. The idea exists principally among young non-Party intellectuals of the Mongolian, Korean, Hui, Uighur and other nationalities. But it exists in more serious proportions in a few national minorities where it is entertained not only by those outside the Party, but also by some within the Party, and not only by Party members in general but also by some high-ranking cadres. They also seriously influenced a considerable part of the Party and non-Party cadres with the idea. . . .

[*Liu Ko-p'ing, Chairman of the Nationalities Committee, NPC. People's Daily. January 11, 1958*

REACTION

" You may ban the expression of wrong ideas, but the ideas will still be there."—*Mao Tse-tung: On the correct handling of contradictions among the people.*

15

THE ANTI-RIGHTIST CAMPAIGN

THERE is no way of knowing when the Communist Party leadership decided to halt the flood of criticisms directed against the régime. As early as May 25, only a week after Peking University students had taken "blooming and contending" into their own hands, Mao Tse-tung was telling delegates to the Youth League Congress that "all words and actions that deviate from socialism are completely mistaken." On the same day, the Standing Committee of the National People's Congress (the Chinese Parliament) postponed the annual congress session from June 3 to June 20. Very possibly, the Chinese leaders felt that in the prevailing atmosphere, the congress might turn out to be an embarrassingly official platform for denunciations of their policies. A breathing-space would enable them to assess the situation and decide what line to adopt. (The congress was again postponed, on June 19, to June 26.)

A third event to occur on that same day turned out to be perhaps the most important. At a forum held by the Kuomintang Revolutionary Committee, Lu Yu-wen, the Assistant to the Secretary-General of the State Council, spoke up in defence of the Communist Party. It was wrong, he said, to say that the Communist Party should not refute incorrect criticisms. He went on to reject some on their behalf. For instance, he said that in cases where non-Communists did not exercise power commensurate with their nominal position—a point raised frequently at the forums of leading non-Communists—the reason was simply that they were incompetent.

The sequel occurred on June 6. Lu Yu-wen told a State Council forum that as a result of his May 25 speech he had received an anonymous threatening letter. It described him as a "shameless rascal" and in effect accused him of being the kind of "activist" —much criticised during "blooming and contending"—who curried favour with the Communist Party by flattery and betrayal of his fellow non-Communists. It warned: "Turn back quickly, or the people will not forgive you."

Lu Yu-wen's story is a plausible one though the letter may have been "planted" to give the Communist Party a justification for turning on its critics. At any rate, on June 8, the *People's Daily* in its first comment on the rectification campaign for three weeks denounced the letter in an editorial prosaically titled: "What is this for?" The episode showed that class struggle had not died down, it averred; and, referring back to a speech by Mme. Ho Hsiang-ning,[1] it claimed that certain "rightists" in the society longed for a Western-type political and economic system and wished to do away with the Communist Party and socialism. For any Chinese intellectual with his experience of the previous eight years the message was clear. The tide had turned; once more the Communist Party would be administering not receiving criticism. That same day, Ch'u An-p'ing tendered his resignation as editor of the *Kuang Ming Daily*.

During the next few days, a series of *People's Daily* editorials pressed the counter-attack and gave the first indications of specific criteria critics should have borne in mind. Reports of forums continued to fill the Press, but instead of attacking the Party all speakers began to attack the rightists.[2] In an attempt to control this trend the *People's Daily* editorial of June 12 adjured Party officials still to accept "correct criticisms." Understandably, few seemed to want to test the definition of "correct."

However, a definition was soon forthcoming. On June 18, the NCNA released the text, admitted to be amended, of Mao's February 27 speech, five days after an enterprising American journalist had cabled home extracts that were exciting Polish Communists. Perhaps the Warsaw "leak" forced the hand of the Chinese; perhaps Mao Tse-tung felt it necessary to publicise an amended version as a result of the events of the previous six weeks. At any rate, the published version contained six criteria for assessing correct criticism—the most important were support for Communist Party

1 See the section on leading non-Communists, p. 54.

2 Part Two of this book makes it clear, however, that rightist activities, in particular student riots, occurred after June 8 although not reported at the time.

leadership and socialism—which would probably have kept many critics quiet if they had been in the original text. (An even more convincing reason for believing the six criteria to be part of the admitted " additions " was discussed in the prelude of this book. It is worth adding that a European of the editor's acquaintance was told by a disillusioned Chinese intellectual when visiting Peking that the criteria were not in the tape-recorded version of the original speech.) The text of the speech also revealed the effect of the Hungarian revolt on Chinese intellectuals and the admission that collectivisation had not been proceeding smoothly. The first section was an elaboration of the theory of contradictions discussed by the *People's Daily* in April; it did not apparently contain any modifications. In some of the other sections, however, Mao Tse-tung seemed to be arguing with critics of the previous weeks. It is important to note, too, that Mao suggested a commission for rectifying injustices in substantially the same terms as earned Lo Lung-chi violent denunciation as a rightist.

Perhaps Lo's critics were too busy criticising him to notice. Members of the Democratic League held session after session at which they denounced him and Chang Po-chun and dissociated the League from the activities of these two deputy chairmen. Gradually the accusation emerged that they had led a nation-wide clique to overthrow the Party. Neither of the two men publicly admitted this to be true (though they were prepared to say they had worked together within the League). Lo in fact denied it. But the campaign against them was pushed relentlessly forward until finally in January 1958, Mme. Shih Liang (who had clashed with Lo Lung-chi at a forum as early as May 10) claimed that they had confessed their crimes and that their clique had been destroyed. The following month Chang and Lo lost their ministerial posts at the National People's Congress.[3]

Endless sessions of denunciation of the kind to which Chang Po-chun and Lo Lung-chi were subjected occurred everywhere that people had been unwise enough to pour out their grievances. The sessions were held normally by the rightist critic's associates, the

[3] A total of fifty-four congress delegates were recalled for rightist activities. Chang Nai-ch'i, Minister of Food, also lost his governmental post.

Communist Party being content to direct from the background with editorials in the *People's Daily*—except, of course, where the rightist was in fact a member of the Party. The other prong of this anti-rightist campaign was a vigorous programme of political education for all, designed to eradicate doubts and erroneous thoughts that the rightists might have inspired.

Perhaps the most interesting aspect of the campaign was the very determined treatment of the students. A thousand senior Party officials were transferred to work in universities and middle schools, 200 being assigned to top posts such as president or vice-president. Regulations were passed to ensure that no graduate would get a job unless he were politically reliable. And as the 1957–58 academic year started, the New China News Agency reported from Wuhan that Wang Chien-kuo, Chang Yu-wen and Yang Huan-yao had been sentenced to death for leading the riot at the Hanyang First Middle School and been executed in front of 10,000 people. That the only announced executions resulting from the events of May and June were of student leaders underlines the seriousness of the student situation then. They were presumably a warning to any future student rioters.

This strong reaction to student activities supports the argument that they, and not the existence of a rightist "plot," were the reason behind the decision to halt criticism. Indeed, the plot was probably thought up to explain away this embarrassing phenomenon; it would have been too damaging to admit that it was a spontaneous outburst. No real evidence for the plot was ever produced; and it was certainly odd, if there was a plot, that Lo Lung-chi, one of its supposed leaders, should be allowed out of the country as a member of an official delegation to Ceylon in the second week of June after the anti-rightist campaign had started.

Lo and Chang Po-chun seem to have wanted to make sure that if the democratic parties were to get more power they personally would benefit. But the speeches they made in March after hearing Mao on contradictions indicates that they were well aware there was to be no fundamental change in the state system, whatever others may have thought. Chang's "two chamber" proposal, which significantly was regarded as quite harmless when first advanced, was certainly an attempt to increase the role of the democratic parties; but it did not in any apparent way conflict with the Communist Party's official policy which was to do just that.

Presumably Chang and Lo were selected as the major scapegoats because of their prominence among the non-Communists who were voicing criticisms and their obvious eagerness to grasp the little extra power the Party was offering them. If they *had* been guilty, trial and at least imprisonment should have been their fate. No complete statistics of the number of rightists exist but some idea of the numbers involved was given when some 26,000 had their rightist " label " removed as a result of the amnesty granted on the occasion of the régime's 10th anniversary in October 1959. If Chang and Lo in fact controlled so large an anti-Communist organisation —and most provincial " cliques " were linked with their name—they have indeed got off lightly. They have been restored to most of their leading positions in their democratic parties and took part in the session of the People's Political Consultative Conference which discussed the question of a successor to Mao Tse-tung in April 1959.

A much harder fate was meted out to senior Communists who sympathised with the rightists or were " soft " on counter-revolutionaries. In late 1957 and early 1958 a number of provincial officials, including the Governor of Chekiang Province, the Governor of Chinghai Province and a Deputy Governor of Anhwei Province, and a number of judicial officials, including a Deputy Minister of Supervision, were dismissed and expelled from the Party as rightists. Clearly the hundred flowers episode caused heart-searching among more idealistic Communists. Apart from extracts from Mao's speech, this section includes Chou En-lai's answers to the rightists (p. 278) and documents to illustrate the tone of the anti-rightist campaign (p. 284).

MAO TSE-TUNG

ON THE CORRECT HANDLING OF CONTRADICTIONS AMONG THE PEOPLE

(1) *Two different types of contradictions*—Never has our country been as united as it is today. The victories of the bourgeois-democratic

revolution and the socialist revolution, coupled with our achievements in socialist construction, have rapidly changed the face of old China. Now we see before us an even brighter future. The days of national disunity and turmoil which the people detested have gone for ever. Led by the working class and the Communist Party, and united as one, our six hundred million people are engaged in the great work of building socialism. Unification of the country, unity of the people and unity among our various nationalities—these are the basic guarantees for the sure triumph of our cause. However, this does not mean that there are no longer any contradictions in our society. It would be naïve to imagine that there are no more contradictions. To do so would be to fly in the face of objective reality. We are confronted by two types of social contradictions—contradictions between ourselves and the enemy and contradictions among the people. These two types of contradictions are totally different in nature.

If we are to have a correct understanding of these two different types of contradictions, we must, first of all, make clear what is meant by " the people " and what is meant by " the enemy."

The term " the people " has different meanings in different countries, and in different historical periods in each country. . . . At this stage of building socialism, all classes, strata and social groups which approve, support and work for the cause of socialist construction belong to the category of the people, while those social forces and groups which resist the socialist revolution, and are hostile to and try to wreck socialist construction, are enemies of the people. . . .

In the conditions existing in China today, what we call contradictions among the people include the following: contradictions within the working class, contradictions within the peasantry, contradictions within the intelligentsia, contradictions between the working class and the peasantry, contradictions between the working class and peasantry on the one hand and the intelligentsia on the other, contradictions between the working class and other sections of the working people on the one hand and the national bourgeoisie on the other, contradictions within the national bourgeoisie, and so forth. Our people's government is a government that truly represents the interests of the people and serves the people, yet certain contradictions do exist between the Government and the masses. These include contradictions between the interests of the state, collective interests and individual interests; between democracy and centralism; between those in positions of leadership and the led, and contradictions arising from the bureaucratic practices of certain state functionaries in their relations with the masses. All these are contradictions among the people. Generally speaking, underlying the contradictions among the people is the basic identity of the interests of the people. . . .

Ours is a people's democratic dictatorship, led by the working class and based on the worker-peasant alliance. What is this dictatorship for? Its first function is to suppress the reactionary classes and elements and those exploiters in the country who range themselves against the socialist revolution, to suppress all those who try to wreck our socialist construction; that is to say, to solve the contradictions between ourselves and the enemy within the country. . . .

The second function of this dictatorship is to protect our country from subversive activities and possible aggression by the external enemy. . . .

Who is to exercise this dictatorship? Naturally it must be the working class and the entire people led by it. Dictatorship does not apply in the ranks of the people. . . . What applies among the people is democratic centralism . . . democracy operates within the ranks of the people, while the working class, uniting with all those enjoying civil rights, the peasantry in the first place, enforces dictatorship over the reactionary classes and elements and all those who resist socialist transformation and oppose socialist construction. By civil rights, we mean, politically, freedom and democratic rights.

But this freedom is freedom with leadership and this democracy is democracy under centralised guidance, not anarchy. Anarchy does not conform to the interests or wishes of the people.

Certain people in our country were delighted when the Hungarian events took place. They hoped that something similar would happen in China, that thousands upon thousands of people would demonstrate in the streets against the People's Government. Such hopes ran counter to the interests of the masses and therefore could not possibly get their support. In Hungary, a section of the people, deceived by domestic and foreign counter-revolutionaries, made the mistake of resorting to acts of violence against the People's Government, with the result that both the state and the people suffered for it. The damage done to the country's economy in a few weeks of rioting will take a long time to repair. There were other people in our country who took a wavering attitude towards the Hungarian events because they were ignorant about the actual world situation. They felt that there was too little freedom under our people's democracy and that there was more freedom under

Western parliamentary democracy. They ask for the adoption of the two-party system of the West, where one party is in office and the other out of office. But this so-called two-party system is nothing but a means of maintaining the dictatorship of the bourgeoisie; under no circumstances can it safeguard the freedom of the working people. . . .

While we stand for freedom with leadership and democracy under centralised guidance, in no sense do we mean that coercive measures should be taken to settle ideological matters and questions involving the distinction between right and wrong among the people. . . . We cannot abolish religion by administrative orders; nor can we force people not to believe in it. We cannot compel people to give up idealism any more than we can force them to believe in Marxism. In settling matters of an ideological nature or controversial issues among the people, we can only use democratic methods, methods of discussion, of criticism, of persuasion and education, not coercive, high-handed methods. . . .

In 1942 we worked out the formula "unity-criticism-unity" to describe this democratic method of resolving contradictions among the people. To elaborate, this means to start off with a desire for unity and resolve contradictions through criticism or struggle so as to achieve a new unity on a new basis. . . . The essential thing is to start with a desire for unity. Without this subjective desire for unity, once the struggle starts it is liable to get out of hand. Wouldn't this then be the same as "ruthless struggle and merciless blows"? . . . Now our task is to continue to extend and make still better use of this method throughout the ranks of the people; we want all our factories, co-operatives, business establishments, schools, government offices, public bodies, in a word, all the six hundred million of our people, to use it in resolving contradictions among themselves.

Under ordinary circumstances, contradictions among the people are not antagonistic. But if they are not dealt with properly, or if we relax vigilance and lower our guard, antagonism may arise. . . .

Quite a few people fail to make a clear distinction between these two different types of contradictions—those between ourselves and the enemy and those among the people—and are prone to confuse the two. It must be admitted that it is sometimes easy to confuse them. We had instances of such confusion in our past work. In the suppression of counter-revolution, good people were sometimes mistaken for bad. Such things have happened before, and still happen today. We have been able to keep our mistakes within bounds because it has been our policy to draw a sharp line between our own people and our enemies and where mistakes have been made, to take suitable measures of rehabilitation. . . .

This is how things stand today: The turbulent class struggles waged by the masses on a large scale characteristic of the revolutionary periods have, in the main, concluded, but class struggle is not entirely over. While the broad masses of the people welcome the new system, they are not yet quite accustomed to it. Government workers are not sufficiently experienced, and should continue to examine and explore ways of dealing with questions relating to specific policies. . . .

(2) *The suppression of counter-revolution*—The question of suppressing counter-revolutionaries is a question of the struggle of opposites in the contradiction between ourselves and the enemy. . . .

If we want correctly to evaluate the results of our efforts to suppress counter-revolution here, let us see what effect the Hungarian events had in our country. These events caused some of our intellectuals to lose their balance a bit but there were no squalls in our country. Why? One reason, it must be said, was that we had succeeded in suppressing counter-revolution quite thoroughly. . . .

After liberation, we rooted out a number of counter-revolutionaries. Some were sentenced to death because they had committed serious crimes. This was absolutely necessary; it was the demand of the people; it was done to free the masses from long years of oppression by counter-revolutionaries and all kinds of local tyrants; in other words, to set free the productive forces. If we had not done so, the masses would not have been able to lift their heads.

Since 1956, however, there has been a radical change in the situation. Taking the country as a whole, the main force of counter-revolution has been rooted out. . . .

Steps have been or are being taken to correct mistakes which have already been discovered in the work of suppressing counter-revolutionaries. Those not yet discovered will be corrected as soon as they come to light. Decisions on exoneration and rehabilitation should receive the same measure of publicity as the original mistaken decisions. I propose that a comprehensive review of the work of suppressing counter-revolution be made this year or next to sum up experience, foster a spirit of righteousness and combat unhealthy tendencies. Nationally, this task should be handled by the Standing Committee of the National People's Congress and the Standing Committee of the People's Political Consultative Conference; and locally, by the provincial and municipal people's councils and committees of the People's Political Consultative Conference. In this review, we must help and not pour cold water on the large numbers of functionaries and activists who took part in the work. . . .

The present situation with regard to counter-revolutionaries can be stated in these words: There still are counter-revolutionaries, but not many. . . .

[*NCNA. June 18*

From the Warsaw version

The first section was devoted to the problem of conflict within a Communist society. It includes the following excerpts:

" These problems are new in Marxism-Leninism. Marx and Engels did not know about these problems for obvious reasons. Lenin mentioned them but did not enlarge upon them because during his lifetime, as a result of foreign intervention, it was difficult to speak about internal problems only.

" As for Stalin, his opinions can be considered only negatively. The experience of the Soviet Union in this respect shows that Stalin made the mistake of substituting internal differences for external antagonism, which resulted in a rule of terror and the liquidation of thousands of Communists.

" In dealing with enemies it is necessary to use force. We in China also have used force to deal with enemies of the people. The total number of those who were liquidated by our security forces numbers 800,000. This is the figure up to 1954.

" Since then we are no longer using methods of terror. Instead we have substituted persuasion and education. If one persists in using the methods of terror in solving internal antagonisms, it may lead to transformation of these antagonisms into antagonisms of the nation-enemy type, as happened in Hungary.

" But the method of persuasion must go together with an analysis of the bad side of the problem, with the making of suggestions that take root in the mistakes committed. This is the old method of meetings and discussions. Many people laugh at us because we have too many meetings. But this old and tried custom of allowing everyone to have his say has frequently given good results and is the most democratic procedure.

" The internal differences are not and must not be antagonistic even if they are the antagonisms between the proletariat and the bourgeoisie. If we stand on the platform of national unity, the solution of these differences must be based on criticism designed to strengthen that unity. . . ."

[*Sidney Gruson. New York Times. June 13*

(3) *Agricultural co-operation*—Who are the staunch supporters of the co-operatives? They are the overwhelming majority of the poor peasants and lower middle peasants. These together account for more than 70 per cent. of the rural population. Most of the rest also cherish hopes for the future of the co-operatives. Only a very small minority are really dissatisfied. But quite a number of persons have failed to analyse this situation. They have not made a comprehensive study of the achievements and shortcomings of the co-operatives and the causes of these shortcomings; they take part of the picture for the whole. And so, among some people a miniature typhoon has whirled up around what they call the co-operatives having no superior qualities.

How long will it take to consolidate the co-operatives and end these arguments about their not having any superior qualities? Judging from the actual experience of many co-operatives, this will probably take five years or a bit longer. . . .

(4) *The question of industrialists and business men*—The year 1956 saw the transformation of privately owned industrial and commercial enterprises into joint state-private enterprises as well as the organisation of co-operatives in agriculture and handicrafts as part of the transformation of our social system. The speed and smoothness with which this was carried out are closely related to the fact that we treated the contradiction between the working class and the national bourgeoisie as a contradiction among the people. Has this class contradiction been resolved completely? No, not yet. A considerable period of time is still required to do so. However, some people say that the capitalists have been so remoulded that they are now not much different from the workers, and that further remoulding is unnecessary. Others go so far as to say that the capitalists are even a bit better than the workers. Still others ask, if remoulding is necessary, why doesn't the working class undergo remoulding? Are these opinions correct? Of course not. . . .

I myself had all sorts of non-Marxist ideas before. It was only later that I embraced Marxism. I learned a little Marxism from books and so made an initial remoulding of my ideas, but it was mainly through taking part in the class struggle over the years that I came to be remoulded. And I must continue to study if I am to make further progress, otherwise I shall lag behind. Can the capitalists be so clever as to need no more remoulding? . . .

(5) *The question of intellectuals*—Most of our intellectuals have made marked progress during the past seven years. They express themselves in favour of the socialist system. Many of them are diligently studying Marxism, and some have become Communists. Their number, though small, is growing steadily. There are, of course, still some intellectuals who are sceptical of socialism or who do not approve of it, but they are in a minority. . . .

Many of our comrades are not good at getting along with intellectuals. They are stiff with them, lack respect for their work, and interfere in scientific and cultural matters in a way that is uncalled for. We must do away with all such shortcomings.

Our intellectuals have made some progress, but they should not be complacent. . . .

There has been a falling off recently in ideological and political work among students and intellectuals, and some unhealthy tendencies have appeared. Some people apparently think that there is no longer any need to concern themselves about politics, the future of their motherland and the ideals of mankind. It seems as if Marxism that was once all the rage is not so much in fashion now. This being the case, we must improve our ideological and political work. . . . Ideological remoulding in the past was necessary and has yielded positive results. But it was carried on in a somewhat rough and ready way and the feelings of some people were hurt—this was not good. We must avoid such shortcomings in future. . . .

(7) *Overall planning, all-round consideration and proper arrangements*—In drawing up plans, handling affairs or thinking over problems, we must proceed from the fact that China has a population of six hundred million people. This must never be forgotten.

Now, why should we make a point of this? Could it be that there are people who still do not know that we have a population of six hundred million? Of course, everyone knows this, but in actual practice some are apt to forget it and act as if they thought that the fewer people and the smaller their world the better. . . .

We have this large population. It is a good thing, but of course it also has its difficulties. Construction is going ahead vigorously on all fronts; we have achieved much, but in the present transitional period of tremendous social change we are still beset by many difficult problems. . . . No matter whether it is the question of food, natural calamities, employment, education, the intellectuals, the united front of all patriotic forces, the national minorities, or any other question—we must always proceed from the standpoint of overall planning and all-round consideration for the whole people; we must make whatever arrangements are suitable and possible at the particular time and place and after consultation with all those concerned. On no account should we throw matters out of the back door, go around grumbling that there are too many people, that people are backward, and that things are troublesome and hard to handle. . . .

[*NCNA. June 18*

From the Warsaw version

The third part of the speech considers the population problem. According to official Chinese statements made earlier this year the annual population increase is between 13,000,000 and 15,000,000.

Mr. Mao said that the number of births, now 30,000,000 a year, was a " sign of great progress made in medical service and the general rise in living standards, especially in the countryside and of the faith people have in the future."

" But this figure must also be of great concern to us all," he said, continuing.

" I will quote two other figures. The increase in grain harvest for the last two years has been 10,000,000 tons a year. This is barely sufficient to cover the needs of our growing population.

" The second figure concerns the problem of education. It is estimated that at present 40 per cent. of our youth have not been placed in primary schools. Steps must therefore be taken to keep our population for a long time at stable level, say, of 600,000,000. A wide campaign of explanation and proper help must be undertaken to achieve this aim. . . ."

[*Sidney Gruson. New York Times. June 13*

(8) *On " letting a hundred flowers blossom," and " letting a hundred schools of thought contend," and " long-term co-existence and mutual supervision "*—The policy of letting a hundred flowers blossom and a hundred schools of thought contend is designed to promote the flourishing of the arts and the progress of science; it is designed to enable a

socialist culture to thrive in our land. . . . Questions of right and wrong in the arts and sciences should be settled through free discussion in artistic and scientific circles and in the course of practical work in the arts and sciences. They should not be settled in summary fashion. A period of trial is often needed to determine whether something is right or wrong. In the past, new and correct things often failed at the outset to win recognition from the majority of people and had to develop by twists and turns in struggle. Correct and good things have often at first been looked upon not as fragrant flowers but as poisonous weeds. Copernicus' theory of the solar system and Darwin's theory of evolution were once dismissed as erroneous and had to win through over bitter opposition. Chinese history offers many similar examples. In socialist society, conditions for the growth of new things are radically different from and far superior to those in the old society. Nevertheless, it still often happens that new, rising forces are held back and reasonable suggestions smothered. . . .

People may ask: Since Marxism is accepted by the majority of the people in our country as the guiding ideology, can it be criticised? Certainly it can. As a scientific truth, Marxism fears no criticism. . . .

What should our policy be towards non-Marxist ideas? As far as unmistakable counter-revolutionaries and wreckers of the socialist cause are concerned, the matter is easy: we simply deprive them of their freedom of speech. But it is quite a different matter when we are faced with incorrect ideas among the people. Will it do to ban such ideas and give them no opportunity to express themselves? Certainly not. It is not only futile but very harmful to use crude and summary methods to deal with ideological questions among the people, with questions relating to the spiritual life of man. You may ban the expression of wrong ideas, but the ideas will still be there. . . .

There can be no doubt that we should criticise all kinds of wrong ideas. . . . But such criticism should not be doctrinaire. . . . We must learn together with the masses of the people how to make this careful distinction, and use the correct methods to fight poisonous weeds. . . .

In the political life of our country, how are our people to determine what is right and what is wrong in our words and actions? Basing ourselves on the principles of our Constitution, the will of the overwhelming majority of our people and the political programmes jointly proclaimed on various occasions by our political parties and groups, we believe that, broadly speaking, words and actions can be judged right if they:

(1) Help to unite the people of our various nationalities, and do not divide them;

(2) Are beneficial, not harmful, to socialist transformation and socialist construction;

(3) Help to consolidate, not undermine or weaken, the people's democratic dictatorship;

(4) Help to consolidate, not undermine or weaken, democratic centralism;

(5) Tend to strengthen, not to cast off or weaken, the leadership of the Communist Party;

(6) Are beneficial, not harmful, to international socialist solidarity and the solidarity of the peace-loving peoples of the world.

Of these six criteria, the most important are the socialist path and the leadership of the Party. These criteria are put forward in order to foster, and not hinder, the free discussion of various questions among the people. . . .

The slogan "long-term coexistence and mutual supervision" is also a product of specific historical conditions in our country. . . .

Why should the democratic parties of the bourgeoisie and petty bourgeoisie be allowed to exist side by side with the party of the working class over a long period of time? Because we have no reason not to adopt the policy of long-term coexistence with all other democratic parties which are truly devoted to the task of uniting the people for the cause of socialism and which enjoy the trust of the people. . . .

Why should the other democratic parties be allowed to exercise supervision over the Communist Party? This is because for a party as much as for an individual there is great need to hear opinions different from its own. . . .

[*NCNA. June 18*

From the Warsaw version

"The opinions against the policy of a hundred flowers are the result of a fear of criticism, fear of losing the monopolistic position. They are an example of dogmatism. Marx never said that he should not be criticised. To those who do not follow that teaching of Marx, I would address an old saying: 'He who does not allow himself to be criticised during his life will be criticised after his death.' . . ."

"There need be no fear that the policy of a hundred flowers will yield poisoned fruit. Sometimes it is necessary even to have this poisoned fruit to know what it is that we are fighting against. For this reason, too, it has been decided to publish the full works of Chiang Kai-shek and even a volume of some of the Voice of America broadcasts. It is not enough to attack reactionaries. We must know exactly what the reactionaries want and what they represent. . . ."

[*Sidney Gruson. New York Times. June 13*

(9) *Concerning disturbances created by small numbers of people*—In 1956, small numbers of workers and students in certain places went on strike. The immediate cause of these disturbances was the failure to satisfy certain of their demands for material benefits, of which some should and could be met, while others were out of place or excessive and therefore could not be met for the time being. But a more important cause was bureaucracy on the part of those in positions of leadership. In some cases responsibility for such bureaucratic mistakes should be placed on the higher authorities, and those at lower levels should not be made to bear all the blame. Another cause for these disturbances was that the ideological and political educational work done among the workers and students was inadequate. In the same year, members of a small number of agricultural co-operatives also created disturbances, and the main causes were also bureaucracy on the part of the leadership and lack of educational work among the masses.

It should be admitted that all too often some people are prone to concentrate on immediate, partial and personal interests, they do not understand or do not sufficiently understand long-range, nation-wide and collective interests. Because of their lack of experience in political and social life, quite a number of young people can't make a proper comparison between the old and new China. . . .

We do not approve of disturbances, because contradictions among the people can be resolved in accordance with the formula "unity-criticism-unity," while disturbances inevitably cause losses and are detrimental to the advance of socialism. . . .

(1) In order to get rid of the root cause of disturbances, we must stamp out bureaucracy, greatly improve ideological and political education, and deal with all contradictions in a proper way. If this is done, there won't usually be any disturbances.

(2) If disturbances should occur as a result of bad work on our part, then we should guide those involved in such disturbances on to the correct path, make use of these disturbances as a special means of

improving our work and educating the cadres and the masses, and work out solutions to those questions which have been neglected in the past. In handling any disturbances, we should work painstakingly, and should not use over-simplified methods, nor declare the matter closed before it is thoroughly settled. The guiding spirits in disturbances should not be removed from their jobs or expelled without good reason, except for those who have committed criminal offences or active counter-revolutionaries who should be dealt with according to law. In a big country like ours, it is nothing to get alarmed about if small numbers of people should create disturbances; rather we should turn such things to advantage to help us get rid of bureaucracy. . . .

[*NCNA. June 18*

From the Warsaw version

"The internal antagonisms should be dealt with as soon as they appear. But what to do if this is hampered by bureaucracy, which in turn leads to demonstrations and strikes? Such incidents should be considered as warning signals to sectors of the administration where bureaucracy has made its nest. . . .

"Of course big general strikes cannot be considered in the same way because they are not fought to rectify mistakes or satisfy rightful grievances but are directed against the régime itself. . . .

"Another aspect of this situation is the question of pay. We do not have at present enough funds to increase the pay even for those who rightly claim more for their work. It is known that the wages given to three workers must suffice for five persons at least. So what can be done? The best solution seems to divide the work so that everyone gets something, both in the way of work and pay. . . ."

[*Sidney Gruson. New York Times. June 13*

THE PARTY'S CASE

Justification of the anti-rightist campaign

Not that the bourgeois rightists who made mistakes had received no warning beforehand. . . . Even in Chairman Mao's speech it is expressly stated that the contradictions between the working class and the bourgeoisie are originally antagonistic contradictions and if the bourgeoisie do not accept the policy of the working class, will still be turned into contradictions between the enemy and ourselves, that we must reject bourgeois democracy and anarchism and must adhere to the democracy of the proletariat and the working people and to democracy under centralised guidance, that it is entirely erroneous to deny the great achievements in the suppression of counter-revolution and entirely erroneous to deny the victory of agricultural co-operation and the improvement of the living standard of the peasants, that bourgeois elements still have a dual character and need continual reform and intensified Marxist political education, and that erroneous views must be criticised while Marxism must develop in the struggle against anti-Marxist thoughts. . . . Some ask: why does the Party, which invites others to rectify its working style, now rectify others? True, the Party will continue to ask the broad masses of the people to help its rectification campaign and there is absolutely no doubt that this must be and can be carried to the end. But can it be said that the reactionary words and deeds of anti-socialist bourgeois rightists should be given protection and must not be criticised? . . .

Others ask: why is the question of class struggle raised now after it has been claimed that large-scale class struggle has in the main been concluded? It is true that large-scale class struggle has in the main been concluded. But it is also true that class struggle will continue for a long time to come on the political front and ideological front. As everybody can see, this struggle is not provoked by the working class. . . .

["The Unusual Spring." People's Daily editorial. June 22

Chou En-lai puts the case for the defence [4]

[*Unified purchase and sale*]—Some people say that unified purchase and sale [*i.e.*, of agricultural commodities] has been a pretty mess. This is a direct attack on the socialist economic system. . . . In agriculture, the harvests may be good this year and bad the next, and often good here and bad there. To make up for this unbalance, in a good year or in bumper-crop areas, provision has to be made against the bad years and for less fortunate areas, and also against serious natural calamities or

[4] Readers will be able to make their own comparison of Chou En-lai's defence with the criticisms that occasioned it. But it may be worth noting that the Chinese Prime Minister in most cases adopts the familiar method (itself deplored by critics) of admitting mistakes, but claiming that basically the situation is sound (unified purchase and sale, selection of students for study abroad, the legal system, non-Communists' lack of power, etc.). Where the criticism is more basic—for instance, that "sectarianism" springs directly from Communist Party dictatorship—he simply denies that it is true without attempting to discuss the arguments offered for the assertion.

other unforeseen circumstances. In industry and transportation, large-scale construction is proceeding. The urban population is steadily growing.

These are reasons why, in a country like ours, if we do not introduce unified purchase and sale and reasonable distribution of food grain and other principal consumer goods, we shall be unable to ensure the livelihood of the great masses of the working people, or to carry on socialist construction successfully. . . .

In criticising this erroneous view, however, we do not deny certain shortcomings in the carrying out of unified purchase and sale. For instance, in the unified purchase and sale of grain, for a time, since the supply quota was excessive, we could not but increase our purchases, and as a result we purchased far too much in some areas, and left not enough reserves for the peasants. Another case is the planned marketing of cotton cloth. Since there was an increase in the production of cotton cloth last year, supply to consumers was rather generous. This year, as production decreased, we had to reduce the supply a little bit. . . .

[*Learning from Russia*]—Some people are against learning from the experience of the Soviet Union and even say that the mistakes and shortcomings in our construction work are also the result of learning from the Soviet Union. This is a very harmful point of view. We believe that learning from the Soviet Union has been absolutely necessary. The question lies in how we ourselves do the learning. If we do not learn well, the responsibility lies wholly with us. . . .

[*The Educational problem*]—Let me now turn to the subject of students joining in labour after graduation. Our growing national economy requires that the cultural level of the workers and peasants be constantly raised, with large numbers of cultured and educated youth joining the ranks of the labourers. Since the liberation, the number of primary and secondary schools and higher educational institutions has greatly increased. To meet the pressing national need for the upper and medium categories of construction personnel, the higher educational institutions and secondary technical schools took in an especially large number of new students. . . .

It must be pointed out, however, that this situation was temporary and abnormal. As the state makes proper arrangements in this matter, the situation will gradually normalise. In 1957, both higher educational institutions and secondary schools will enrol fewer students, according to plan. . . . Young persons and students should regard participation in industrial and agricultural production as the greatest of honours. . . .

[*Selection of students for study abroad*]—In order to train higher intellectuals loyal to the cause of socialism, we used to stress the importance of examining one's political qualifications when sending students abroad before the basic victory of the socialist revolution—this was absolutely necessary. But at the same time there was formalism in the examination of the student's political qualifications, and there were a few cases where the political character of the student sent abroad proved to be bad. We must draw a lesson from this shortcoming in our work.

Then, too, inadequate attention was sometimes paid to examining the student's scholastic and physical qualifications. . . .

[*Party leadership of science*]—Some people hold that the Communist Party and the People's Government are not able to direct scientific work. They say that, at present many of the leaders are not scientists, and that "laymen" are not qualified to lead the "experts. . . ."

If the idea that the "laymen" are not qualified to lead the "experts" implies that only specialists are qualified to lead in their own field, this not only negates political leadership over science but is tantamount to ruling out the possibility of any unified leadership in scientific research, because scientific pursuits are highly specialised, and there could not be a leader of scientific work who was himself a master of all branches of science. Such an idea can only sow the seeds of disintegration in the ranks of scientific workers and is therefore harmful to the development of scientific work. . . .

[*Living standards*]—Some people . . . say that our living standards have gone down since the liberation. But as workers and peasants constitute the vast majority of our people, and their living standards have improved, how can we say our people's livelihood has deteriorated? It should be admitted that in the case of a small number of highly qualified intellectuals and a small number of workers and employees, although their livelihood now is better than during the years just before the liberation, their standards of living have not yet regained the level before the outbreak of the war against Japanese aggression. However, as the living standards of the masses of workers and peasants are still rather low, it is not possible to raise the living standards of the intellectuals too much or too rapidly. . . .

[*Discrepancy between living standards of workers and peasants*]—Some people say there is too great a discrepancy between the living standards of our workers and peasants. . . . In the old Chinese countryside, the majority of our peasants wore rags and were half-famished, feeding on husks for six months out of the year. Since the liberation, as a result of land reform and the co-operative movement, 20 to 30 per cent. of our peasants today have a little more than enough, about 60 per cent. make an adequate living, and 10 to 15 per cent. are short of food and clothes and need aid from the state or the agricultural producers co-operatives. The average peasant's net income from agricultural production for the country as a whole is about seventy yuan a year, so that each peasant household gets about 300 yuan. . . .

In 1956, the average yearly wage of workers and employees was 610 yuan, more than twice the income of a peasant household. If we simply compare these figures, there does appear to be too great a discrepancy. But if we take into consideration the different conditions in villages and towns, that puts a different complexion on the matter. To keep yourself clothed and fed in the country you need on the average only five yuan a month, while to live at a comparable standard in the city costs ten yuan. So we believe although there is a difference between the living standards of workers and peasants it is not too great. Moreover, as the labour productivity of the workers is much higher than that of peasants, it is proper that there should be a reasonable difference in income. . . .

[*Discrepancies between salaries of higher and lower officials*]—Some people say that there is also a great discrepancy between the life of high-ranking and low-ranking employees. This is correct if it means that our country is very poor. The living standards of workers and peasants are still very low, and therefore there should not be too great a difference between the pay of high-ranking and low-ranking employees. The criticism is wrong, however, if it aims at denying that there should be a reasonable difference in pay for different types of work. . . . Last year, during and after the wage reform, in order to suitably reduce the discrepancy in wages between high-ranking and low-ranking employees, the state took steps to control or lower the salaries of heads of enterprises and high-ranking personnel of state organisations. . . .

[*Admitted defects of wage and apprenticeship systems*]—There are still unrealistic and unfair practices in the grading of wages, in the system of piece-work wages, in the apprentice system, the system of subsidies and rewards, as well as in the regulations governing the workers' welfare, as in labour insurance, free medical service, welfare funds and so forth. We should continue to make readjustments here. There were so many shortcomings in the work of wage reform. While learning from the advanced experience of other socialist countries in this respect we did not combine it enough with the actual condition in our country. We did not carefully study of what was useful in our former wage system and we even simply ignored them. . . .

[*Shortcomings of the legal system*]—It must be said that while the legal system in our country is not all it should be, neither is it a question of " there is no law to go by," as some people make it out to be . . . we have drawn up and put into force many important laws, such as the trade union law, labour insurance regulations, land reform law, regulations governing national regional autonomy, electoral law, marriage law, national service law, model regulations for agricultural producers' co-operatives, regulations governing the punishment of counter-revolutionaries, regulations governing punishment for corruption, regulations governing arrest and custody, etc. . . .

In the early days of the foundation of our state, and throughout the period of transition, political and economic conditions changed rapidly, and it was, and continues to be, difficult to draw up laws of a fundamental character suited to long-term periods. For instance, it is difficult to draft the civil and criminal codes before the completion in the main of the socialist transformation of the private ownership of the means of production and the full establishment of socialist ownership of the means of production. Under these circumstances, it is necessary and proper for the state to issue provisional regulations, decisions and directives as terms of reference for general observance. . . . For example, a draft criminal code is now ready and a draft civil code and regulations governing public security are in process of being drafted by the departments concerned.

[*The state system*]—The right-wing elements . . . slandered the people's democratic dictatorship, describing it as the root of all mistakes and shortcomings. . . . We welcome criticisms of shortcomings and mistakes offered with the purpose of perfecting and developing our socialist system. But what the right-wing elements are in fact trying to do is to drive our country from the path of socialism to the path of capitalism. This will not be permitted by the broad masses of the people. . . .

[*Freedom and democracy*]—The right-wing elements say there is far too little freedom in our country, and speak as if there is freedom only when facilities are granted and guarantees are provided by the state for those who want to oppose the basic state system laid down in the constitution, and to oppose socialism in words and deeds. It is quite clear that the people will not agree to give them this sort of freedom. . . .

The suffrage is only one of the democratic rights enjoyed by our people. The democratic life of our country has a much richer content than this. . . . Many important laws are fully deliberated upon and discussed by the masses while they are being drawn up. The state economic plans were finalised only after control figures or draft plans put forward by the departments concerned had been discussed by the rank and file members of production units at the basic levels. . . .

Under no circumstances should we completely repudiate centralised leadership merely because we have extended democracy. . . .

[*Leadership of the Communist Party*]—The leading role of the Chinese Communist Party in the political life of the state is set forth in clear terms in our constitution. . . . Certain rightist elements describe this leading position of the Communist Party in the political life of the state as a "monopoly of the state by the Party." This is a malicious slander. . . .

The workers of Peking said recently: "China under the leadership of the Communist Party is a country where the working class 'monopolises' the state." This is the best reply to the hue and cry about the "Communist Party's monopoly of the state. . . ." Some rightist elements have further declared that the Communist Party is the root cause of sectarianism. . . .

As a matter of fact, the Communist Party has at all times opposed sectarianism. . . .

When I was entrusted by the first session of the National People's Congress in 1954 to form a government, I drew up the composition of the State Council in accordance with the principle of the people's democratic united front led by the Communist Party as stipulated in the Constitution. At that time, members of the democratic parties and groups other than the Communist Party and non-party democrats made up something over one-fourth of the total membership of the Government. This ratio was also largely maintained when the Government membership was later enlarged. . . .

[*The merging of Party and Government*]—Some people have criticised the lack of a clear division of function between the Party and the Government. . . . In directly issuing political calls and announcing policy-making decisions to the masses, the Party, far from hampering the work of the Government, renders it great help. . . . Inspections in certain fields of work were made jointly by the Party and Government organisations concerned. . . . These methods have been found helpful in improving work and should continue to be used in the future. But, in some departments, there have indeed been cases where Communist Party organisations have monopolised the work and taken over administrative control; on some specific questions, they have by-passed the administration and directly interfered with the work. This sort of thing befits neither the work of the Government nor the work of the Party and should be corrected.

[*Positions without authority*]—Some people have raised the issue that non-Communist leading members in state organisations, schools or enterprises do not have the authority that should go with their posts. There were, indeed, a number of facts to support what they said. But a detailed analysis of the question will show that several different cases are involved.

The first case is where Communists and non-Communists co-operate closely and are not divided by " walls " or " moats." The second case is where some Communist Party organisations and officials do not have sufficient respect for the functions and powers of non-Communists and even adopt an attitude which is discriminative or keep them at arm's length. This is a grave mistake of a sectarian character. The third case is where some non-Communists fail to devote enough effort to the duties that go with their posts. They stand aloof from and look askance at Communist Party organisations and members; but in these cases, on the other hand, the Communist Party organisations and leading officials concerned have often made inadequate efforts to approach and help them. The two latter cases deserve our serious attention. We must make energetic efforts to correct them. . . .

[*Report to the NPC. Peking. June 26. NCNA. June 26*

METHODS OF THE CAMPAIGN

Ch'u An-p'ing denounced by his son

I am Ch'u An-p'ing's son. I was recently demobilised and have returned home.

Since the publication of his anti-socialist views, Ch'u An-p'ing has met with the stern reproaches of the whole nation. I myself, a soldier of the revolutionary army and a socialist youth, resolutely stand on the side of the nation in opposition to his canards against the Communist Party, socialism and the people's leadership.

Many of his anti-Party and anti-socialist views have been exposed by the Press. It has been adequately proved that he has entertained such vicious ideas for a long time, that he has political ambitions and that he exploited the *Kuang Ming Daily* as a base for launching anti-socialist attacks. I have thus become aware of his anti-Party visage.

I wish to offer Mr. Ch'u An-p'ing one word of advice: I hope that you will repent in time; listen to the opinions of the people; uproot your anti-socialist thoughts; render a thorough account of yourself; in this way you may find grace with the people.

Ch'u Wang-ying,
June 26, 1957.

[Letter in the Wen Hui Pao. June 29

Lo Lung-chi attacked in his village

The members of the Chetien Agricultural Co-operative in Fengtien hsiang, Anfu hsien, Kiangsi, met on the evening of June 24 to denounce the fallacious representations made by the right-wing elements of the bourgeoisie against socialism and the leadership of the Communist Party and to unveil the reactionary words and deeds perpetrated by Lo Lung-chi in his home village.

Fengtien hsiang is the home village of Lo Lung-chi. The co-operative members revealed that when Lo Lung-chi returned to his home village in the summer year before last, he never asked the peasants what benefit they had got under the leadership of the Party, but devoted himself exclusively to fault-finding. When talking with other people, he always asked meaningfully: " What is wrong with co-operation? " " What is wrong with planned buying and marketing? . . ."

[NCNA. Nanchang. June 30

Confessions at the National People's Congress

Ch'u An-p'ing: " Surrender to the people "

To begin with, my view that the Party dominates the world today is completely at variance with the facts. After the liberation, the people led by the Party have risen to the status of owners. The world today is the people's world with a tremendous people's power growing everywhere. . . . In the little more than two months during which I was Editor-in-Chief, the *Kuang Ming Daily* published many vicious, one-sided and destructive reports, attacking Party leadership and damaging Party prestige. I sent many correspondents to Shanghai, Nanking, Wuhan, Canton, Sian, Lanchow, Shenyang, Changchun and Tsingtao to call forums at which persons dissatisfied with the Party and courageous enough to attack the Party were specially invited to make speeches. My plan was to use this concentrated form to damage the prestige of the Party. I published the wrong reports from the bulletins issued by the students of Peking University. Outwardly I gathered news but actually I stirred up disturbances. . . .

The damage done by these erroneous speeches and actions was immense. They created ideological confusion among some backward members of the masses, as a result of which some people were for a very short time unable to see the truth. They aggravated the grievances of certain people who were already dissatisfied with the Party. They damaged the prestige of the Party among the masses and encouraged attacks on the Party. . . .

Outside our country, my erroneous speeches were exploited by our enemies, the Americans and Chiang, who gained the wrong impression that many intellectuals in China stood against the Party and Government. . . .

At this solemn session today and through this congress I sincerely admit my mistakes, ask punishment from the people and surrender to the people. . . . From now on I will honestly accept Party leadership and wholeheartedly follow the socialist road.

[*From a speech delivered to the NPC. July 13.*
People's Daily. July 15

A tearful confession

One of the rightists to confess today, Wang Chi-hsiang, a vice chairman of the Peasants and Workers party, broke down and cried as he addressed the congress. Sobbing loudly and blowing his nose lustily with a large blue handkerchief, he ended "Long live the unity of all Chinese, Long live the Communist Party." Chinese leaders who sat on the platform at the back of the speaker seemed unmoved by his performance and for much of the time he was speaking the Premier, Mr. Chou En-lai, was carrying on an animated conversation with Deputy

Premier Ch'en Yun. Each rightist speaker was met with stony silence, but at the end were greeted with a little applause in which none of the leaders joined.

[*David Chipp. Reuter. Peking. July 13*

Lo Lung-chi : " My preliminary examination "

I am a guilty creature of the Chinese People's Republic. I have spoken and acted against the Communist Party and socialism. I stand on this august rostrum to bow my head before the deputies, and the people of the country. . . .

I am to be held culpable for egging on and adding fuel to the subversive acts of rightists and even reactionary and counter-revolutionary elements against the Party through the speech I made on May 22 at the conference of the United Front Work Department. . . . I did not ask the original Party organs to reverse the wrongs done but worked for the establishment of a new organ to do it. Here I attempted to negate the leadership of the basic level of the Party. . . .

Following the convening of the 20th Congress of the Soviet Communist Party and the outbreak of the Polish and Hungarian incidents, I had for a while doubts about Communism. But I did feel that the advocacy by the Chinese Communist Party under Chairman Mao's leadership of " co-ordination of the practices of the Chinese revolution " was, after all, different from the situations in Poland and Hungary. China, under the leadership of the Communist Party, had a bright future. Of this I was deeply convinced. . . . I had attempted to ingratiate myself into the fever of the intellectuals, especially old intellectuals, counting on this to expand the organisation and raise the position of the China Democratic League, thereby acquiring a relatively big voice in decisions on national affairs. This was where my dream stopped. I do not have and have never had any scheme for the overthrow of the Party and socialism or for reinstitution of capitalism in the country. . . .

In the explanations made by many persons in the Press, the term " Chang-Lo alliance " has been freely used and it is believed that this alliance is the supreme directing organ for the rampant offensive against the Party and that it is the well-planned central organisation of the plot. I wish to offer no explanation today. I have given the truth about the sinful deeds I have done in co-operation with Chang Po-chun. I suggest that the leadership Party and the people make thorough investigations. If anything is found that tends to show my deliberate concealment of various plots in my joint activities with Chang Po-chun, I am prepared to receive the due punishment. . . .

[*From a written statement presented to the NPC. July 15. People's Daily. July 16*

Chang Po-chun: "I bow my head and admit my guilt before the People"

I am an offender guilty of serious political mistakes. . . .

At a forum called by the Communist Party United Front Work Department this year, I erroneously proposed the establishment of a "political planning council" and advocated more study of state policies and guiding principles and a strengthening of the rights of democratic parties. . . . It was simply an attempt to substitute bourgeois democracy for proletarian dictatorship and the system of people's congresses. It was a violation of the Constitution. . . .

The question of the Chang-Lo alliance. Since last year, he has backed me in the work of the Democratic League, and on personnel matters of the League like the appointment of Fei Hsiao-t'ung, Fan Pu-chai, Pan Kuang-tan, Tseng Chao-lun and Wu Ching-chao I accepted the wishes of Lo. The work of the China Democratic League was divided in such a way that he took charge of propaganda and I took charge of culture and education. . . . Thus I needed Lo's support in order to expand my influence among the higher intellectuals. In this respect, it can be said that our ideological affinity led to a political alliance. . . .

The whole nation is demanding stern punishment of me, a rightist. This is what should be done and I am prepared to accept it. I hate my wickedness. I want to kill the old and reactionary self so that he will not return to life. I will join the whole nation in the stern struggle against the rightists, including myself. The great Chinese Communist Party once saved me, it saved me once more today. I hope to gain a new life under the leadership and teaching of the Party and Chairman Mao and to return to the stand of loving the Party and socialism. I will mend my ways and wholeheartedly serve socialism. . . .

[*From a written statement presented to the NPC. July 15. People's Daily. July 16*

Criticism and Self-Criticism

The Central Committee of the Democratic League held its Sixth Enlarged Rectification Forum at the People's Political Consultative

Conference's Cultural Club this afternoon to expose the persistent criminal, anti-Communist and anti-people words and deeds of Lo Lung-chi. Over 200 members attended the forum. . . .

Lo Lung-chi spoke for more than thirty minutes, but without disclosing anything new. He said: "If everybody thinks I should confess, I am willing to make another confession." He admitted only two things today: One, he and many of his friends had become rightists and there had been invisible, spiritual and ideological links between them; and, Two, his two statements, made on May 10 and May 22, respectively, this year, were anti-Communist. . . . He also said that he had made use of legitimate organisations in doing illegal things, and that he could not say that his clique was not anti-Communist in the least.

Other members who attended the meeting then followed with speeches accusing Lo Lung-chi. . . .

As far back as 1929, according to Liang Ssu-ch'eng, Lo Lung-chi had written two articles for *New Moon Magazine*, one of which was entitled, "My 'Unreserved' Criticism of [the] Party Affairs [of the Kuomintang]" and the other, "What Sort of Political System Do We Want?" He malignantly called the dictatorship of the proletariat a one-party dictatorship and likened the Communist Party of the Soviet Union to the Fascist Party of Italy. He said: "The Russian Communists were the first to experiment with one-party dictatorship." Lo Lung-chi declared on the one hand that he was opposed to one-party dictatorship, but said at the same time: "If there were such a man as Mussolini in China . . . the common people would surely and willingly sing his praises, flatter him, obey and support him. Unfortunately there is no such man in China. . . ." He also said: "If the Chinese political parties really carry on the English or American type of politics . . . China would be free and on the same footing as the other Powers, and the Chinese people would be happy and at peace. . . . Such a course . . . may very well prove promising." So, according to Lo Lung-chi, "The British or American way would certainly be smoother and safer in a country where Lenin is dead and Mussolini is not yet born." It was merely because there was no such man as Mussolini in China and China was a country "where Mussolini was not yet born," that Lo Lung-chi temporarily chose the British or American way while waiting for a Mussolini to be born. . . .

Wu Han said that Lo Lung-chi not only opposed the Communist Party himself, but had also proposed to the Japanese imperialists—the enemy of the Chinese people—that they should oppose the Communists together. He once wrote in *New Moon* monthly: "Victory of the Chinese Communists would be a disaster not only to China, but also to Japan. . . ."

After the liberation of the country in 1949 and before the People's Political Consultative Conference was held, Lo Lung-chi arrived in Peking. He was received by both Chairman Mao Tse-tung and Premier Chou En-lai. It has now been disclosed that after his meeting with Chairman Mao Tse-tung, Lo Lung-chi spoke slanderously of Chairman Mao Tse-tung to his friends, saying: "Chairman Mao is a very shrewd and crafty man, much more ruthless than any other ruler in our history." In his meeting with Lo Lung-chi, Premier Chou En-lai told him that the democratic parties represented the national bourgeoisie and petty bourgeoisie while the Communist Party represented the proletariat. Lo Lung-chi disagreed. He asked: "Why should Chou En-lai, who had come from Nankai [University], and Mao Tse-tung, who had come from Peking University, represent the proletariat, while he, whose *alma mater* was Tsinghua University, must represent the bourgeoisie and petty bourgeoisie?" Lo Lung-chi suggested to Premier Chou En-lai that a Popular Front should be inaugurated. He said: "You represent part of the people, while we represent another party, and so we should come to an agreement on a coalition government and co-operate in its organisation." These words fully revealed Lo Lung-chi's unwillingness to accept the leadership of the Communist Party. He wanted to take over the reins of government from the Communists on a rotation basis. He also unashamedly called himself a representative of part of the people and tried to bargain with the Communist Party on that basis. . . .

Tseng Chao-lun accused Lo Lung-chi of persistently trying to stir up enmity between the Party and the intellectuals after the liberation and to wrest the leadership of the intellectuals from the Party, and substantiated his accusations with much evidence. According to Tseng Chao-lun, Lo Lung-chi once said: "Intellectuals are feeling very uncomfortable in the new society" and "Many college professors opposed the readjustment of colleges and departments, but they could do nothing else but obey." Tseng Chao-lun said that Lo Lung-chi was obviously trying to stir up enmity between the Party and the intellectuals by saying such things. Continuing, Tseng Chao-lun said that Lo Lung-chi opposed the study of Marxism-Leninism by intellectuals, declaring that "middle-aged people are difficult to reform and unlikely to be converted to Marxism-Leninism, and therefore should not waste their efforts on Marxism-Leninism. . . ."

Miss P'u Hsi-hsiu [a good friend of Lo's and attacked as a member of his clique for her activities on the *Kuang Ming Daily*] said: "Lo Lung-chi has always wanted to rely on United States imperialism for carrying out his comprador-capitalist ideas, that is, the so-called 'Third Force' line favoured by the Americans. Before the liberation, when the Democratic League Headquarters on the mainland was forcibly dissolved and most of the progressive people had gone either to Hongkong or to the liberated areas, Lo Lung-chi continued to stay in Shanghai awaiting his opportunity. . . ."

Speaking immediately before the meeting concluded, Hu Yu-chih said: "Instead of confessing, Lo Lung-chi is still trying to deny his guilt. Lo Lung-chi is deeply anti-Party and anti-socialist, which is evident from his family and social background. . . . Lo Lung-chi has opposed agrarian reform, the 'three-anti,' the 'five-anti,' the ideological reform, and the eradication of counter-revolution movements. His reactionary thinking has not changed a bit today. . . ."

Hu Yu-chih said: "Lo Lung-chi's attitude today was extremely vicious. Lo Lung-chi calls the accusations against him fabrications, and has brought disorder to the meeting. That is intolerable. In his next confession, Lo Lung-chi should give an account especially of his secret anti-Communist organisation and his secret anti-Communist activities."

[*NCNA. Peking. August 10*

EPILOGUE

by

G. F. HUDSON

16

CHINA AND THE COMMUNIST "THAW"

by G. F. Hudson

In November 1957, the twelve ruling Communist Parties of the Sino-Soviet *bloc*, gathered together in Moscow to celebrate the 40th anniversary of the Bolshevik seizure of power in Russia, issued a joint declaration violently denouncing revisionism. This denunciation may be taken as marking the end of the "liberal" course of general Soviet policy which began with Khrushchev's visit of conciliation to Belgrade in May 1955, if not in the period immediately following Stalin's death two years earlier. In spite of short-term oscillations, the main line of this policy follows a well-marked curve of relaxation and liberality—in a very relative sense—increasing up to the 20th Congress of the Soviet Communist Party in February 1956 and decreasing after the upheavals in Poland and Hungary in October of the same year. At the outset the major factor of influence appears to have been Russian. But from the time of the Hungarian revolt we find China playing a far more active role and intervening with vigorous initiative in the affairs of European Communism, to such an extent that it has sometimes seemed as if Peking had replaced Moscow as the ideological centre of the Communist world. In order to understand how this has come about it is necessary to survey briefly the course of Soviet policy since the death of Stalin, with special reference to the points at which it involved relations with China.

The death of Stalin, like the death of Lenin, was followed by a period of collective leadership. By the constitutional theory of Communist Party organisation—the principle of democratic centralism—the collegiate authority of the highest Party organ, the Presidium of the Central Committee, was indeed the proper depository of supreme power; the theory had no place for an official leader or personal head of the Party. Nevertheless, on each occasion when the demise of a supreme personality and the absence of an obvious successor left the leadership collectively in the hands of the highest Party organ, the factional conflicts that ensued finally led to a fresh concentration of power in the hands of one man, if only because a Party suppressing all opposition to itself and exercising dictatorial rule over the people could not afford the luxury of uncontrolled dissensions at the top, and the mass of Party members not directly involved in the factional struggles instinctively looked for a single personal leadership which would resolve all inner-Party conflicts. In both instances, however, it was very difficult for such a leader to emerge quickly, for the deceased leader left behind him a number of lieutenants of approximately equal standing in the Party and intensely jealous of one another. It was this fear of a new Stalin and unwillingness to place too much power again in the hands of any one man that compelled Malenkov, as initially the strongest candidate for the succession to Stalin, to resign from the secretariat after he had been appointed Prime Minister, so that he might not combine, as Stalin had done since 1941, control of the Party apparatus with control of the state bureaucracy. Moreover, Khrushchev, who was put at the head of the secretariat, was denied the title of General Secretary, which had been Stalin's original office, and was merely entitled First Secretary, so as to emphasise the collegiate character of the secretariat.

However, Khrushchev, like Stalin before him, succeeded in building up a strong body of personal supporters in the Central Committee through his patronage of appointments in the Party apparatus. But he still had to reckon with the established major figures of the Party such as Malenkov, Molotov, Kaganovitch and Mikoyan, and could only advance to power by political alliances with one clique against another on issues of policy.

He engineered the downfall of Malenkov in alliance with the "Stalinists" in the name of Stalin's principle of the priority of heavy industry. But after Malenkov had been replaced by Bulganin as Prime Minister at the beginning of 1955, Khrushchev appeared in the new light of a reverser of the policies pursued by Stalin in the field of foreign affairs during the last years of his life. The most spectacular manifestation of this was his visit to Belgrade and reconciliation with Tito in May of 1955; then came the Geneva summit conference in the summer and the tour of India and Burma in the autumn. All this diplomatic activity was part of an attempt to get out of the rut of isolation and barren intransigence into which Soviet foreign policy had fallen and to exert a new influence in the world under the banner of " peaceful coexistence," lulling the West into disarmament and dissolution of its alliances through a new creation of confidence and winning over the nationalist leaders of Asia and Africa—Nehru, Sukarno and Nasser—instead of promoting efforts at Communist revolution in countries not yet ripe for it. The purposes of the reconciliation within this larger design appear to have been, first, to close a scandalous breach in the unity of the Communist world, secondly to further the creation of confidence in the West by the liquidation of one of Stalin's most truculent and menacing policies, and thirdly to make use of Yugoslavia's special contacts with neutralist countries and with socialist circles in Western Europe to extend Soviet influence.

But Tito had no intention of abandoning the position of an independent oracle of the Maxist faith which he had acquired since 1948, and he even demanded that the individuals, whether in the Soviet Union or the satellite countries, who had been specially concerned in the Cominform campaign against him, should be removed from high office as proof of the sincerity of Moscow's repentance. This attitude of Tito was to become an increasingly serious matter for the Soviet leadership as time went on. As long as Yugoslavia was an outcast from the Communist world and Tito labelled a Fascist and an imperialist agent, Titoism could be fought in Communist countries by propaganda and police action without reservations. But now that he had been forgiven and rehabilitated, his heresy was condoned and it became difficult for the guardians of Marxist-Leninist orthodoxy to treat it as anything but permissible comradely dissent. Thus it began to spread widely in the satellite countries and even to exert influence in the Soviet Union itself.

The Chinese Communist leadership was sympathetic to the new direction of Soviet foreign policy and particularly to the endeavour to establish a new relationship between Moscow and the satellite governments of Eastern Europe looser than that which had existed in Stalin's time. They considered that they themselves had successfully adapted the principles of Marxism-Leninism to the particular national conditions and problems of China and they thought that " different roads to socialism " should similarly be allowed elsewhere. They were thus in favour of a relaxation of Soviet control over the European satellites and approved of Khrushchev as the leading advocate of it in Moscow.

The 20th Congress of the Soviet Party found Khrushchev firmly in command of the Party organisation, but it revealed a serious contradiction in his political position which could be dangerous to him. His reforming policies had made him dependent for support on the more liberal wing of the Party in which Mikoyan was the principal figure. But this faction was also the one which was most anxious to prevent any return to Stalin's autocracy and rule by terror. Khrushchev, on the other hand, had been trying for some time to build up for himself through suitable publicity a kind of apostolic succession to Stalin.

When the Congress opened, Khrushchev spoke of the " loss " sustained by the Party through Stalin's death and gave no indication that the demotion of the former *Vozhd* from his unique eminence was to be carried any further. What then caused Khrushchev to take so momentous a step as the devastating attack on Stalin in the " secret speech " without previously consulting the leaders of other Communist Parties and after having himself spoken of Stalin in terms of at least moderate eulogy at the opening of the Congress? The only explanation that fits the facts of this astonishing episode is to be found in the speech of Mikoyan on February 16. He was the first to denounce Stalin before the Congress and he did so publicly; further, by naming Kossior (whom Khrushchev had been appointed by Stalin to succeed in his post as First Secretary in the Ukraine after his execution as one of Stalin's victims) he directed attention to Khrushchev's unsavoury past. The attack on Stalin was not simply a polemical condemnation of a dead dictator; it was a practical move to rouse the Party against a revival of Stalin's tyranny in the person of Khrushchev. The applause which this speech evoked showed how much the delegates had been stirred by the thought of a return of the nightmare times of Stalin's purges. Feeling the ground insecure under his feet, Khrushchev evidently decided to act on the principle of "If you can't break 'em, join 'em," and to take the lead in the movement against himself. By his speech to the secret session at the close of the Congress he committed himself before the Party to the repudiation of Stalin's methods, to abolition of the "cult of personality" and to affirmation of the principle that Party members should not be subject to arbitrary arrest and execution by the secret police as had happened in Stalin's time.

It was a masterpiece of tactical improvisation, but its consequences were serious and far-reaching. Although the speech was delivered to a secret session, the audience was too numerous for it to be kept entirely hidden and a text was soon published on the other side of the Iron Curtain. The disclosures had their minimum effect within the Soviet Union, where the main facts about Stalin's rule were well known, though never mentioned; they were shattering in their impact on Communist morale and the reputation of the Soviet régime in other countries. In China they embarrassed the Communists both by giving the lie to the *couleur de rose* picture of the Soviet Union which they had been doing their best for years to project before the Chinese people and by their indirect rebuke to the flourishing cult of personality in China itself. Mao lost face by having paid his tribute to the memory of Stalin a few days before the latter was hurled from his pedestal by the man who had been hoping to inherit his mantle, and apart from his personal annoyance must have felt doubt about Khrushchev's capacity to lead the Communist *bloc*, since he had shown himself so ready to hazard the cause of Communism throughout the world for an immediate tactical gain in domestic politics.

Eight months later the Communist world was shaken to its foundations by the revolts in Poland and Hungary. One of the main consequences of the events of October and November 1956 was a long-drawn-out crisis in the leadership of the Soviet Union; another was China's first active intervention in the political affairs of Europe. There were two possible explanations of what had happened. The liberalisers, with whom Khrushchev had now identified himself, could argue that the outbreaks were the delayed result of Stalinist policies of excessive rigour and oppression which had isolated the Communist Parties from the broad masses and deprived them of the popular support which should have been theirs; reform had come too late to avert the explosions of popular resentment. To this the advocates of the firm hand—concentrated round Molotov, who had been dismissed from the post of Foreign Minister just before Tito's visit to Russia—replied that it was precisely the reforms that had caused the trouble; Poland and Hungary had been kept effectively in line under Bierut and Rakosi, but the condonation of Titoist heresy, the new toleration for subversive writers and journalists, and such measures as the public reburial of Rajk, had confused and demoralised loyal Party cadres while giving encouragement to all hostile elements. To an outside observer, it must appear that the Molotov faction had the better of the argument.

But the controversy between the Khrushchev and Molotov factions was not a discussion among professors of history; it was an issue to be settled by " organisational " means within the Soviet Communist Party, and after Khrushchev had been defeated in the Presidium—on a complex of issues, of which international Communist policy was only one—he used his control of a packed Central Committee to remove his opponents from the Presidium altogether and replace them with his own nominees.

Meanwhile, Peking had been trying both to mediate between the Soviet Union and Poland and to provide the Communist world as a whole with the new formulations of Marxist-Leninist doctrine which the critical and unprecedented situation demanded, but which Moscow during the months following the Polish and Hungarian outbreaks signally failed to produce. Chou En-lai was ordered to break off a goodwill tour of Asian capitals on which he was engaged and go to Moscow, Warsaw and Budapest and use his good offices to promote a compromise between Gomulka and the Soviet leaders; he was at the same time to throw the weight of Chinese prestige behind the effort to restore Communist authority in Hungary. Mao and Chou already had good personal relations with Polish Communist leaders arising from the visit of Ochab and Cyrankiewicz to Peking in September of 1956, and it was reported that the Chinese had then encouraged the Poles to follow their own "road to socialism" and had promised them support in their aspirations for greater independence from Moscow. In the crisis of Soviet-Polish relations Chinese pressure is believed to have been brought to bear on the Soviet Government to abstain from any use of force against Gomulka. These moves were no mere improvisations of diplomacy to meet a confused and changing situation, but were in accordance with principles systematically expounded both in an official Chinese pronouncement on the events in Europe at the end of 1956 and in Mao Tse-tung's February speech on contradictions among the people. The characteristic feature of both these declarations was the attempt to reconcile the need to win popular support with the requirements of Party dictatorship, and the principle of distinct national roads to socialism with the demands of the international solidarity of the "camp." The Chinese restatement of the Marxist-Leninist doctrine sought to provide a certain flexibility within the system, to allow for conflicts of interest and opinion within definite limits. Mao drew from the indirect experience of the Hungarian revolution the lesson that a Communist Party would be found ineffective in a moment of crisis if through excessive rigidity of policy, reliance on coercion and failure to distinguish loyal criticism from counter-revolutionary hostility it lost contact with the masses; in other words, the Chinese Communists must avoid the mistake of governing in the manner of Rakosi. Mao was only too well aware that there was much in the current Communist administration of China which was closely comparable to the methods of government which had earned for the Party so much popular hatred in Eastern Europe, and he was anxious to eradicate from it as far as he could the trio of evils known by the names of subjectivism, sectarianism and bureaucratism. But he was also aware—though not quite sufficiently, as events were to show—of the risk that any relaxation of control from above might endanger the Party's monopoly of power, and the basic orthodoxy of Marxism-Leninism. He also recognised that the theory of different roads to socialism could be used to justify in any particular country a lapse into multi-party democracy and neutralism in foreign policy. He therefore laid it down that all reforms must be contained within the bounds set by the principles of the dictatorship of the proletariat (now identified for the first time in China with the "People's Democratic Dictatorship" established by Mao) and of proletarian internationalism as embodied in a unified camp of socialist states against imperialism.

Even though there was no very profound thought in these and other Chinese pronouncements of the period, they attracted widespread attention in the Communist world and gained for Peking an ascendancy of ideological influence because of the lack of any comparable guidance from Moscow, whence all Communists had hitherto been accustomed to expect it.

An appeal for transplanting Chinese flowers

POLAND

The contradictions within the people—in spite of the specific differences between the countries—also appear in our country. To overcome them through persuasion and discussion requires a decided struggle against bureaucracy, an improvement of the state machinery and an elastic policy towards political and class allies. . . .

The Chinese flowers are certainly different from ours and not all of them could blossom in our climate. But it is worth while trying to transplant to our soil those which could. . . .

[S. Brodzki. *Sztander Mlodych*. Warsaw. May 7

"A bold step forward"

Our Party is watching with profound sympathy the activity of the Communist Party of China, which with greatest boldness is developing the creative teachings of Marxism-Leninism. An expression of the great strength of the Communist Party of China and of its close unity with the nation is the introduction in this country of new methods in solving non-antagonistic contradictions. Similarly, the thesis about the hundred blossoming flowers is a bold step forward, so far unknown in the practice of socialist construction in other countries. . . .

[W. Gomulka. Speech to 9th plenum, central committee, Polish United Workers' (Communist) Party. May 15

In the initial Chinese response to the events of October and November 1956 there was never any hesitation in endorsing the Soviet action in crushing what was by Marxist-Leninist criteria a counter-revolution in Hungary, but the emphasis was on the responsibility of Rakosi's rule for creating the conditions in which such a breakdown of the régime had become possible, and there was approval for the new course in Poland as likely to revive and strengthen Communist power there by gaining the confidence of the masses.

In China itself the main preoccupation in the spring of 1957 was with correcting misrule by officials and encouraging criticism of the Party's "style of work"; this was the era of "rectification." But after the alarming consequences of the new freedom had become apparent, policy veered sharply to confront the "bourgeois rightists" (linked with international revisionism) as the main enemy to be fought. This corresponded to a similar transition which took place, though less abruptly, in the Soviet Union. Superficially, the purge of Khrushchev's critics from the higher organs of the Party should have strengthened him for carrying out further the policy of liberalisation with which he had come to be identified. But in fact the note of reaction towards Stalinism became more and more marked from the time the leaders usually classified as Stalinist were expelled from the seats of power.

The explanation appears to be that by the middle of 1957 Khrushchev himself had become convinced that the relaxation of controls and tolerance of dissent had gone too far, but while he remained under fire from men who were his rivals for supreme power in the Party, he could not afford to admit that his general policy had been unsound; only after Molotov, Malenkov and Kaganovitch were out of the way could he reverse himself without making himself dangerously vulnerable to political attack. Be that as it may, the occasion of the fortieth anniversary of the Bolshevik Revolution found both Khrushchev and Mao Tse-tung in accord on the need, not for further relaxation, but for a great tightening-up of the Communist system, both internally in each country and internationally in the relation of the national parties to the "camp."

After the fortieth anniversary, three outstanding episodes in Communist affairs illustrated the new relations between the Soviet Union and China—the onslaught on Tito, the execution of Imre Nagy and his associates in Hungary, and the Khrushchev-Mao meeting in Peking at the end of July 1958. China certainly took the initiative in the major offensive against Tito, for although the Yugoslav Communists' programme for their Congress at Ljubljana in April 1958 had been condemned in the Soviet Union, and Moscow had persuaded most other Communist Parties not to send fraternal delegates to the Congress, it was the editorial in the Peking *People's Daily* on May 5, 1958, which first launched an all-out attack on the Yugoslav régime in terms reminiscent of the former invectives of the Cominform.

The record indicates that it was the zeal of Chinese anti-revisionism which gave momentum to the change in Soviet policy, and that, but for the thrust from Peking, Khrushchev might have continued to vacillate for some time longer.

With regard to the executions in Hungary, there is no direct evidence of any Chinese intervention in the matter, but the glee with which the news of them was received by the Chinese Communist Press suggests that the influence of China had been exerted in favour of meting out an exemplary punishment to those who

---

No transplantation of Chinese flowers

HUNGARY

Of Chinese movements in recent months that which has spread in the field of literature, art and science, i.e., *"let every flower bloom," is the most widely spread in Hungary. . . . In its first stage it was attacked for leading to the liberalisation of intellectual life and the repression of Marxism. . . . Comrade Mao Tse-tung, who is familiar with the Chinese intelligentsia and knows that its majority is loyal to socialism, defended the slogan of "a hundred flowers" . . . after the sad experiences of the past it is perhaps just as well to guard ourselves against the idea of realising Chinese methods in Hungary. The Chinese comrades would protest against it most vehemently. . . .*

[Anna Bebrits. *Nepszabadsag*. Budapest. May 26

were held to have translated the principles of revisionism from words into deeds. It was indeed insufficient to carry on a verbal war against revisionism unless it was to be made clear that death would be the penalty for serious cases of such treason to the Communist cause. The warning was directed above all to the hotbed of revisionism in Poland.

In the subsequent phase of Soviet-Chinese relations internal tension in China, due to a ferocious anti-revisionism combined with an immense pressure on the masses for the " great leap forward " in industrialisation, was reflected in a new truculence towards the West which Khrushchev appeared not so much to have instigated as to have been persuaded to support. His visit to Peking was followed by the cancellation of the summit conference " within the framework of " the Security Council, which he had originally been willing to accept, and the commencement soon afterwards of the deliberate challenging of America in the Formosa straits. It was clear that the external tension was being utilised in China for an internal mobilisation and tightening of political control, and it may indeed have been created partly with that object. This was a long cry indeed from the year of the hundred flowers and the relative degree of reasonableness that then seemed for a moment to be emerging in China.

The violence of the reaction in China from the hundred flowers ideal is partly, perhaps, to be explained by the fact—for it seems to have been a fact—that Mao Tse-tung himself shared to some extent in the illusions that others held on China's behalf—the belief that China could carry through a Communist revolution without the rigours and repressions it involved in Russia. He has now learnt the lesson that a dictatorial party cannot relax its rule beyond a certain point without endangering its monopoly of power. To abandon this monopoly is something that Mao Tse-tung has never had the slightest intention of doing—though it is just what the more radical revisionists in Europe, who have virtually turned themselves into social democrats, are prepared to do, and that is why revisionism has to be fought with such fury by those who are resolved to maintain the Party's total control over society and the state. The idea, so widely entertained in some quarters since the death of

Stalin, that a Communist political order can be peacefully transformed and mellowed into something like democracy is a vain dream, for every such trend must sooner or later come up against the vested interest of the Party in the retention of its own power, and then either the system collapses—as it had done in Hungary

---

Mao's contradictions not for Russia

MOSCOW

Daniel Schorr (*Moscow correspondent, CBS News*): *" Mr. Khrushchev, to come back to your remark about not being divided, the Government and the people, it reminds me of a recent statement from Peking, which I believe was also published in* Pravda, *that in a socialist state there can exist contradictions between the masses and the leaders. I wonder if in republishing that in* Pravda, *whether the Soviet Communists accept this idea, and what are the implications for the Soviet Union ?"*

Nikita Khrushchev: *" Each socialist or capitalist country has its own course of development and its own stages of development, and therefore socialist countries, we, for instance, our country, has been in existence forty years; the Chinese People's Republic has been in existence eight years. Therefore, a stage through which we passed does not necessarily have to be repeated in other socialist countries. Then each people have their own habits, customs, its own history, and the Communist Party of the country concerned should take that into account, of course, and our Chinese friends have many original ideas, which they are implementing in the course of socialist construction in their country. They are giving birth to new ideas, too, which take into consideration the specific conditions in China. We look upon that as perfectly normal, and we lend support to many of these things. We publish these ideas in our Press, but each one has to base oneself on the conditions existing in one's own country. There is no contradiction with any Marxist-Leninist ideas in this respect."*

Daniel Schorr: *" But are you saying these contradictions do not exist in the Soviet Union today ?"*

Nikita Khrushchev: *" We believe that we have no contradictions of that nature. . . ."*

[From " Face the Nation," CBS Television and Radio. June 2 (NCNA, June 4, omitted the last question and answer.)

before the Soviet Army brought back Kadar—or it must be saved from dissolution by a new period of repression and persecution. What has happened in China is part of the common experience of the Communist world, but it has happened there with a violence in the swing of the pendulum greater than anywhere else.

Ideologically, however, Mao Tse-tung, by his speech on contradictions among the people, may himself have provided a text for subversive agitation against his own régime.

His admission that there can be contradictions between the Government and the governed in a Communist state was indeed a novelty as far as explicit Communist doctrine was concerned and was the cause of some dismay in Moscow, where it seemed to provide too much theoretical justification for popular discontent. The official teaching had been that since the Communist Party represented the inevitable march of history and the real interests of the masses, no opposition to it, even if provoked by genuine grievances, could possibly be justified; certainly anything in the nature of strikes and demonstrations must be treated as counter-revolutionary. Mao's more indulgent attitude towards such popular manifestations, even if only the outcome of a temporary mood, made a breach in the defences of orthodoxy which it will not be easy to repair. In practice, no doubt, it can be held that the scope given theoretically to these contradictions is not of much importance, for since it is the Party which in the last resort must decide whether any particular contradiction is one " among the people " or " with the enemy," any discontent which appears dangerous to the authorities can always be classified as counter-revolutionary and thus subjected to the full rigours of repression. But for a political system based on a revolutionary ideology, the theoretical formulation of doctrine can never be without significance, and Mao's ideas of contradictions among the people, no less than his declaration that erroneous ideas cannot be eliminated by coercion, is unhelpful for the Party in a period of aggravated tension and intolerance. For the extreme rigours and regimentation of the " people's communes " what is needed is not the teaching of even a very limited right of rebellion, but an unqualified emphasis on the infallibility of the Party and the citizen's duty of unquestioning obedience to its commands. In this new context, Mao's speeches of 1957 are already an embarrassment; in Orwell's perfected totalitarian state they could be consigned to oblivion as required, but it is doubtful whether this is yet possible even in Communist China. The Mao of yesterday survives to reproach the Mao of today.

BIOGRAPHICAL NOTES

Lo Lung-chi: Born 1896. Graduated from Tsinghua University and then went to the U.S.A., where he took an M.A. (Wisconsin) and PH.D. (Columbia, 1928) in political science. On returning to China he did some university teaching and filled senior editorial posts on a number of publications. On a magazine, he collaborated with the noted scholar, Dr. Hu Shih (now in Formosa; vilified by the Communists for his pragmatic philosophy), and P'an Kuang-tan, another Columbia PH.D. who, in the summer of 1957, was accused of being a member of Lo's rightist clique.

Lo made his first forays into politics after the outbreak of war with Japan with other intellectuals attempting to form a democratic "third force" between the Nationalists and Communists. He helped to organise the Democratic League in Chungking in 1941 and became one of its leading figures. When the Nationalists dissolved the League for leftist leanings, Lo retired to Shanghai until the Communists took over. He has been Standing Committee member of the People's Political Consultative Conference, member of the Government Administration Council, Standing Committee member of the National People's Congress and Minister of the Timber Industry (from May 1956). As a leading member of the Chinese Committee for World Peace he represented his country in Ceylon at the World Peace Council meeting from June 10 to June 17, 1957.

Chang Po-chun: Born 1896. On graduating in foreign languages at Wuchang Normal College, he became principal at a normal school; in 1920 he took up a post at an agricultural school, but a short time later was in Berlin on a government scholarship studying philosophy. There he joined the local branch of the Kuomintang (Nationalists) along with Chu Teh, now Vice Chairman of the Communist Republic. After the split between the Nationalists and the Communists in 1927, Chang, now back in

China, joined one of the groups of Communist troops. When it broke up, he took refuge in the foreign concessions of Shanghai and there helped to organise a new party, known from 1930 as the Provisional Action Committee of the Kuomintang, eventually becoming its Chairman. He was still Chairman of it until this period under its new name the Peasants' and Workers' Democratic Party. After taking part in an abortive anti-Nationalist uprising in Fukien Province—he was Minister of Education in the short-lived "Chinese Republic" that was set up there—he fled abroad.

With the rallying of all political forces for the anti-Japanese war, he was able to return home and was one of the organisers of the Democratic League. During the post-war Nationalist crack-down on democratic politicians he took refuge in Hongkong. He returned to join the Communist-sponsored People's Political Consultative Conference in 1949. He was made a member of the Government Administration Council, of its Financial and Economic Committee, and Minister of Communications. In 1953, he accompanied Premier Chou En-lai to Moscow for Stalin's funeral and in 1956, as a Standing Committee member of the National People's Congress, was deputy leader of a parliamentary delegation to the Soviet Union, Roumania and Czechoslovakia.

Chang Nai-ch'i: The third Minister to be attacked as a rightist, Chang Nai-ch'i, was never seriously charged with joining the Chang Po-chun-Lo Lung-chi clique. In his confession to the National People's Congress he vigorously rejected most of the criticisms levelled at him, admitting only to "serious bourgeois individualism."

Born 1898. Graduating from a commercial school, he displayed marked financial acumen and by 1931 had become Vice President of the Chekiang Industrial Bank and had written two books on monetary problems. In 1936, he was imprisoned with six other leading members of the National Salvation Association which advocated allying with the Communists against the Japanese. (Among the others were the rightist Futan University professor, Wang Tsao-shih, and the non-Communist leaders of the anti-rightist campaign, Shen Chun-ju, noted lawyer and Chairman of the Democratic League, and Mme. Shih Liang, Minister of Justice.) This "Case of the Seven Gentlemen" aroused widespread protest and the following year the seven were released. (This stand did not prevent Mao Tse-tung from citing Chang Nai-ch'i as an example of a political capitulator to the Nationalists in 1937.) Towards the end of the war, Chang was in business in Chungking. Later he went to Hongkong, where he became prominent in the Democratic National Construction Association, of which he became a Vice Chairman. In 1949 he went as one of its representatives to the People's Political Consultative Conference in Peking. He has been a member of the Government Administration Council (1949), Minister of Food (1952), Vice Chairman, All-China Federation of Industry and Commerce (1953), People's Congress Deputy and Director of the Bank of China (1954).

Ch'en Ming-shu: Born 1892. One-time Buddhist monk. Fought for the Nationalists in Northern Expedition 1926–27. Governor, Kwangtung Province 1928–31. Nationalist Deputy Prime Minister and Minister of Communications. Prime Minister in the independent Fukien Government, 1933 (see Chang Po-chun).

Lung Yun: Born 1888. Graduate of Yunnan Military Institute, 1926. Governor, Yunnan Province, 1928–45. Member, Kuomintang Central Executive Committee, 1931–49. Expelled from latter on fleeing to Hongkong to defect to the Communists. Under them has been Vice Chairman, National Defence Council and Standing Committee member, National People's Congress.

Fei Hsiao-t'ung: Eminent sociologist and former student of Professors Malinowski and Firth. Author of *Peasant Life in China* and *Earthbound China*. Vice President, Central Nationalities College; Professor of Sociology, Tsinghua University; member, Scientific Planning Commission of State Council; National People's Congress Deputy.

Mme. Ting Ling: Born 1907. Entered National Peking University in 1924 and later the Masses University in Shanghai. Here she got a reputation as a female rebel advocating the emancipation of her sex. Her first husband, a revolutionary writer, was executed by the Nationalists in 1931. Ting Ling then joined the Communist Party. From 1933 to 1936 she was in a Nationalist prison. After her release she went to the Communist-controlled areas in the northwest, where she taught literature and worked as a journalist. Since publishing her first collection of short stories in 1928, she has written a number of novels, one, *The Sun shines on the Sangkan River*, being awarded the Stalin Prize in 1951. Among her posts under the present régime have been member of the Board, Sino-Soviet Friendship Association; member, All-China Federation of Literary and Art Circles' committee; Vice Chairman, Chinese Writers' Union.

Liu Shao-t'ang: Communist Party member; aged twenty-two at this period. Author of two novels and numerous short stories. Had been regarded by official critics as a writer of brilliant promise.

Miss Lin Hsi-ling: Communist Party member; aged twenty-one at this period. Joined the army in 1951, leaving as a " cultural teacher " in 1953, and going to the People's University. In 1954, published an essay on Balzac and Tolstoy in the *Journal of Literature and Arts* (*Wen Yi Pao*).

INDEX